ACCOUNTING

AUDITING RESEARCH

TOOLS AND STRATEGIES

6e

THOMAS R. WEIRICH
Central Michigan University

THOMAS C. PEARSON
University of Hawaii

ALAN REINSTEIN
Wayne State University

THOMSON
——★——™
SOUTH-WESTERN

Australia · Canada · Mexico · Singapore · Spain · United Kingdom · United States

Accounting & Auditing Research: Tools and Strategies, 6/e

Thomas R. Weirich, Thomas C. Pearson, & Alan Reinstein

VP/Editorial Director:
Jack W. Calhoun

Publisher:
Rob Dewey

Executive Editor:
Sharon Oblinger

Sr. Developmental Editor:
Craig Avery

Marketing Manager:
Keith Chasse

Production Editor:
Margaret M. Bril

Technology Project Editor:
Amy Wilson

Media Editor:
Kelly Reid

Manufacturing Coordinator:
Doug Wilke

Production House/Compositor:
DPS Associates

Printer:
Globus Printing
Minster, Ohio

Design Project Manager:
Anne Marie Rekow

Internal Designer:
Justin Klefeker

Cover Designer:
Christy Carr

Cover Images:
© Alamy Images

BRIEF CONTENTS

CONTENTS

CHAPTER 3 | WEB-BASED PROFESSIONAL RESEARCH   **41**

CHAPTER 4 | THE ENVIRONMENT OF ACCOUNTING RESEARCH   **55**

PREFACE

With the continuing expansion of various accounting and reporting authorities, increased penalties for incomplete research and erroneous positions—and even the change in the CPA examination designed to test basic research skills—planning and performing accounting and business research is more important than ever. Conducting applied research is essential for accounting graduates and professionals. In fact, we believe that *your success depends on learning and practicing these key business skills.*

Accounting & Auditing Research: Tools & Strategies, Sixth Edition is an invaluable, step-by-step guide to research sources and methodology. Revised for greater readability and flexibility—and enhanced by a new, integrated **ResearchLink** web suite of research tools and demonstrations, the Sixth Edition is designed to assist the reader in conducting practical professional research in accounting, auditing, and taxation. Additionally, the text concludes with a chapter on **fraud investigations**, an increasingly demanded professional service that requires careful research skills.

The Sixth Edition of *Accounting & Auditing Research* is more user-friendly, interactive, and powerful than ever. The new subtitle, *Tools and Strategies*, hints at the text's awesome integration of teaching and learning capabilities with the new **ResearchLink** suite of online research tools.

In fact, this edition focuses on electronic research tools and strategies. It also enhances the reader's critical thinking and effective writing skills in conducting research by providing extensive practice exercises throughout the text. The text further helps prepare the student who must conduct research using electronic databases both for future practice and for the CPA exam simulations that comprise approximately 20% of the Uniform CPA Examination. This edition enables users to find justifiable authoritative solutions to accounting, auditing, or tax questions.

Adopted over the years by a number of universities and staff training courses in public accounting firms and corporations, the text in its Sixth Edition guides the reader, step-by-step, through the research process. The basic objective, however, remains the same as to the "how-to" of conducting practical professional research—that of a do-it-yourself, understand-it-yourself manual. However, this new edition focuses on greater utilization of electronic databases and the use of the Internet in conducting the research. Besides accounting and auditing research, the text includes basic tax research and fraud investigations.

Including Research Skills in the Accounting Curriculum

The Sixth Edition can be used as a comprehensive text for a basic accounting/auditing research course. It can also contribute as a supplemental text to any intermediate accounting, advanced accounting, governmental accounting, tax, theory, or auditing course. The book web site, *http://weirich.swlearning.com*, provides additional cases and assistance in using the text for various classes.

New, Revised, and Enhanced Features of the Sixth Edition

While the emphasis of the text remains on providing useful guidance and information in conducting practical professional research, the Sixth Edition has been **enhanced and updated to reflect changes in research sources, technological advancements, and common professional practices**. Moreover, up-to-date guidance is provided for research stemming from legal changes particularly in the **Sarbanes-Oxley Act** and its implications for the auditing profession. The new edition also stresses the importance of the standards issued by the **Public Company Accounting Oversight Board** and current standards on **fraud investigations**.

The Sixth Edition includes more interactive, user-friendly learning and teaching features for accounting, auditing, and taxation than ever before. From its online tools to its integrated, mid-chapter practice exercises that use these tools to reinforce learning, this edition is the most extensive revision yet.

- **NEW: ResearchLink** online research suite integrates all the research tools and demonstrations provided with the Sixth Edition. ResearchLink makes research easier and faster, provides access to powerful electronic databases and demos, and is one link away from the text website. (Read more about ResearchLink below.)

- **NEW: Quick Facts** sidebar boxes throughout the text summarize and expand on chapter concepts to provide new and useful research information. Quick Facts help readers do a better, faster, more effective research job.

- **NEW: Research Tips** sidebar boxes throughout the text provide help in doing common research tasks effectively and efficiently.

- **NEW: Practice Exercises**, located following sections in most chapters, provide immediate reinforcement of concepts, databases, and research techniques presented in the preceding section. These exercises, using fill-in areas for notes and answers with solutions found on the text's web site, allow users to practice the key skills immediately after they are presented. These new exercises use a combination of ResearchLink tools, URLs, and other widely available data sources discussed in the text.

- **NEW: Simulation appendices** help users preview and practice the research skills they will use on the Computerized Uniform CPA Examination.

- **REVISED:** Many new and revised end-of-chapter discussion questions and exercises require the user to explore various data sources in developing solutions, including tools available on ResearchLink and other widely available databases discussed in the text.

- **NEW: Product Web Site.** The text's web site, *http://weirich.swlearning.com*, not only contains access and registration to **ResearchLink** but provides suggested solutions to practice exercises, instructor's solutions manual downloads, and links to the many web sites discussed throughout the book. **NEW Web cases** help develop effective and efficient research skills in the online environment. This site is truly an accounting researcher's dream come true.

ResearchLink

With the growing importance of database research tools and strategies, as well as prominent internet web sites, the Sixth Edition has expanded its integration of databases. The new edition presents an overview of many of these tools, with certain ones available for use with the text at *http://weirich.swlearning.com*. These tools are highlighted throughout the text by a **Research Tools** icon. Many universities and colleges have access to other tools reviewed in this edition but not available at the text's website that can be utilized to provide powerful learning tools in teaching applied professional research.

Available at ResearchLink are the following resources:

FARS Online—The Sixth Edition devotes Chapter 5 to the use of the **FARS** (Financial Accounting Research System) database, created by the Financial Accounting Standards Board. FARS now has an online version as well as a CD version for conducting research. By special permission, ResearchLink provides the FASB's new **FARS Online demo** of this tool that highlights the functionality of the new version FARS for schools and organizations which have access to the FARS system.

LexisNexis® Academic—This dynamic research tool, available only to the academic community, is a Web-based subset of the widely recognized commercial LexisNexis® database. In addition to various topical areas, this database provides access to U.S. authoritative accounting and auditing literature, accounting journals, and various tax sources. LexisNexis Academic is featured in Chapter 6. ResearchLink provides access as well as a demo for this tool.

PricewaterhouseCoopers' EDGARSCAN™—This Internet-based applet, created by PricewaterhouseCoopers, is an excellent tool for performance measurement or benchmarking. Edgarscan™, presented in Chapter 8, is very powerful for anyone researching a company and making performance comparisons with competitors. ResearchLink provides handy access and a demo for this tool.

Thomson ONE™ Business School Edition—Thomson ONE, discussed in Chapter 6, is a Web-based portal product that provides integrated access to Thomson Financial content for the purpose of financial analysis. This is an educational version of the same financial resources used by Wall Street analysts on a daily basis. ResearchLink provides access to 500 companies via the Business School Edition.

RIA Checkpoint® Student Edition—This professional tax database covered extensively in Chapter 7 of the text is a total tax database that contains research libraries for federal, state and local, and international taxation, estate planning, pensions, payroll, and Financial Reporting and Management Services by WG&L (Warren Gorman & Lamont). ResearchLink provides access to the student edition along with a demo.

ACL™ Desktop Edition (Full Educational Version)—One of the most widely used audit software package in the world, ACL™ Desktop Edition (Full Educational Edition) is a major software product used by fraud examiners and auditors. Most audit and accounting firms and internal audit departments use ACL. ResearchLink provides a downloadable executable file of the full educational version, covered with in-chapter practice exercises that use the software, as well as an in-depth demo **(ACL in Practice)** for those interested in fraud investigations.

i2—Analyst's Notebook, created by i2 Inc. and discussed in Chapter 10, is a visual investigative analysis software product that assists investigators by uncovering, interpreting, and displaying complex information in easily understood charts. More than 1,400 organizations in over 80 countries rely on i2 for investigations and intelligence analysis. ResearchLink provides a demo of this tool.

Other Major Research Tools Highlighted in the Sixth Edition

Many universities and colleges have access to other tools discussed in this edition but not available at the text's website that can provide powerful learning tools in applied professional research. Using introductions, screen shots, URLs, and descriptions in the text, the Sixth Edition also introduces users to these major research tools:

AICPA reSOURCE—This database as presented in Chapter 8, includes a comprehensive compendium of the AICPA literature consisting of Professional Standards, Accounting Trends and Techniques, Technical Practice Aids, Auditing and Accounting Guides, and Audit Alerts. Chapter 8 presents an overview with screen shots of how to use this powerful database in research.

Thomson Research—This professional database, presented in Chapter 6, contains more than 6,000,000 source documents. The database also contains full-text keyword searching capabilities of SEC filings in EDGAR.

Westlaw—This comprehensive legal database, highlighted in Chapter 6, is considered the best database for case law research. Westlaw Campus™, the academic version of Westlaw geared toward business law research, may be bundled with the Sixth Edition for instructors who wish to emphasize business law research. Instructors should contact their Thomson sales representative for more information.

Acknowledgments

The authors express appreciation to the many faculty members and former students that have utilized previous editions of this text and who have made valuable comments in the development of this new edition. Also, we would like to thank the accounting firms who have incorporated this text into their staff training programs. A specific thank you is extended to all those granting permission to utilize their databases and demonstrations: The Financial Accounting Foundation, Thomson Financial, RIA, LexisNexis, PricewaterhouseCoopers, ACL Services Ltd., and i2 Inc. We also thank those who have allowed us to use screen images of their products, including the American Institute of Certified Public Accountants.

Special thanks go to the technical support provided by the staff of Thomson Business & Professional Publishing, especially Craig Avery (senior developmental editor), Marge Bril (production editor), and Amy Wilson (technology project editor), as well as Crystal Bullen from DPS. We are grateful to Sharon Oblinger (executive editor) and Rob Dewey (publisher) for their support of this project. Special thanks also to our supportive wives and other family members, who provided special encouragement during the writing of this edition.

Thomas R. Weirich
Central Michigan University

Thomas C. Pearson
University of Hawaii

Alan Reinstein
Wayne State University

ABOUT THE AUTHORS

Thomas R. Weirich

Thomas R. Weirich, Ph.D., CPA, is currently Professor of Accounting at Central Michigan University and former chair of its School of Accounting. He earned a Doctorate in Accountancy from the University of Missouri–Columbia, as well as an M.B.A. and B.S. degrees from Northern Illinois University. Dr. Weirich has public accounting experience with both an international firm and a local firm. He has served as the Academic Fellow to the Office of Chief Accountant at the U.S. Securities and Exchange Commission and a sabbatical with Arthur Andersen, LLP, in their Business Fraud and Investigative Services Division. Dr. Weirich has also served as a consultant to the Public Oversight Board's Panel on Audit Effectiveness, and as an expert witness for the SEC and several other organizations.

Professor Weirich has written numerous articles in professional journals and assisted others, such as by serving on the Editorial Advisory board to the *Journal of Accountancy*. Professor Weirich has received many teaching and professional awards, including the College of Business Dean's Teaching Award, the Michigan Association of Governing Boards' Distinguished Faculty Award, the Michigan Association of CPAs Distinguished Achievement in Accounting Education Award, and Beta Alpha Psi's Outstanding Faculty Advisor Award. He has extensive committee experience including the American Accounting Association's Education Committee and the SEC Liaison Committee, the AICPA's SEC Regulation's Committee, the AIPCA's Ethics Subcommittee, and the AICPA's Board of Examiners' Content Committee and Auditing Subcommittee that aid in the development of the CPA examination. Dr. Weirich has also served as mayor of Mt. Pleasant, Michigan, and spent many years on its City Commission.

Thomas C. Pearson

Thomas C. Pearson, LL.M., J.D., CPA is a Professor of Accounting at the University of Hawaii at Manoa and former Director of its School of Accountancy. He earned his Masters of Letters of Law in tax from the University of Denver, Doctorate of Jurisprudence and M.B.A. from Vanderbilt University, and an A.B. from Dartmouth College. Professor Pearson has previously taught at the University of Wyoming and National Taiwan University. While on sabbatical, he is also affiliated with New York University. Professor Pearson has previously worked at Hospital Corporation of America.

Professor Pearson has published numerous articles, mostly in professional publications such as *Taxes* and the *Tax Advisor*. He has also published in leading academic publications such as *Accounting Horizons*, *Journal of Accounting Education*, and *Journal of the American Taxation Association*. Professor Pearson has received numerous teaching awards including the University of Hawaii's Board of Regents Teaching Excellence Award. He has served as President of the College of Business Faculty Senate and on numerous university committees. He has also served on Hawaii's Tax Review Commission and is involved in several professional organizations.

Alan Reinstein

Alan Reinstein, DBA, CPA, is the George R. Husband Professor of Accounting and former Chair of the Department of Accounting, School of Business Administration, at Wayne State University in Detroit, Michigan. He received his Doctorate in Accounting from the University of Kentucky, an M.B.A degree from the University of Detroit, and M.S. and B.A. degrees from the State University of New York (New Paltz). Professor Reinstein has conducted many seminars for the AICPA, several State Auditors Generals' Offices, state CPA societies, and other professional groups.

An author of many professional articles, Dr. Reinstein has served on the editorial boards of four major academic and professional journals and served as Editor of *Issues in Accounting Education*. Professor Reinstein has also held many board and committee chair positions, and other leadership roles in such professional and academic organizations as the Michigan Association of CPAs, Financial Executives International, Institute of Internal Auditors, and the American Accounting Association. He has also served as a Commercial Panel Member "Neutral" for the American Arbitration Association and to the Board of Arbitrators of the National Association of Securities Dealers (NASD).

Introduction to Professional Research

LEARNING OBJECTIVES

After completing this chapter, you should understand:

- The importance of research in the daily activities of the professional accountant.

- The definition and nature of professional accounting research.

- The U.S. Securities & Exchange Commission's view on the importance of research.

- The role of research within a public accounting firm or within an accounting department of a business or governmental entity.

- The basic steps of the research process.

- The importance of critical thinking and effective communication skills.

- The importance of research on the U.S. CPA exam.

The accounting profession, like other professions, is witnessing major changes due to changes in the law, new services, technologies, and an ever-increasing number of professional standards. In addition to accounting, auditing, and tax compliance services, accountants are involved in such services as attestation reviews, forensic accounting, fraud examinations, and tax planning. Today's professional accountant must possess the knowledge to remain current and the skills to critically analyze various problems. Additionally, the accounting professional must be able to listen effectively and understand opposing points of view, and then present and defend his or her own views through formal and informal presentations. Professional research and communication skills are essential in this environment.

Varying views and interpretations exist as to the meaning of the term **research**. In the accounting profession, *research* points to what the accounting practitioner does as a normal, everyday part of his or her job. In today's environment, to become proficient in accounting, auditing, and tax research one must also possess the skills to use various professional databases, which are increasingly available on the Web. Using professional databases for research is even required on the computerized CPA exam.

The professional accountant, whether in public accounting, industry, or government, frequently becomes involved with the investigation and analysis of an accounting, auditing, or tax issue. Resolving these issues requires a clear definition of the problem, using professional databases to search for the relevant authorities, reviewing the authoritative literature, evaluating alternatives, drawing conclusions, and communicating the results. This research process often requires an analysis of very complex and detailed issues. Therefore, researching such issues will challenge the **critical thinking** abilities of the professional. That is, the professional must possess the expertise to understand the relevant facts and render a professional judgment, even in some situations where no single definitive answer or solution exists. In such cases, the researcher would apply reasonable and reflective thinking in the development of an answer to the issue or problem at hand.

QUICK FACTS

Accounting Research is a combination of using accounting theory and existing authoritative accounting literature.

WHAT IS RESEARCH?

The objective of conducting any type of research, including professional accounting, auditing, and tax research, is a systematic investigation of an issue or problem utilizing the researcher's professional judgment.

Below are two examples of generalized research problems that can provide insight as to the types of research questions confronting the accounting practitioner:

1. A client is engaged in land sales, primarily commercial and agricultural. The company recently acquired a retail land sales project under an agreement stating that, if the company did not desire to pursue the project further, the property could be returned with no liability to the company.

    After the company invests a considerable amount of money into the project, the state of the economy concerning retail land sales declines and the company decides to return the land. As a result, the client turns to you, the CPA, and requests the proper accounting treatment of the returned project. At issue is whether the abandonment represents a disposal of a segment of the business, an unusual and nonrecurring extraordinary loss, or an ordinary loss. The client may also want to understand the tax consequences.

2. As controller for a construction contracting company you are faced with the following problem. The company pays for rights allowing it to extract a specified volume of landfill from a project for a specified period of time. How should the company classify the payments for such landfill rights in its financial statements?[1]

Research is often classified as either theoretical research or applied research. **Theoretical research** investigates questions that appear interesting to the researcher, generally an academician, but may have little or no practical application at the present time. In conducting theoretical research, one attempts to create new knowledge in a particular subject. Sometimes theoretical research uses empirical data based upon experimentation or observation. For example, a theoretical researcher may create a model predicting the change in an analyst's information in relation to a business's earnings announcement.[2] Thus, theoretical research adds to the body of knowledge in a particular field and may ultimately contribute directly or indirectly to practical problem solutions. Theoretical research using empirical research studies based on experimentation or observation are frequently reviewed and evaluated by standard-setting bodies in drafting authoritative accounting and auditing pronouncements.

Applied research, which is the focus of this text, investigates an issue of immediate practical importance. One type of applied research is known as *a priori* (before the fact) research. This research is conducted before the client actually enters into the transaction. For example, assume that a public accounting firm needs to evaluate a client's proposed new accounting treatment for environmental costs. The client expects an answer within two days as to the acceptability of the new method and its impact on the financial statements. In such a case, a member of the accounting firm's professional staff would investigate to determine if the authoritative literature addresses the issue. If no authoritative pronouncement exists, the accountant would develop a theoretical justification for, or against, the new method.

---

[1] *AICPA Technical Practice Aids*, Vol. 1, (Chicago: Commerce Clearing House, Inc.)

[2] Barron, Orie E., *et al.*, "Change in Analysts' Information around Earnings Announcements," *The Accounting Review*, Vol. 77, No. 4 (October 2002): 821–846.

Applied research relating to a completed event is known as *a posteriori* (after the fact) research. For example, a client may request assistance preparing his or her tax return for a transaction that was previously executed. Frequently, many advantages accrue to conducting a priori rather than a posteriori research. For example, if research reveals that a proposed transaction will have an unfavorable impact on financial statements, the client can abandon the transaction or possibly restructure it to avoid undesirable consequences. These options are not available, however, after a transaction is completed.

Society needs both theoretical and applied research. Both types of research require sound research design to resolve the issue under investigation effectively and efficiently. No matter how knowledgeable a professional becomes in any aspect of accounting, auditing, or tax, he or she will always have research challenges. However, using a systematic research approach will greatly help in resolving the problem.

RESEARCH QUESTIONS

Individual companies and CPA firms conduct research to resolve specific accounting, auditing, and tax issues relating to a company or client. The results of this research may lead to new firm policies or procedures in the application of existing authorities. In this research process, the practitioner (researcher) must answer the following basic questions:

1. Do I have complete knowledge to answer the question, or must I conduct research to consult authoritative references?

2. What is the law (tax law), or the authoritative literature?

3. Does the law or the authoritative literature address the issue under review?

4. Where can I find the law or authoritative literature and develop a conclusion effectively and efficiently?

5. If there exists more than one relevant authority, what is the hierarchy of authoritative support?

6. If there is no law or authoritative literature directly addressing the topic at issue, what approach do I follow in reaching a conclusion?

7. What professional databases or other sources on the Internet should I access for the research process?

8. If more than one alternative solution exists, what alternative do I select?

9. How do I document my findings or conclusions?

> **RESEARCH TIPS**
>
> Successful research requires answering various questions to find and apply relevant authorities.

The purpose of this text is to provide the understanding and the research skills needed to answer these questions. The "whats," "whys," and "hows" of practical professional accounting, auditing, and tax research are discussed with emphasis on the following topics:

• How do I research effectively?

• How do I apply a practical research methodology in a timely manner?

• What are the generally accepted accounting principles, auditing standards, and tax authorities?

• What constitutes substantial authoritative support?

• What are the available sources and hierarchy of authority for accounting, auditing, and tax?

- What databases are available for finding relevant authorities or assisting in researching a particular problem?

- What role does the Internet (the information superhighway) have in the modern research process?

This text presents a practical research approach along with discussions of various research tools and demonstrates this research approach through the use of a number of practice exercises presented throughout the chapters, as well as end-of-chapter questions and exercises. The text also addresses the importance of critical thinking and effective writing skills that the researcher should possess in executing the research process. Specific tips on these skills are presented in subsequent chapters.

NATURE OF PROFESSIONAL RESEARCH

This text focuses on applied research, known as professional accounting research. Today's practitioner must be able to conduct research effectively and efficiently to arrive at appropriate and timely conclusions regarding the issues at hand. Effectiveness is critical in order to determine the proper recording, classification, and disclosure of economic events; to determine compliance with authoritative pronouncements; or to determine the preferability of alternative procedures. Efficiency is needed to meet deadlines and manage research costs.

Additional examples of issues frequently encountered by the practitioner include such questions as

- What are the accounting, auditing, or tax implications of a new transaction?

- Does the accounting treatment of the transaction conform with generally accepted accounting principles? Does the tax treatment conform with the law?

- What are the disclosure requirements for the financial statements or tax returns?

- What is the auditor's responsibility when confronted with supplemental information presented in annual reports but not as part of the basic financial statements?

- What responsibilities and potential penalties exist for tax accountants?

- How does an accountant proceed in a fraud investigation?

Responding to these often complex questions has become more difficult and time consuming as the financial accounting and reporting requirements, auditing standards, and tax authorities increase in number and complexity. The research process often is complicated further when the accountant or auditor researches a practical issue for which no authoritative literature exists, or the authoritative literature does not directly address the question.

As a researcher, the practitioner should possess certain desired characteristics that aid in the research process. These characteristics include inquisitiveness, open-mindedness, thoroughness, patience, and perseverance.[3] Inquisitiveness is needed while gathering the relevant facts to obtain a clear picture of the research problem. Proper problem definition or issue identification is the most critical component in research. An improperly stated issue usually leads to the wrong conclusion, no matter how carefully the research process was executed. Likewise, the researcher should avoid drawing conclusions before the research process is completed. A preconceived solution can result in biased research in which the researcher merely seeks evidence to support a preconceived position, rather than search for the most appropriate solution. The researcher

---

[3] Wallace, Wanda, "A Profile of a Researcher," *Auditor's Report, American Accounting Association*, (Fall 1984): 1–3.

must carefully examine the facts, obtain and review authoritative literature, evaluate alternatives, and then draw conclusions based upon research evidence. The execution of an efficient research project requires thoroughness and patience. This is emphasized in both the planning stage, where all relevant facts are identified, and the research stage, where all extraneous information is controlled. Finally, the researcher must work persistently in order to finish the research on a timely basis.

Perhaps the most important characteristic of the research process is its ability to "add value" to the services provided. A good auditor not only renders an opinion on a client's financial statements, but also identifies available reporting alternatives that may benefit the client. A good tax accountant not only prepares the returns, but suggests tax planning for future transactions. The ability of a researcher to provide relevant information becomes more important as the competition among accounting firms for clients becomes more intense and the potential significance and enforcement of penalties more common. Researchers who identify reporting alternatives that provide benefits or avoid pitfalls will provide a strong competitive edge for their employers. Providing these tangible benefits to clients through careful and thorough research is essential in today's accounting environment.

CRITICAL THINKING AND EFFECTIVE COMMUNICATION

The researcher needs to know "how to think." That is, he or she should be able to identify the problem or issue, gather the relevant facts, analyze the issue(s), synthesize and evaluate alternatives, and then develop an appropriate solution. Such skills are essential for the professional accountant in providing services in today's complex, dynamic, and changing profession. In this environment, the professional accountant must possess not only the ability to think critically, which includes the ability to understand a variety of contexts and circumstances, but also be able to apply and adapt various accounting, auditing, tax, and business concepts and principles to these circumstances to develop the best solutions. The development and nurturing of **critical thinking** skills will also contribute to the process of life-long learning that is needed for today's professional.

Certain research efforts may culminate in memos or workpapers, letters to clients, journal articles, or company or firm reports. The dissemination of your research, in whatever form, will require you to possess **effective communication skills** for both oral presentations and written documents. Your research output must show coherence, conciseness, good use of standard English, and achievement of the purpose for the intended reader. Critical thinking and effective writing skills are the focus of Chapter 2.

RESEARCH TIPS

Successful research requires critical thinking and effective communication.

ECONOMIC CONSEQUENCES OF STANDARDS SETTING

Various accounting standards have produced far-reaching economic consequences. This was demonstrated by the Financial Accounting Standards Board (FASB) in addressing such issues as restructuring costs, financial instruments, stock options, and post-employment benefits. Various difficulties sometimes arise in the proper accounting for the economic substance of a transaction within the current accounting framework.

Since financial statements must conform to generally accepted accounting principles, the standard setting bodies, such as the FASB or the GASB (the Governmental Accounting Standards Board), will conduct research on the economic impact of a proposed standard. For example, the handling of off-balance sheet transactions has at times encouraged the selection of one business decision over another, producing results that may be less oriented to the users of financial statements.

In today's environment, the researcher conducting accounting and auditing research needs to be cognizant of the economic and social impact that various accepted accounting alternatives may have on society in general and the individual entity in particular. Such economic and social concerns are becoming a greater factor in the evaluation and issuance of new accounting standards, as discussed more thoroughly in Chapter 4.

ROLE OF RESEARCH IN THE ACCOUNTING FIRM

Although research is often conducted by accountants in education, industry, and government, accounting, auditing, and tax research is particularly important in the public accounting firm.

As a reflection of today's society, significant changes have occurred in the accounting environment. The practitioner today requires greater knowledge because of greater complexity in many business transactions and the proliferation of new authoritative pronouncements. As a result, practitioners should possess the ability to conduct efficient research. An accountant's responsibility to conduct accounting/auditing research is analogous to an attorney's responsibility to conduct legal research. Rule One of the Model Rules of Professional Conduct of the American Bar Association states:

> A lawyer should provide competent representation to a client. Competent representation requires the legal knowledge, skill, thoroughness, and preparation reasonably necessary for the representation.

In a California court decision, this rule was interpreted to mean that each lawyer must be able to research the law completely and is expected to know the legal principles "and to discover the rules which, although not commonly known, may readily be found by standard research techniques."[4]

In this case, the plaintiff recovered a judgment of $100,000 in a malpractice suit that was based upon the malpractice of the defendant lawyer in researching the applicable law.

The U.S. Securities and Exchange Commission (SEC) has also stressed the importance of effective accounting research through an enforcement action brought against an accountant. In *Accounting and Auditing Enforcement Release No. 420*, the SEC instituted a public administrative proceeding against a CPA. The Commission charged that the CPA failed to exercise due care in the conduct of an audit. The enforcement release specifically stated the following:

> In determining whether the [company] valued the lease properly, the [CPA] failed to consult pertinent provisions of GAAP or any other accounting authorities. This failure to conduct any research on the appropriate method of valuation constitutes a failure to act with due professional care. . . .

Thus, it is vital that the professional accountant possess the ability to find and locate applicable authoritative pronouncements and to ascertain their current status.

Due to the expanding complex environment and proliferation of pronouncements, certain accounting firms have created a research specialization within the firm. Common approaches used in practice include the following:

1. The staff at the local office conducts day-to-day research with industry-specific questions referred to industry specialists within the firm.

---

4 Smith and Lewis, 13 Cal. 3d 349, 530 P.2d 589, 118 Cal Reptr. 621 (1975).

2. Selected individuals in the local or regional office are designated as research specialists and all research questions within the office or region are brought to their attention for research.

3. The accounting firm establishes at the executive office of the firm a centralized research function that handles questions for the firm as a whole on technical issues.

4. Databases used by the firm provide consolidated expertise on how the firm has handled various issues.

The task of accurate and comprehensive research can be complex and challenging. However, one can meet the challenge by becoming familiar with a research process to solve the accounting, auditing, or tax issue.

A more in-depth look at a typical organizational structure for policy decision making and research on accounting and auditing matters within a multioffice firm that maintains a research department is depicted in Figure 1-1.

The responsibilities of a firm-wide accounting and auditing policy decision function include maintaining a high level of professional competence in accounting and auditing matters, developing and rendering high-level policies and procedures on accounting and auditing issues for the firm, disseminating the firm's policies and procedures to appropriate personnel within the firm on a timely basis, and supervising the quality control of the firm's practice. Research plays an important role in this decision-making process.

A CPA firm's Policy Committee and Executive Subcommittee, as shown in Figure 1-1, generally consist of highly competent partners with many years of practical experience. The Policy Committee's primary function is to evaluate significant accounting and auditing issues and establish firmwide policies on these issues. The Executive Subcommittee function is to handle the daily ongoing policy decisions (lower-level decisions) for the firm as a whole. The responsibility of the accounting and auditing research units is to interpret firm policies in the context of specific client situations. Frequently, technical accounting and auditing issues that arise during the course of a client engagement can be resolved through research conducted by personnel assigned

RESEARCH TIPS

At times, conducting research will require consulting with research specialists.

FIGURE 1-1 | ORGANIZATIONAL FRAMEWORK FOR POLICY DECISION MAKING AND RESEARCH WITHIN A TYPICAL MULTIOFFICE ACCOUNTING FIRM

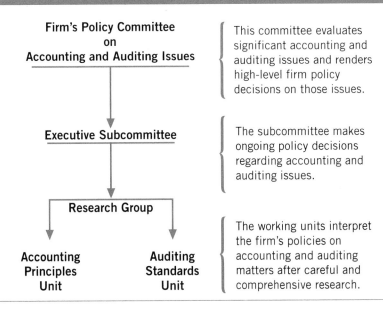

Firm's Policy Committee on Accounting and Auditing Issues
This committee evaluates significant accounting and auditing issues and renders high-level firm policy decisions on those issues.

Executive Subcommittee
The subcommittee makes ongoing policy decisions regarding accounting and auditing issues.

Research Group

Accounting Principles Unit   **Auditing Standards Unit**
The working units interpret the firm's policies on accounting and auditing matters after careful and comprehensive research.

to the engagement. When a local office cannot resolve a research matter satisfactorily, assistance is requested from the firm's research units. These units conduct careful and comprehensive research in arriving at the firm's response to technical inquiries. This response is then disseminated to the various offices of the firm for future reference in handling similar technical issues.

Practical accounting and auditing research is not confined to public accounting firms. All accountants should possess the ability to conduct effective research and develop logical and well-supported conclusions on a timely basis. The basic research process is similar, whether the researcher is engaged in public accounting, management accounting, governmental accounting, auditing, or even taxation.

RESEARCH AND THE CPA EXAM

In licensing a new CPA, state laws or regulations typically require a combination of education, examination, and experience. State legislatures, State Boards of Accountancy, the Public Company Accounting Oversight Board, and the American Institute of Certified Public Accountants (AICPA), have strived to assure the professional competencies of CPAs. The important role that a CPA plays in society is so significant that the AICPA's Board of Examiners have identified certain skills that are necessary for the beginning CPA to possess in order to protect the public interest. These skills and their definition are as follows:

- **Analysis**—the ability to organize, process, and interpret data to develop options for decision making.

- **Judgment**—the ability to evaluate options for decision making and provide an appropriate conclusion.

- **Communication**—the ability to effectively elicit and/or express information through written or oral means.

- **Research**—the ability to locate and extract relevant information from available resource materials.

- **Understanding**—the ability to recognize and comprehend the meaning and application of a particular matter.

For the CPA exam, not only are CPA candidates required to demonstrate their research ability, but also to demonstrate understanding, analysis, and judgment through questions that will require the candidate to

- Interpret and apply the relevant professional literature to specific fact patterns in various cases.

- Identify relevant information and draw appropriate conclusions from searching the professional literature.

- Recognize business-related issues as one evaluates an entity's financial condition.

- Identify, evaluate, analyze and process an entity's accounting and reporting information.

On the computer-based CPA examination, candidates must demonstrate their research abilities by accessing various professional databases and searching through the legal or professional literature in order to identify the relevant authorities and draw conclusions related to the issues at hand. A candidate's research skills are tested by completing various simulations or "case studies" as part of the exam. The appendix to Chapter 1 provides an overview of the basic format of the CPA exam's simulations. Examples of simulations are presented throughout subsequent chapters. This text will help you develop the necessary skills to utilize these databases for the computerized CPA exam and also help you develop and refine the necessary skill sets and competencies necessary for your professional career. The following chapters will further focus on these skills, with particular emphasis on research skills.

OVERVIEW OF THE RESEARCH PROCESS

The research process in general is often defined as a scientific method of inquiry, a systematic study of a particular field of knowledge in order to discover scientific facts or principles. An operational definition of research encompasses the following process:[5]

RESEARCH TIPS

Carefully conduct
each step in the
research process.

1. Investigate and analyze a clearly defined issue or problem.

2. Use an appropriate scientific approach.

3. Gather and document adequate and representative evidence.

4. Employ logical reasoning in drawing conclusions.

5. Support the validity or reasonableness of the conclusions.

With this general understanding of the research process, practical accounting, auditing, and tax research may be defined as follows:

> *Accounting, auditing, or tax research*—A systematic and logical approach employing critical thinking skills to obtain and document evidence (authorities) underlying a conclusion relating to an accounting, auditing, or tax issue or problem.

The basic steps in the research process are illustrated in Figure 1-2, with an overview presented in the following sections. As indicated in the illustration, carefully document each step of the research process. When executing each step, the researcher may also find it necessary to refine the work done in previous steps. The refinement of the research process is discussed more fully in Chapter 9.

Step 1—Identify the Relevant Facts and Issues

The researcher's first task is to gather the facts surrounding the particular problem. However, problem-solving research cannot begin until the researcher clearly and concisely defines the problem. One needs to know the "why" and "what" about the issue in order to begin the research process. Unless the researcher knows why the issue was brought to his or her attention, he or she might have difficulty knowing what to research. The novice researcher may find it difficult to distinguish between relevant and irrelevant information. When this happens, it is advisable to err on the side of gathering too many facts rather than too few. As the researcher becomes more knowledgeable, the researcher will become more skilled at quickly isolating the relevant facts.

QUICK FACTS
The research process
is appropriate to
any type of
accounting or tax
issue confronted.

In most cases, the basic issue is identified before the research process begins; e.g., when a client requests advice as to the proper handling of a specific transaction. However, further refinement of the exact issue is often required. This process of refining the issue at hand is referred to as **problem distillation,** whereby a general issue is restated in sufficiently specific terms. If the statement of the issue is too broad or general, the researcher is apt to waste valuable time consulting sources irrelevant to the specific issue.

Factors to consider in the identification and statement of the issue include the exact source of the issue, justification for the issue, and a determination of the scope of the issue. To successfully design and execute an investigation, state the critical issue clearly

---

[5] Luck, David J., Hugh C. Wales, and Donald A. Taylor. *Marketing Research* (Englewood Cliffs: Prentice Hall, Inc., 1961), 5.

FIGURE 1-2 | THE RESEARCH PROCESS

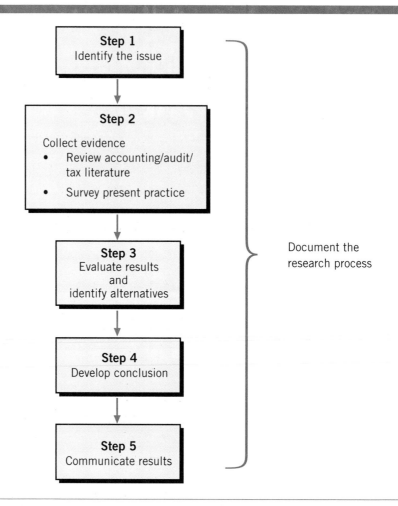

and precisely. As explained in Chapters 5 and 6, many research tools, especially computerized databases, are indexed by a set of descriptive words. Since keywords aid in reference identification, failure to describe the facts (the key words) in sufficient detail can cause a researcher to overlook important sources. Undoubtedly, writing a clear, concise statement of the problem is the most important task in research. Failure to frame all the facts can, and often will, lead to an erroneous conclusion.

Step 2—Collect the Evidence

As previously stated, problem-solving research cannot begin until the researcher defines the problem. Once the issue is adequately defined, the researcher is ready to proceed with step two of the research process, the collection of evidence. This step usually encompasses a detailed review of relevant authoritative accounting or auditing literature and a survey of present practice. In collecting evidence, the researcher should be familiar with the various sources available, and know which ones to use, which ones not to use, and the order in which to examine them.

This early identification of the relevant sources will aid in the efficient conduct of the research. A number of research tools, including electronic databases and the Internet, that will aid in the collection of evidence are available and are discussed in detail in Chapters 3 through 8. In cases where authoritative literature does not exist on a specific issue, the practitioner should develop a theoretical resolution of the issue based upon a logical analysis of the factors involved. In addition, the researcher needs to evaluate the economic consequences of the various alternatives in the development of a conclusion. Note that, in practice, a solution is not often readily apparent. Professional judgment and theoretical analysis are key elements in the research process.

Step 3—Analyze the Results and Identify the Alternatives

Once a practitioner has completed a thorough investigation of the facts and collection of evidence, the next step is to evaluate the results and identify alternatives for one or more tentative conclusions to the issue. Fully support each alternative by authoritative literature or a theoretical justification with complete and concise documentation. One cannot expect to draw sound conclusions from faulty information. Soundly documented conclusions are possible only when the information has been properly collected, organized, and interpreted.

Further analysis and research may be needed as to the appropriateness of the various alternatives identified. This reevaluation may require further discussions with the client or consultations with colleagues. In discussing an issue with a client, the researcher should recognize that management may not always be objective in evaluating alternatives. For example, the issue may involve the acceptability of an accounting method that is currently being used by the client. In such cases, the research is directed toward the support or rejection of an alternative already decided on by management. The possibility of bias should cause the researcher to retain a degree of skepticism in discussions with the client regarding a conclusion.

Step 4—Develop a Conclusion

After a detailed analysis of the alternatives, including economic consequences, the researcher develops a conclusion and thoroughly documents the final conclusion selected from the alternatives identified. The conclusions should be well supported by the evidence gathered. The conclusion and details of the proposed solution are then presented to the client.

Step 5—Communicate the Results

The most important point in the communication is the conclusion reached. The communication often takes the form of a research memorandum, requiring an objective and unbiased analysis and report. The memorandum should contain a statement of facts, a clear and precise statement of the issue, a brief and straightforward conclusion, discussion of the authoritative literature and explanation as to how it applies to the set of facts. The written communication should follow the conventional rules of grammar, spelling, and punctuation. Nothing diminishes credibility faster than misspellings, incorrect grammar, or misuse of words.

In drafting the memo, avoid making common errors such as (1) excessive discussion of the issue and facts, which indicates that the memo has not been drafted with sufficient precision; (2) excessive citations to authoritative sources—cite only the relevant authorities for the conclusion reached; and (3) appearing to avoid a conclusion by pleading the need for additional facts. Novice researchers too often include irrelevant research information. This distracts from the current solution to the problem.

A serious weakness in any part of the research process undermines the entire research effort. Therefore, address each segment of the process with equal seriousness as to its impact on the entire research project.

RESEARCH TIPS

After analyzing the results, develop a conclusion and communicate the results.

SUMMARY

The research work of a practicing professional accountant is very important. Few practitioners ever experience a work week that does not include the investigation and analysis of an accounting, auditing, or tax issue. Thus, every professional accountant should possess the ability to conduct practical research in a systematic way. The goal of this text is to aid the practitioner in developing a basic framework, or methodology, to assist in the research process.

The emphasis of the following chapters is on practical applied research that deals with solutions to immediate issues rather than theoretical research that has little or no present-day application. **Chapter 2** presents an overview of the importance of critical thinking and effective writing skills that every researcher (accountant/auditor/tax professional) must possess to be effective. **Chapter 3** presents how the practitioner can use the Internet for research. **Chapters 4** and **8** provide an overview of the environment of accounting and auditing/attestation research, with an emphasis on the standard-setting process. The hierarchy of the authoritative literature that applies in the research process is also presented. **Chapter 5** presents a discussion of the sources of authoritative literature as well as an explanation of access techniques to the professional literature. **Chapter 6** discusses other available research tools that may aid in the effective and efficient conduct of practical research, with an emphasis on computerized research via various databases that exist. **Chapter 7** provides the basic steps of tax research and valuable databases and web sites. This chapter highlights the RIA tax database, part of which is also utilized on the CPA exam. **Chapter 9** concludes with a refinement of the research process by presenting specific annotated procedures for conducting and documenting the research process via a comprehensive problem.

Chapter 10 will provide an overview of fraud and insights into the basic techniques of fraud investigation, particularly as more practitioners are entering the specialized field of forensic accounting.

DISCUSSION QUESTIONS

1. Define the term *research*.
2. Explain what accounting, auditing, and tax research are.
3. Why are accounting, auditing, and tax research necessary?
4. What is the objective of accounting, auditing, and tax research?
5. What role does professional research play within an accounting firm or department? Who primarily conducts the research?
6. What are the functions or responsibilities of the Policy Committee and Executive Subcommittee within a multioffice firm?
7. Identify and explain some basic questions the researcher must address in performing accounting, auditing, or tax research.
8. Differentiate between *theoretical* and *applied* research.
9. Identify the characteristics that an accounting practitioner should possess.
10. Distinguish between *a priori* and *a posteriori* research. Which research is used more for planning work?
11. Explain the analogy of the California court decision dealing with legal research as it relates to the accounting practitioner.

12. Explain how the research process adds value to the services offered by an accounting firm.

13. What consequences are considered in the standards-setting process?

14. Explain the importance of identifying keywords when identifying relevant facts and issues.

15. Explain the five basic steps involved in the research process.

16. Discuss how research can support or refute a biased alternative.

17. Explain what is meant by problem distillation and its importance in the research process.

18. What skills are important and tested on the CPA exam?

19. Your conclusion to the research will often be presented to your boss or client in the form of a research memorandum. Identify the basic points that should be contained in this memo. Also, identify some common errors to avoid in the drafting of the memo.

20. Explain the necessity of critical thinking in the research process.

21. Why did the SEC bring an enforcement action against a CPA concerning research?

APPENDIX

Research Focus on the CPA Exam

A component of the computerized CPA exam is referred to as simulations. The AICPA defines a simulation as "An assessment of knowledge and skills in context approximating that found on the job through the use of realistic scenarios and tasks, and access to normally available and familiar resources." In other words, simulations are condensed case studies that utilize real life work-related examples. These case studies require the use of tools (computerized databases) and skills that accountants use in the real world. These primary computerized databases are similar in functionality to the AICPA's Professional Standards (Auditing and Attestation literature), the FASB's FARS (Financial Accounting Research System) database, and Thomson's RIA Checkpoint® tax database.

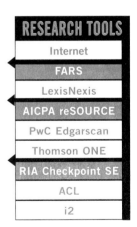

RESEARCH TOOLS

Internet

FARS

LexisNexis

AICPA reSOURCE

PwC Edgarscan

Thomson ONE

RIA Checkpoint SE

ACL

i2

To successfully complete a simulation, the CPA candidate is expected to possess basic computer skills that include the use of spreadsheets and word processing functions. As to the research component of the simulation, the candidate will be required to search various authoritative literature databases in order to answer accounting, auditing, and tax questions to support his or her judgments and also to prepare formal communications.

A typical view of a simulation is presented in Figure A1-1. The tabs across the top of the screen can vary depending on whether the simulation relates to an accounting, auditing, or tax issue. (This figure is for an accounting simulation.) Figure 1 discusses only the main tabs that are common to all three types of simulations. Each simulation will begin with the candidate clicking on the "Directions" tab and then clicking on the "Situations" tab, which presents the case scenario. The "Research" tab, the focus of this text, is where the candidate will be required to search through various authoritative databases.

What the Tabs Mean

As the CPA candidate clicks on the Research tab, the appropriate research questions will be presented. These questions will require an online keyword search of three databases—Accounting Standards, Auditing Standards, or the Tax Code. Clicking on the "Standards" or "Code" icon will open up the authoritative literature for conducting the research. Figure A1-2 illustrates the two opening screens after clicking on the "Standards" icon in Figure A1-1 for accounting standards.

FIGURE A1-1 | VIEW OF FINANCIAL ACCOUNTING AND REPORTING SIMULATION

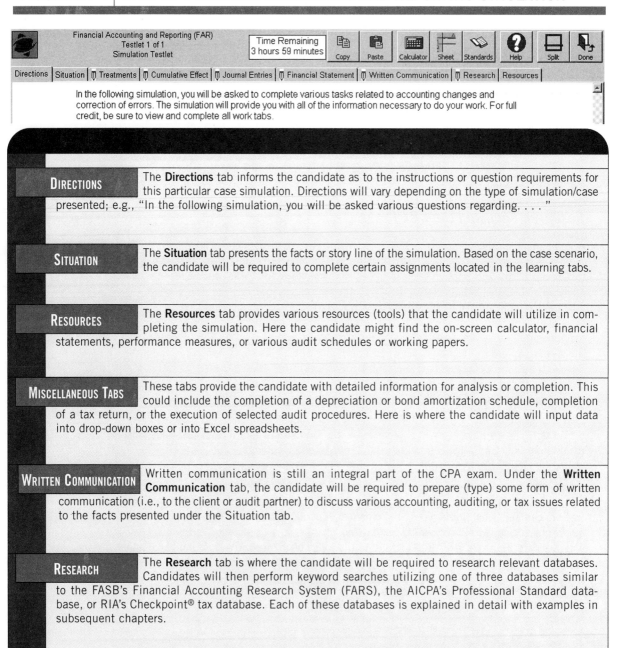

DIRECTIONS — The **Directions** tab informs the candidate as to the instructions or question requirements for this particular case simulation. Directions will vary depending on the type of simulation/case presented; e.g., "In the following simulation, you will be asked various questions regarding. . . . "

SITUATION — The **Situation** tab presents the facts or story line of the simulation. Based on the case scenario, the candidate will be required to complete certain assignments located in the learning tabs.

RESOURCES — The **Resources** tab provides various resources (tools) that the candidate will utilize in completing the simulation. Here the candidate might find the on-screen calculator, financial statements, performance measures, or various audit schedules or working papers.

MISCELLANEOUS TABS — These tabs provide the candidate with detailed information for analysis or completion. This could include the completion of a depreciation or bond amortization schedule, completion of a tax return, or the execution of selected audit procedures. Here is where the candidate will input data into drop-down boxes or into Excel spreadsheets.

WRITTEN COMMUNICATION — Written communication is still an integral part of the CPA exam. Under the **Written Communication** tab, the candidate will be required to prepare (type) some form of written communication (i.e., to the client or audit partner) to discuss various accounting, auditing, or tax issues related to the facts presented under the Situation tab.

RESEARCH — The **Research** tab is where the candidate will be required to research relevant databases. Candidates will then perform keyword searches utilizing one of three databases similar to the FASB's Financial Accounting Research System (FARS), the AICPA's Professional Standard database, or RIA's Checkpoint® tax database. Each of these databases is explained in detail with examples in subsequent chapters.

FIGURE A1-2 | OPENING SCREEN SHOTS OF THE FASB LITERATURE DATABASE

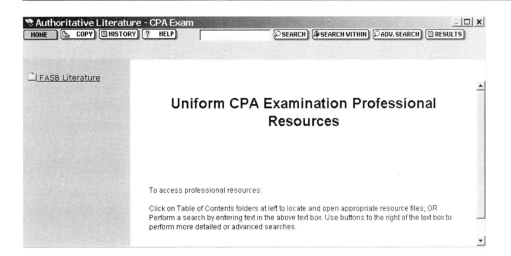

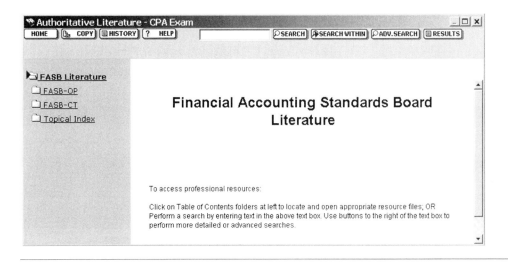

Figures A1-3 and A1-4 illustrate the opening screen shots for the auditing and tax (regulations) simulations followed by the first two screen shots of the auditing standards and tax code databases. Each of these databases is explained in detail, with examples, in Chapters 5, 7, and 8 of this text.

FIGURE A1-3 | VIEW OF AN AUDITING AND ATTESTATION SIMULATION

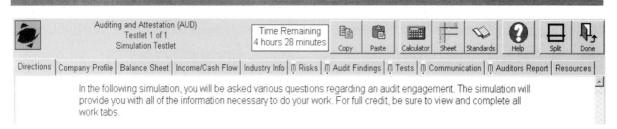

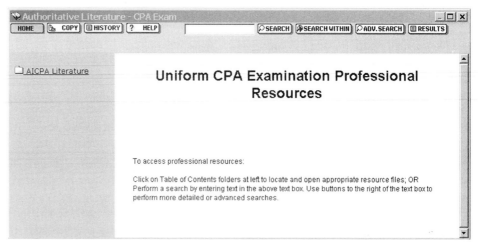

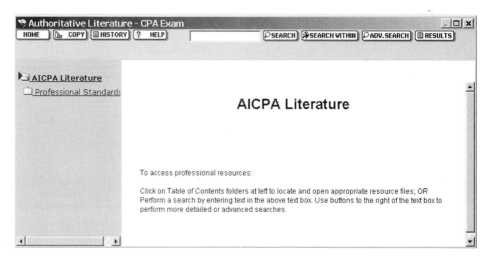

FIGURE A1-4 | VIEW OF A TAX AND REGULATION SIMULATION

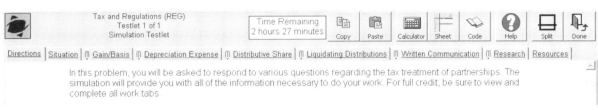

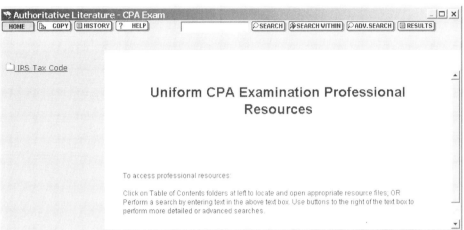

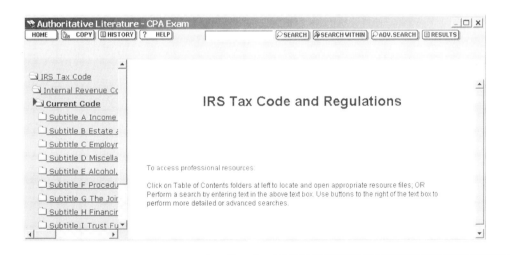

Critical Thinking and Effective Writing Skills for the Professional Accountant

LEARNING OBJECTIVES

After completing this chapter, you should understand:

- Critical thinking skills.

- Levels of thinking.

- How critical thinking skills can help professional accountants "add value" to their services.

- How competent writing forms a key element of critical thinking skills.

- How to strengthen and improve your writing skills.

- A primer on proper punctuation.

- The U.S. Securities and Exchange Commission's "Plain English" initiative.

- How to write effective client letters and e-mails.

- How to write memos to the file.

Change is accelerating in today's environment and the pressure to respond is intensifying. As new technology, new laws, regulatory changes, and global realities work their ways through the accounting profession, these changes and realities are becoming increasingly complex. Critical thinking is necessary for effectively addressing these dynamic changes and is considered an important component of accounting education. All professionals must also know how to write effectively.

Clients now expect professional accountants to "add value" to what they observe, read, and write. Accountants must evaluate complex systems and information, as well as detect, predict, advise, and recommend appropriate courses of action. Critical thinking is the initial step in this process. Effective writing communicates the results to others.

CRITICAL THINKING SKILLS

Today's professional accountants must respond to the progressive diversity and complexity of accounting, auditing, and tax practice and develop life-long learning skills that focus on their ability to think critically. Critical thinking skills are essential to understanding, applying, and adapting concepts and principles in a variety of contexts and circumstances. The accountant's professional skepticism, that of questioning management's responses, involves critical thinking that entails an attitude of examining and recognizing emotion-laden and explicit and hidden assumptions "behind" each question. Accountants must master critical thinking skills particularly because business organizations continue to evolve in response to new information technology and greater worldwide competition.

Descriptions of critical thinking are summarized as follows:

1. Critical thinking is difficult because it is often complex.

2. Critical thinking applies multiple criteria.

3. Critical thinking requires an ability to tolerate ambiguity and uncertainty.

4. Critical thinking involves self-regulation of the thinking process.

5. Critical thinking may impose meaning and find structure in apparent disorder.

6. Critical thinking requires effort. It entails intense elaboration and careful judgment.

7. Critical thinking often yields multiple solutions and requires cost and benefit analysis.

8. Critical thinking involves making interpretations.[1]

RESEARCH TIPS

Use critical thinking to assess issues, problems, data, and other concerns.

Nothing is more important and practical to the accounting practitioner than developing critical thinking skills. Poor thinking will inevitably cause problems, waste time, and ensure frustration. As you become more proficient in critical thinking, you also become more proficient in assessing issues and objectives, problems and solutions, information and data, assumptions and interpretations, different points of view, and frames of reference.

Critical thinking has many definitions. The *American Heritage Dictionary* defines **critical** as "characterized by careful and exact evaluation and judgment." "Critical thinking" points to a positive ability in those who possess it. Critical thinking focuses on problem definition and problem solving; it is a rational response to questions that may lack definite answers or may be missing some relevant information. Its purpose is to explore situations to arrive at justifiable conclusions and optimal solutions. Critical thinking rests on a willingness to take nothing for granted and to approach each experience as if it were unique. Although the purpose of critical thinking is to understand, its goal usually leads to evaluation and, therefore, to judgment. Simply stated, critical thinking is the art of using your best thinking given your knowledge and skills.

Critical thinking is purposeful, goal-oriented, and creative. Critical thinking is an active process involving rethinking the problem, and refusing to merely consider the most obvious or easiest solutions. The qualities that lie behind rethinking are these:

• A willingness to say "I don't know."

• An openness to alternative ways of seeing and doing—alternatives that are based on understanding how things work.

• An interest in the ideas of others shown by paying attention to them—even when others don't agree with your ideas.

• Thoughtfulness that is shown by genuine curiosity, not just idle curiosity.

• A desire to discover what other people have done and thought.

• An insistence on getting the best evidence before making up your mind.

• An openness to your own intuition.[2]

Critical thinking is a process of understanding how thinking and learning work, using *higher order* skills for comprehending issues, analyzing, synthesizing, and assessing those ideas logically. Critical thinking uses higher order reasoning skills, including:

1. **Analysis** of a problem, or breaking ideas into their component parts to consider each of them separately.

2. **Synthesis,** or the connection among different components or ideas in order to derive relationships that tie the parts of an answer together.

---

[1] Resnick, Lauren B., *Education and Learning to Think* (Washington, D.C.: National Academy Press, 1987).

[2] Boostrom, Robert, *Developing Creative and Critical Thinking: An Integrated Approach* (Chicago: National Textbook Co., 1992), 24–25.

3. **Critical assessment** of the conclusions reached, requiring an examination of the conclusions for sound logical reasoning. Accountants must master critical thinking skills in order to engage effectively in the process of research and problem solving.

The ability to reason critically is an essential, fundamental skill that enables one to acquire more knowledge. To summarize, critical thinking includes:

1. Recognizing any explanatory relationship among statements.

2. Recognizing the structure of arguments (the premises, implicit assumptions, and conclusions).

3. Assessing consistency or inconsistency, equivalence among statements, and logical implications.

4. Formulating and identifying deductively and inductively, justified conclusions based on the available evidence.

LEVELS OF THINKING

The difficulty in discussing critical thinking concisely arises from two characteristics of critical thinking itself:

> First, clear thinking results less from practicing skills than from adopting such attitudes as persistence, open-mindedness, thoroughness, and flexibility. . . . Second, thinking is not a single process that can be divided into a series of steps. Instead, it is a family of processes that enlighten and support each other.[3]

The noted nineteenth-century writer Oliver Wendell Holmes characterized people as to their thinking skills. The lowest-level thinkers were fact collectors with no aims beyond the facts; the next level thinkers were able to compare, reason, and generalize using the results of the fact collectors' work; and the highest level thinkers could idealize, imagine, and predict.

One current classification of thought by the Illinois Renewal Institute distinguishes recall, process, and application. The lowest-level thought is **recall**, in which one defines, describes, lists, recites, and selects. The second level of thought is **process**, in which one compares, contrasts, classifies, sorts, distinguishes, explains, infers, sequences, analyzes, synthesizes, and analogizes. The highest level of thought is **application**, in which one evaluates, generalizes, imagines, judges, predicts, speculates, hypothesizes, and forecasts.

Probably the most famous classification of thought is presented in Figure 2-1 using Harold Bloom's taxonomy. Bloom's six-level taxonomy proceeds from knowledge, comprehension, application, analysis, and synthesis to evaluation. Bloom hypothesized that higher-order knowledge occurs when using the higher-level skills (often called critical thinking skills). Practitioners can use higher-level application skills to complement lower-level recall skills by both focusing on "what" successful accountants do to "add value" to their organizations and by always questioning assumptions.

Bloom's taxonomy implies that the levels of thinking are incremental: One must be able to perform at level four, for example, before moving up to level five. (The ideal reader, writer, accountant, or auditor moves up the levels until he or she can perform at the top level.) To exercise the highest level six skills, one must already possess the skills at the other levels. To be able to *infer* properly, for example, one must often first define and describe accurately the objects or situations from which one will infer. The skills

---

[3] *Ibid.*, Teacher's Manual, 1.

FIGURE 2-1 | EXAMPLES OF APPLYING AND UNDERSTANDING BLOOM'S TAXONOMY

Level No.	Major Categories in Bloom's Taxonomy	Illustrative General Instructional Objectives	Illustrative Behavioral Terms for Stating Specific Learned Outcomes
1.	**Knowledge** represents recalling previously learned materials.	Knows common terms, specific facts, basic concepts, and principles.	Defines, describes, labels, lists, reproduces, selects, and states.
2.	**Comprehension** involves "grasping" the material, including translating words into numbers, summarizing or interpreting the materials, and estimating future trends.	Understands facts and principles; translates verbal materials into mathematical formulas; estimates future consequences implied in the data; and justifies methods and procedures.	Converts, defends, distinguishes, estimates, extends, explains, predicts, rewrites, and summarizes.
3.	**Application** of the use of previously learned materials into new situations.	(Correctly) applies laws and theories into new and practical situations.	Changes, computes, demonstrates, discovers, manipulates, modifies, shows, solves, and uses.
4.	**Analysis** breaks down the material into its component parts to understand better its organizational structure.	Recognizes unstated assumptions and logical gaps in reasoning; distinguishes between facts and inferences; and evaluates the relevancy of data.	Breaks down, diagrams, differentiates, discriminates, distinguishes, infers, outlines, selects, relates, separates, and subdivides.
5.	**Synthesis** puts parts together to form a new whole, usually involving creative behaviors and new patterns or structures (e.g., developing a new schema for classifying information).	Writes a well-organized research paper; gives a well-organized speech; integrates learning from different areas into a new plan to solve a problem; and formulates a new schema to classify objects or events.	Categorizes, combines, compiles, composes, creates, devises, assigns, explains, generates, recognizes, plans, revises, reorganizes, rewrites, tells, or writes.
6.	**Evaluation** judges the value of the statement (based upon definite criteria) for a given purpose. The criteria can be internal (organization) or external (relevant to the given purpose).	Judges the logical consistency of the presented material, how well the data "support" the "conclusions" and how well the end product adheres to the internal. and external criteria.	Appraises, compares, concludes, criticizes, contrasts, explains, justifies, interprets, relates, summarizes, and supports.

increase in complexity as the level rises. To analyze a situation, for example, is a far more complicated process than simply to recall a situation, while to evaluate a situation (using definite criteria and for a given purpose) is more complicated than either of the others. The basic differences between the levels are largely a matter of attitude, not procedure. That is, the ability to progress up through the levels partly depends on one's ability to internalize the qualities noted on page 20.

Bloom's framework of thought has had a practical impact on accountants. It has influenced many professional accounting examinations to modify their exam questions and format in order to test higher-level critical thinking skills of candidates (levels four, five, six). For example, the Uniform CPA Exam, now completely computerized, emphasizes more heavily the critical thinking and research skills that accountants need in the workplace.

Critical thinking also depends on the ability to make certain specific decisions, such as:

1. Deciding on the meaning (and intent) of a statement.

2. Deciding whether a definition is adequate.

3. Deciding whether an observation statement is reliable.

4. Deciding whether a statement is an assumption.

5. Deciding whether a statement made by an alleged authority is acceptable.

6. Deciding whether a conclusion follows necessarily from the underlying data.

7. Deciding whether an inductive conclusion is warranted.

In critical thinking "you decide first what the words mean, then whether they make sense, and finally whether you believe them."[4] Figure 2-2 provides a simplified example that helps to reinforce the critical thinking process.

UNIVERSAL ELEMENTS OF REASONING

It is helpful for the professional accountant/researcher to concentrate on the universal elements of reasoning when using critical thinking to reason out a solution to a problem. The eight elements of purpose, issue, information, concepts, assumptions, interpretation, implications, and conclusions provide a central focus in critical thinking.[5] Whenever we think, we should use these eight elements of analysis as depicted in Figure 2-3.

RESEARCH TIPS

As you analyze a problem, you need to proceed through the eight elements of reasoning.

AN EXAMPLE OF USING CRITICAL THINKING SKILLS

Using critical thinking skills in a business organization is illustrated in Goldratt and Cox's[6] best selling business book, *The Goal*. This book describes a company that has "floundered" because it conducted its business under certain constant, time honored assumptions, such as:

1. Keep all employees busy all of the time.

2. Order materials in the largest quantities possible to receive the lowest price.

3. Keep the manufacturing robots working all the time (to minimize downtime).

4. Measure the "cost" of an idle machine as its depreciation expense.

5. Allow management to change the priority of jobs in process to meet customer needs.

Goldratt demonstrates that the company could operate much more profitably by challenging these assumptions (i.e., by using higher-order critical thinking skills), thereby

---

[4] Boostrom, *op. cit.,* 198.

[5] Paul, Richard, *Critical Thinking: Basic Theory & Instructional Structures,* Foundation for Critical Thinking, 1998.

[6] Goldratt, E.M. and J. Cox, *The Goal* (New Haven, Conn.: North River Press, 1992).

FIGURE 2-2 | CRITICAL THINKING ACCOUNTING EXAMPLE

Purpose: To prepare a report based upon your research to answer the following client request.

Issue/Question: A major client, who maintains homes in both New York and Florida and uses both frequently throughout the year, asks you, from an economic standpoint, which state would be the best for her to establish residency in.

Answering this question quickly, intelligently, and accurately requires critical thinking to identify all the relevant factors regarding this decision and to develop proper conclusions, including focusing on such issues as (a) income tax rates of both states, (b) state sales tax rules and rates (e.g., buying and using such "discretionary" assets as a new car), (c) property taxes (e.g., buying or selling a home), unemployment/welfare taxes, municipal taxes, inheritance taxes (e.g., considering the client's age), and (d) costs of other essentials (e.g., food, clothing, and shelter).

After identifying the relevant factors, you should focus this analysis by asking specific questions to narrow the scope of this decision to such relevant issues as:

1. Does the client anticipate selling one of the homes? If so, which one?
2. Where will the client purchase and use her assets (e.g., the new car)?

The answers to these and other similar questions will affect how you proceed with this analysis, while fully considering all of the relevant factors. Considering relevant issues and eliminating irrelevant ones forms the crux of critical thinking.

This example can also help you better understand such critical thinking skills. For example, the researcher must analyze, synthesize, and critically assess the relevant factors. This process requires using the available evidence effectively. Specifically, the accountant should ascertain that the evidence is

1. **Sufficient.** Does the accountant have adequate evidence to reach a proper conclusion or should he or she ask further questions (e.g., are state inheritance tax rates under review by the respective state legislatures)?
2. **Representative.** Is the evidence provided objective (e.g., will the client actually spend the requisite days in Florida to be considered a legal resident of that state)?
3. **Relevant.** Does the evidence relate directly to the provided assertion (e.g., will the client's plans to spend much time visiting her grandchildren in California impact her legal residence status)?
4. **Accurate.** Does the evidence come from reliable primary or secondary sources (e.g., can CPA firm employees observe the times spent in Florida or New York)?

Thus, the ability to reason critically is essential to the acquisition of knowledge in any discipline and may, therefore, be appropriately regarded as a fundamental skill, one that new accountants should acquire as soon as possible. Critical thinking includes:

1. Formulating and identifying deductively and inductively warranted conclusions from available evidence.
2. Recognizing the structure of arguments (premises, conclusions and implicit assumptions).
3. Assessing the consistency, inconsistency, logical implications, and equivalence among statements.
4. Recognizing explanatory relations among statements.

FIGURE 2-3 | EIGHT ELEMENTS OF REASONING

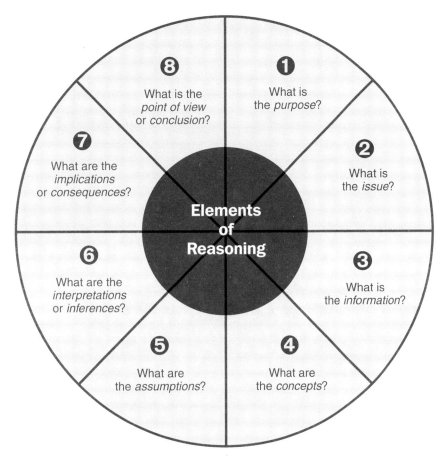

1. **Purpose.** You reason things out in order to meet some specific end, goal, or objective. If the purpose or goal is unclear or unrealistic, various problems can occur as you proceed. As an accountant/researcher, your primary goal or purpose is to complete accounting/auditing research in order to develop an answer to a particular practical issue/problem. You should select clear and realistic purposes and evaluate your reasoning periodically to make sure you still are on target with your stated purpose.

2. **Issue.** The second element is to reason out a question or issue. This requires the formulation of the issue in a clear and relevant way. Because accounting/auditing authoritative literature is organized on keywords or concepts, clearly identifying the issue will greatly aid you in researching it.

3. **Information.** Data or information exists concerning the issue about which you are reasoning. Any defect in the data or information is a possible source of problems in conducting research. As an accounting practitioner, you will use client-provided data and both authoritative and nonauthoritative sources in reasoning out a solution. Therefore, you need to be mindful that the data or information may contain defects or contradictions, especially in the client data or nonauthoritative sources.

4. **Concepts.** Reasoning uses concepts that include theories, principles, or rules. A basic understanding of the concepts is important as you reason out an accounting/auditing issue.

5. **Assumptions.** All reasoning begins somewhere. Incorrect assumptions in your reasoning can be a source of problems and can bias your research. You must determine that your assumptions are justifiable and how they will shape your point of view in conducting research.

6. **Interpretation.** The sixth element of reasoning requires that what you infer from your research is based upon the evidence gathered. All reasoning requires some type of interpretation of the data in order to draw conclusions from the research process.

7. **Implications.** As you conclude the research process and begin to develop conclusions, you need to consider the various implications or consequences that arise from your reasoning. Consider both negative and positive implications as you develop your conclusions.

8. **Conclusion.** The final element of reasoning is the conclusion to the research question or issue. As you develop the conclusion, be careful to have the proper point of view—one that is not too narrow or broad, or based on misleading information or contradictions.

FIGURE 2-4 | BASIC CRITICAL THINKING SKILLS

Skill	Description
Value Added Services	Advise, predict, detect, recommend, and evaluate.
Wariness	Take nothing for granted. Approach each experience as a "unique" event.
Rethinking	Do not perform tasks in an obvious and routine manner. Use innovative, alternative ways to perform the necessary jobs. Insist on obtaining the "best" available evidence, considering the related costs.
Evaluation and Judgment	Use definitive criteria to obtain the goal of the assignment, and then apply reasonable judgment after this evaluation.
Incremental Levels of Thinking	Apply lower levels of thinking before progressing to higher ones.

RESEARCH TIPS

Use careful analytical reasoning (critical thinking skills) for effective research.

yielding dramatically improved results. He showed that adhering to these "old" policies made the company more inefficient. Some "new" results included:

1. Because busy employees produce unneeded inventory, thus wasting large resources, have certain production employees perform quality control and preventive maintenance, rather than produce nonessential parts.

2. Because ordering large amounts of materials increases unnecessary inventory, order smaller quantities of parts inventory.

3. Because robots, like employees, only increase unneeded inventory, consider the cost of the inventory they produce in deciding whether to allow the robots to work.

4. Because "bottlenecks" often prevent a factory from working to its full potential, focus on reducing such operating bottleneck constraints.

5. Because rush orders generally impair the optimal timing of the production process, rarely alter the normal work flow for "special" jobs.

Similarly, professional accountants should develop and use critical thinking skills to add value to their services, an important task for all professionals—including newly hired employees. A summary of some necessary, basic critical thinking skills appears in Figure 2-4.

Practice Exercises | *Critical Thinking Skills*

A-1. Utilizing your critical thinking skills, answer the following concern.

Three auditors check into a hotel under one reservation. After paying $100 each to the hotel manager, they went to their individual rooms. The manager discovers that the total rate for the three rooms is $250 and therefore gives $50 to the bellboy to return to the three auditors. On the way to the rooms, the bellboy reasons that $50 would be difficult to share among three individuals, so he pockets $20 and gives each auditor $10. Now each person paid $100 and got back $10. So they paid $90 each, totaling $270. The bellboy kept $20, totaling $290 (270 + 20)! Where is the remaining $10?

_____

_____

_____

_____

Practice Exercises   *Critical Thinking Skills (continued)*

A-2. Critical thinking applications:

a. Critically analyze why an asset is an asset.

b. Critically evaluate the pros and cons of the following statements:

1) Financial statements are useless because they are incomplete. Not all assets or liabilities are included.

2) Financial statements are useless because they present assets at historical cost rather than fair market values.

c. When should a liability first be reported? When should reporting of a liability cease?

d. What benefits exist for utilizing a contra "accumulated depreciation" account rather than crediting the asset account directly?

EFFECTIVE WRITING SKILLS

The ability to communicate effectively, in both oral and written communication, is essential for today's practitioner. In the workplace, an accountant may write to a supervisor, a shareholder, a company's management, government agency, or others. Strong communication skills are emphasized in the following personal statements shared by two leading business professionals:

In accounting and all other professions, we must have the appropriate technical skills. But if we cannot communicate what we know, the value of technical skills is lessened. For example, knowing how to compute corporate income taxes is a valuable skill. Being able to tell others how to do it magnifies the value of that technical skill. Others can capitalize on your knowledge only if you can communicate it.

Dennis R. Beresford, Former Chair of the Financial Accounting Standards Board

Learning to communicate well should be a top priority for anyone aspiring to lead or advance in a career. Strong technical skills are needed, but technical ability alone will not result in career advancement. Those who develop only technical skills always will work for people who have both technical and leadership abilities, and communication is the key ingredient in leadership.[7]

Hugh B. Jacks, President, BellSouth Services

Accounting practitioners have ranked written communication as the most important skill out of 22 skills to develop in students, according to research conducted by Albrecht and Sack.[8] Similarly, writing skills are among the most important attributes in the hiring process, according to a survey of Fortune 500 senior tax executives.[9] Thinking and writing are somewhat related: Thinking determines what one wants to say, while writing records these ideas for future communication. However, effective writing is more than making a draft, jotting down isolated ideas, writing reminders to one's self, making outlines, or charting different sides of an issue. Writing is a process that enables one's knowledge to become more precise and effective, rather than merely relying on reading or discussion.

Since thinking and writing are somewhat related, it follows that critical thinking and effective writing are also connected. Effective writing is not just a matter of form but of quality content arising from critical thought. One must think critically in order to write effectively.

Writing as a Process

Writing is a way to make meaning of our experiences and knowledge. Writers perform many functions at the same time, such as:

- Remembering past experience or readings while determining what they intend to write.

- Trying to convey major concepts while at the same time supplying supporting evidence and details.

- Considering their own knowledge while considering what the audience needs to know for its unique purposes.

- Continually changing their minds and revising accordingly while trying to retain their central idea and purpose while writing.

Envisioning the intended, final product helps to bring logical order to the writing. The AICPA defines effective writing in essay answers for the CPA examination as requiring the following six characteristics:

1. **Coherent organization.** Organize responses so that the ideas are arranged logically and the flow of thought is easy to follow. Generally, knowledge is best expressed by using short paragraphs composed of short sentences. Moreover, short paragraphs, each limited to the development of one principal idea, can better emphasize the main points in the answer. Place each principal idea in the first sentence of the paragraph, followed by supporting concepts and examples.

---

[7] From Himstreet, William C., Wayne M. Baty, and Carol M. Lehman, *Business Communications: Principles and Methods*, 10th edition. © 1993. Reprinted with permission of South-Western, a division of Thomson Learning: *http://www.thomsonrights.com*. Fax 800 730-2215.

[8] Albrecht, W. S., and R.J. Sack, *Accounting Education: Charting the Course Through a Perilous Future. Accounting Education Series*, vol. 16 (Sarasota, FL; American Accounting Association, 2000).

[9] Paice, G. and M. Lyons, "Addressing the People Puzzle," *Financial Executive*, September 2001. Available Online: *http://www.fei.org/magazine/articles/9-2001_corptaxes.cfm*.

2. **Conciseness.** Conciseness requires that candidates present complete thoughts in as few words as possible, while ensuring that important points are covered adequately. Short sentences and simple wording also contribute to concise writing.

3. **Clarity.** A clearly written response prevents uncertainty concerning the candidate's meaning or reasoning. Clarity involves using words with specific and precise meanings, including proper technical terms. Well-constructed sentences also contribute to clarity.

4. **Use of standard English.** Standard English is characterized by exacting standards of punctuation and capitalization, by accurate spelling, by exact diction, by an expressive vocabulary, and by knowledgeable usage choices.

5. **Responsiveness to the requirements of the question.** Answers should directly address the requirements of the question and demonstrate the candidate's awareness of the purpose of the writing task. Avoid making broad expositions on the general subject matter.

6. **Appropriateness for the reader.** Writing that is appropriate for the reader takes into account the reader's background, knowledge of the subject, interests, and concerns. The requirements of some essay questions may ask candidates to prepare a written document for a certain reader, such as an engagement memorandum for a CPA's client. When the intended reader is not specified, the candidate should assume the intended reader is a knowledgeable CPA.[10]

RESEARCH TIPS

Write concisely and clearly, using standard English and coherent organization.

Any professional accountant should apply these same six criteria of coherent organization, conciseness, clarity, use of standard English, responsiveness to the requirements of the question, and appropriateness for the reader to his or her writing. Thus, let us further examine these six criteria.

Three criteria are linked to **editing** skills, while the other three are essential **composing** skills. Composing skills are essential for the actual drafting of a paper. The composing skills include:

- **Organization:** Is the writing organized in a logical manner?

- **Responsiveness:** Does the writing respond to what is being asked?

- **Appropriateness:** Is the writing appropriate for the reader, considering his or her capacity and experience?

While composing skills are also used in revising, the primary value of composing skills is for a focused first draft. Revising primarily relies on editing skills. Editing is what one does to the draft; it is largely a matter of rewriting. Editing skills include:

- **Conciseness:** The writing contains no extraneous matter and does not repeat itself.

- **Clarity:** The right word choices and the most effective sentence patterns are used.

- **Use of standard English:** The writing reflects standard English both in usage and mechanical exactness

Writers making a first draft should not worry about conciseness, clarity, and standard English until it is time to revise the draft. Some basic suggestions for revising word selection and sentence structure for effective writing are presented in Figure 2-5.

Success in critical thinking and effective writing comes from life-long learning. The skills develop from practice and experience. If effective writing is not developed, the accountant may lose business or potential career advancement. Clients who are unable to judge the quality of work may form impressions based on the quality of the accountant's writing. Bad writing may indicate poor thinking.

---

10 Examination Division, AICPA, *Report of the Testing of Writing Skills Subtask Force of the CPA Examination Change Implementation Task Force,* September 18, 1990.

FIGURE 2-5 WORD SELECTION AND SENTENCE STRUCTURE GUIDELINES

1. Visualize your reader and select words familiar to him or her.
2. Use the active voice in your writing.
3. Choose short words.
4. Use technical words and acronyms with caution.
5. Select your words for precise meanings.
6. Limit your sentence content. Use short sentences.
7. Use proper punctuation in sentence development.
8. Arrange your sentences for clarity and unity.

PUNCTUATION PRIMER

QUICK FACTS

Effective writing is a process that includes proper grammar as well as proper punctuation.

Successful writing requires proper grammar and punctuation. Figure 2-6 provides a basic primer on the main punctuation issues with examples. Remember that proper punctuation is very important not only for business writing, but also on the CPA exam; proper punctuation on the CPA exam essays affects one's grade.

IMPROVED WRITING SKILLS REQUIRED

RESEARCH TIPS

Use plain English with short sentences, everyday language, active voice, tabular presentation of complex material, limited legal jargon, and no multiple negatives.

Improved writing skills are required by many key accounting organizations, including the AICPA, and the managing partners of the country's largest public accounting firms. Improved writing skills will enhance an organization's productivity and lower training costs. Thus, the Uniform CPA Examination now requires CPA candidates to possess more effective research and writing skills.

The Securities and Exchange Commission (SEC) criticized the dense writing styles, legal jargon, and repetitive disclosures in various prospectuses. A prospectus is a document provided to the public when a company is issuing new stock. The prospectus outlines the business and principal purposes for the company's proposed use of the capital funds raised from the stock offering. Therefore, the SEC issued Rule #33-7380: "Plain English Disclosures," which requires the public company registrants to use "Plain English" in a prospectus's cover page, summary, and risk factor sections. The SEC also issued *A Plain English Handbook: How to Create Clear SEC Disclosure*, which specifies six principles for clear writing: active voice, short sentences, everyday language, tabular presentation of complex material, limited legal jargon, and no multiple negatives.

The SEC plain writing concepts apply to any writing. However, let's first discuss the concepts in the context that most concerns the SEC.

Active Voice

QUICK FACTS

The active voice helps to keep the reader's attention.

The active voice uses strong, direct verbs. The active voice follows how we think and process information. In the active voice, the subject of the sentence performs the action described by the verb. The active voice is often easier to understand than the passive voice. The passive voice is easy to spot because it uses the words "be" or "been" as part of the verb. In the passive voice, the action is done to somebody or something by another agent that might not always be identified in the sentence. Did you notice how the previous sentence included an example of the passive voice: "be identified?" The passive voice is less effective because it often forces the reader to reread information, particularly if it is part of a long, complex sentence.

FIGURE 2-6 | PUNCTUATION PRIMER

PERIODS

Rule 1. Use a period after a declarative sentence (one that states a fact) or an imperative sentence (one that states a command).

Examples: Our accountant resigned yesterday. Get me the reconciliation report immediately.

Rule 2. Use a period with abbreviations and initials. If the last word in the sentence ends in a period, do not follow it with another period.

Examples: Robert received his M.B.A. from Harvard.
The meeting will begin at 2:00 p.m.

COMMAS

Rule 1. Use commas when a sentence contains words in a series.

Examples: Her previous employers were the SEC, AICPA, and FBI.
The auditor requested support for the accounts payable balance, the accounts receivable balance, and the vacation accrual balance.

Rule 2. Use a comma when two or more adjectives describe the same noun.

Examples: That was a long, tiring meeting.
Susan is a loyal, dedicated employee.
Note: If the word "and" can be inserted between the two adjectives, a comma is needed.

Rule 3. Use a comma to separate two independent clauses that are joined by a conjunction. An independent clause is a group of words that can stand alone as a sentence.

Examples: The audit has been concluded, but an opinion has not been issued.
We are pleased to have you join our firm, and we hope this will be a rewarding experience for you.

SEMICOLONS

Rule 1. Use a semicolon to separate two independent clauses when no conjunction is used.

Examples: The president declined the raise; he was already making $2 million a year.
Fifty people attended the conference; most of them were accountants.

Rule 2. Use a semicolon to avoid confusion where commas are already present.

Examples: The auditors traveled to Los Angeles, California; Chicago, Illinois; and Little Rock, Arkansas, to conduct the fraud investigation. Will, partner of the firm, interviewed three potential staff members; but not one of them was hired.

COLONS

Rule 1. Use a colon after a complete sentence to show that something is to follow.

Examples: Please get me the following items: payroll register, list of vendors, and list of accounts payable.
Please get the payroll register, a list of vendors, and a list of accounts payable. (No colon after get because *Please get* is not a complete sentence.)

Rule 2. Use a colon after the salutation of a business letter.

Example: Dear Mr. Williams:

FIGURE 2-6 | PUNCTUATION PRIMER (CONTINUED)

QUESTION MARKS

Rule 1. Use a question mark after a direct question.

Examples: Are you sure the tax forms were filed before the deadline?
I asked John if he was sure the tax forms were filed before the deadline. (No question mark because it is not a direct question.)

Rule 2. When quotation marks are used, place the question mark inside the final quotation mark only if the quoted part of the sentence is a question.

Examples: The partner asked, "Will you be at the audit committee meeting tomorrow?"
Did Thomas say, "Can we push the deadline back until Friday"? (The question mark is placed outside the quotation mark because the entire sentence is a question.)

EXCLAMATION POINTS

Rule 1. Use an exclamation point to show emphasis or surprise.

Example: Help me!

Rule 2. Do not use an exclamation point in formal business letters.

QUOTATION MARKS

Rule 1. Periods and commas always go inside quotation marks.

Examples: Jill said, "I will not have time to reconcile the bank statement tomorrow."
The professor said, "Remember the accounting equation for tomorrow's test."

Rule 2. Use single quotation marks for quotes within quotes. Remember that the period goes inside all quote marks.

Examples: He said, "The boss said, 'Make sure to disclose the inventory method used in our notes to financial statements.'"
Bob said, "The professor said, 'The quiz tomorrow only covers the journal entries regarding cash and accounts receivable.'"

APOSTROPHES

Rule 1. Use an apostrophe to show singular possession by placing the apostrophe before the *s.*

Examples: Today's assignment will involve performing some tax research on the Internet.
Bill's presentation was excellent.

Rule 2. Do not use an apostrophe with possessive pronouns—his, her, our, their, etc.

Examples: His accounting professor was one of the best.
Our company should have caught the error—not theirs.

Rule 3. Use an apostrophe with contractions. Replace the omitted letters with the apostrophe.

Examples: Sue doesn't care if you use LIFO or FIFO.
Don't assume that the financial statements are free of error.

HYPHENS

Rule 1. Use a hyphen in a compound expression when a noun follows the expression.

Examples: The vendor has a past-due account.
The vendor's account is past due. (No hyphen because a noun does not follow *past due.*)

FIGURE 2-6 | PUNCTUATION PRIMER (CONTINUED)

Rule 2. Use a hyphen in compound numbers and fractions.

Examples: Sixty-three employees signed the code of ethics.
Please sell me the 10-year-old bonds.

Rule 3. Use a hyphen with a word that may be confusing.

Examples: Joe remarked that he will re-mark the goods tomorrow.
Please re-create the original invoice.

CAPITALIZATION

Rule 1. Capitalize the first word in a sentence.

Examples: The balance sheet presents information for a certain date.
The income statement presents information over a period of time.

Rule 2. Capitalize the first word of a direct quote.

Examples: The manager said, "Please have the statement of cash flows ready by tomorrow."
Peter asked, "Should we expense this item or capitalize it?"

Rule 3. Capitalize proper nouns.

Examples: During our business trip we saw the Golden Gate Bridge.
The SEC office is close to the Washington Monument.

The SEC provides the following example of how to change from the passive voice to the active voice to achieve effective writing. The "before" material is from an actual corporate filing with the SEC.

> *Before:* No person has been authorized to give any information or make any representation other than those contained or incorporated by reference in this joint proxy statement/prospectus, and, if given or made, such information or representation must not be relied upon as having been authorized.

The SEC's proposed revision not only changes the voice, but strengthens the clarity, conciseness, and use of standard English:

> *After:* You should rely only on the information contained in this document or incorporated by reference. We have not authorized anyone to provide you with information that is different.

Short Sentences

Short sentences help to reduce such problems as run-on sentences and sentence fragments, which represent just part of a sentence. Typically, in a sentence fragment, either the subject or verb is left out. Run-on sentences have two independent clauses joined without any punctuation; this makes the sentence difficult to read. The SEC suggests that a registrant should strive to use shorter sentences of 25 to 30 words, as in the following "before and after" example.

> *Before:* Machine Industries and Great Tools, Inc., are each subject to the information requirements of the Securities Exchange Act of 1934, as amended (the "Exchange Act"), and in accordance therewith file reports, proxy statements, and other information with the Securities and Exchange Commission (the "Commission").

> *After:* We must comply with the Securities Exchange Act of 1934. Accordingly, we file annual, quarterly and current reports, proxy statements, and other information with the Securities and Exchange Commission.

RESEARCH TIPS

Divide long sentences into short sentences to convey your research results.

Definite, Concrete, Everyday Language

Clearer communication results when writers and readers use definite and concrete words. Similarly, providing examples using one investor helps make complex information more understandable. The SEC provided the following "before and after" example to help registrants communicate in clearer, less vague language. The SEC uses greater specificity in the "after" example.

> *Before:* History of Net Losses. The Company has recorded a net loss under generally accepted accounting principles for each fiscal year since its inception, as well as for the interim nine months of this year. However, these results include the effect of certain significant, non-cash accounting transactions.

> *After:* History of Net Losses. We have recorded a net loss under general accounting principles for each year since we started business, and for the interim nine months of this year. Our losses were caused, in part, by the annual write-off of a portion of the goodwill resulting from the ten acquisitions we made during this period.

Tabular Presentation

Tabular presentations often help to organize complex information. SEC registrants using "if-then" tables also present a clearer presentation of complex information. For example, the following table has two columns to enhance the readability of information that might not stand out in a paragraph:

The Event of Default (if)	Remedy (then)

Limited Legal Jargon and Technical Terms

Use legal jargon sparingly in registration statements, since it often forces readers to learn a new vocabulary that inhibits their understanding of the information. In certain circumstances, jargon is unavoidable. Technical terms are sometimes needed to communicate technical information as efficiently as possible; however, the writer should define or explain the technical terms. The SEC suggests clear and common terms for better understanding, as demonstrated in the following example.

> *Before:* The following description encompasses all the material terms and provisions of the Notes offered hereby and supplements, and to the extent inconsistent therewith replaces, the description of the general terms and provisions of the Debt Securities (as defined in the accompanying Prospectus) set forth under the heading "Description of Debt Securities" in the Prospectus, to which description reference is hereby made.

> *After:* We disclose information about our notes in two separate documents that progressively provide more detail on the notes' specific terms: the prospectus, and this pricing supplement. Since the specific terms of notes are made at the time of pricing, rely on information in the pricing supplement over different information in the prospectus.

No Multiple Negatives

The SEC suggests that registrants' filings avoid multiple negatives. Comprehending documents is more difficult when readers must "decipher" the meaning of the negatives. Avoidance of negatives clarifies the writing, as in the following example.

> *Before:* Except when an applicant has submitted a request for withdrawal without the appropriate tax identification number, the request will be honored within one business day.

> *After:* We will send your money within one business day if you include your tax identification number in your withdrawal request.

Elements of Plain English

The SEC also stated that using plain English means writing well. Plain English uses common language; however, it is not overly simplified English. Plain English is the opposite of obscure language, for it seeks to have the message understood on the first reading. Successful plain English depends on whether the writing is clear, straightforward language for that audience. The use of plain English aids in writing well.

The SEC has identified the following four basic requirements for plain English.

1. **Know your audience.** Successful communicators first identify the investor groups for whom they write. Effective writing includes analyzing the readers' needs and expectations. Writers should tailor their tone and style to their intended audience, select words that contribute to an effective writing style, and choose language based on current and future investors' educational and financial knowledge.

   Other pertinent factors in audience targeting include investor demographics (e.g., job experience, age, and income) and how the investors will read and use the document. Authors should remember that the least sophisticated investors often have the greatest need for an "understandable" disclosure document.

2. **Know what material information needs to be disclosed.** After identifying the readers' needs and expectations, the author should gather the necessary information to communicate. The SEC has stated that too many disclosure documents combine material and immaterial information into long, dense sentences; they do not prioritize the information and organize it logically for the reader. The SEC notes that prospectus cover pages typically include very dense printing with sentences running 60 to 100 words in length and include superfluous information. They do not "invite" the investor to read the remainder of the prospectus for key information concerning the offering.

   In coherent writing, main points should stand out. Registrants should emphasize these main points by placing them where they will attract the reader's attention. Therefore, the cover page should provide a clear, concise, and coherent "snapshot" of the offering. Subsequent sections of the prospectus would then present the details in a logical fashion.

3. **Use clear writing techniques.** Two overriding themes in clear and effective writing are **conciseness** and **clarity**. In writing documents, one should eliminate digressions and irrelevant detail. Precise diction is an important element of clear writing.

4. **Design and structure the document for ease of readability.** Readers demand properly designed documents, but typical dense printing in most prospectuses discourages reading them. Good use of white space and margins increases the readability of documents. Headings, bullet points, and graphic illustrations make a long document more pleasing to the eye.

Plain English writing does not delete complex information. Rather, it presents information in an orderly and clear fashion so that the reader can better understand it.

A summary table of some elements of effective writing is presented in Figure 2-7.

> **QUICK FACTS**
> The SEC requires plain English for clear, straightforward language.

Practice Exercises   *Proper Grammar and Punctuation*

B-1. Insert the correct punctuation.

   a. The professor received his PhD from the University of Illinois and he continued teaching there after he was finished with the program

   b. The general ledger does not balance it must balance before we leave

   c. Did Robert say Can this item be classified as an asset

   d. Susans investigation didn't discover any fraud but theres new evidence that might keep the investigation going

   e. Dear Mr Smith

B-2. Correct the capitalization needed in the following sentences.

   a. the auditor said, "we must have these work papers completed by tomorrow."

   b. when do we have to file our taxes?

   c. is the conference in dallas or austin, texas?

WRITING EFFECTIVE CLIENT LETTERS AND E-MAILS

Written communication is used if the information is complex and will warrant repeating, or a copy helps for later reference. Oral communication, such as telephone calls or in-person meetings, are used if an immediate response is needed, if one needs to hear the voice to read between the lines, or if a greater concern about privacy exists.

Written communication by today's accountants includes both letters and e-mails. The increased use of e-mail has reinforced the need to develop strong writing skills, as well as technological skills in the security of the transmissions, as well as the sophistication of the presentation. Apply the writing and thinking concepts previously discussed in the context of typical written communications with clients. Also, strive to maintain a cordial and respectful tone, which connects with the client. While one might use a little conversational style in a client letter, it should be limited for most letters. Write directly and clearly.

Four basic types of business letters, which are often delivered via e-mail, are transmittal letters, status up-date letters, action requested letters, and opinion letters. Before discussing each type, review the basic letter contents: the date, address, greeting, message, a polite closing, signature, and special notations, such as for attachments.

QUICK FACTS

Business letters include transmittal, status update, action requested, and opinion letters.

FIGURE 2-7 | KEY POINTS OF EFFECTIVE WRITING

Content	Effective writing should contain relevant, "value added" content matter, a process enhanced with critical thinking skills.
Chain of Processes	To add meaning from your experiences, convey "large" concepts, while supplying supporting evidence to these ideas.
Coherent Organization	Organize ideas logically, making the flow of thought easy to follow.
Conciseness	Use as few words as necessary to convey "complete thoughts."
Clarity	Select "effective" words to state ideas with "certainty."
Use of Standard English	Use appropriate punctuation and grammar, perhaps with the help of a computer-based spell/grammar checker.
Responsiveness	Ascertain that the answers directly address the research question.
Appropriateness for the Reader	Consider the intended reader's background and experience.

A transmittal letter merely transmits information; it does not seek an action An effective transmittal letter must quickly summarize any information the accountant is delivering in more detail. The letter often closes with an offer to provide additional assistance. A firm newsletter is a common transmittal letter example. Since the accountant's real goal is to impress clients and potential clients with the firm's knowledge and potential services, it's essential to assure that the newsletter and its transmission meets the firm's quality standards. If the transmittal occurs via e-mail, it is particularly important that the subject line state the contents accurately, so as not to provide any surprise.

A status update letter typically reminds the client about a situation by providing an update. In writing such a letter, assume that not everyone reading the letter will remember everything about the past events. Thus, reference previous correspondence on a subject or summarize major actions already taken. Then summarize new developments or activities. You might close the status update letter with a suggestion to call if the reader has any questions.

A letter requesting action needs to make the request for action clearly and up-front. List precisely what is needed from the client, so as to help minimize his or her burden. Briefly mention why the information is needed, so as to help motivate the desired response. Close the letter by politely mentioning an approaching deadline or likely follow-up.

An opinion letter summarizes the situation very briefly, but should restate the critical facts that are the basis for the advice provided. While the client is primarily interested in the conclusions and planning implications, provide some detail depending upon the sophistication of the client. Include language limiting potential misunderstanding, such as "based on the facts provided" or "based on a due diligence review" as of a given date.

WRITING MEMOS TO THE FILE

Writing a memo to the file is often an important part of documentation that is required in accounting, auditing, and taxation. Memos should provide important information up-front. For example, the top of the memo will list the date, whom the memo is written to, whom the memo is from, and the subject matter. Similarly, the content of the memo states important conclusions early. A memo rarely waits until the end to provide a conclusion. Busy business people do not always read the entire memo.

In tax, the typical memo will have the following headings: Facts, Issues, Conclusion, and Reasoning. Sometimes the reasoning is divided by the issue. The reasoning must discuss both the law or authorities, as well as apply the law or authorities to the client's set of facts. Writing the application so that each sentence integrates some aspect of the facts with some aspect of the law is difficult, but is a necessary skill to develop. Some firms will want to separate discussion of the law and authority from the analysis. In such cases, every law and authority explained in the discussion should be referenced in the application. Don't just provide conclusions; state how each element of the legal test or authority applies in that case.

Thus, a memo should not provide an academic lecture about a topic. Instead, it should be carefully written to provide only the potentially relevant facts, laws, and authorities. However, it is generally better to err on the side of providing too many facts than too few. Potentially relevant authority is sometimes referred to as "colorable authority." Colorable authority is discussed but distinguished from having any real relevance to the problem. The distinction is made in the application.

Make the discussion of the facts, as well as the law and authorities, proceed logically. Thus, the facts are often provided in chronological order. A tax memo may need to discuss both the client's position and the government's position. Generally, the strongest authority is discussed first, before going to other authority that may interpret the strongest authority. Most firms will want the writer to discuss objectively all relevant authorities. Do not omit discussion of law or authorities that may prevent the client from achieving the desired results.

A strong memo provides great insight when identifying the issues. Thus, the issue statement is refined to include the most critical facts, along with pinpointing where in the law the real issue arises. For example, even if an accountant is told that the issue is whether the client gets a home office deduction, the accountant must refine that issue with more precision using the facts and law. In this case, detailed knowledge of the law on home offices will help determine which facts are critical. Then pinpointing precisely where in the law, or what phrase in the law is at issue, enables the reader to assess the situation much more quickly and accurately.

A memo is a formal document. Use the third person in the memo (the name, he, she, it, they) to keep the consistent focus on the subject. Avoid using the first person (I, we, our) and the second person (you, yours), which creates a less objective appearance. The length of the memo may vary, but edit it for conciseness. A chit-chatty writing style does not go over well in a memo.

SUMMARY

Accounting professionals—whether in auditing, management accounting, not-for-profit accounting, or taxation—provide value-added services to others in a dynamic, complex, expanding, and constantly changing profession. Therefore, accountants must learn to *rethink*, to develop lifelong learning skills to think critically (to grasp the meaning of complex concepts and principles), and to judge and apply these concepts and principles to specific issues.

Additionally, quality writing needs continual practice. Just as SEC registrants must recognize the importance of developing strong writing skills, accountants must also expect to follow many of the above suggestions to better meet their goals.

Critical thinking and effective writing are essential tools for accounting, auditing, and tax research. The concepts outlined in this chapter are used throughout the remainder of this text.

DISCUSSION QUESTIONS

1. Define *critical thinking*.
2. Discuss the highest level of thinking according to Bloom's taxonomy.
3. Discuss what *grasping the meaning of a statement* or *comprehension* implies.
4. Discuss how critical thinking relates to the term *professional skepticism*.
5. What are the qualities that lie behind rethinking?
6. Discuss the three levels of thought as defined by the Illinois Renewal Institute.
7. Discuss the AICPA list of effective writing characteristics. Which are editing skills and which are composing skills?
8. What six principles of clear writing does SEC Rule #33-7380 identify?
9. Explain why plain English writing does not mean deleting complex information.
10. What are the elements of plain English?
11. What is the difference between the active and passive voice? Give an example.
12. What are special concerns with e-mails?

13. What types of client letters exist?

14. How does writing a client letter differ from writing a memo to the file?

15. How is a tax memo usually organized?

EXERCISES

1. There are five houses in a row, each of a different color, and inhabited by five people of different nationalities, with different pets, favorite drinks, and favorite sports. Use the clues below to determine who owns the monkey and who drinks water. Utilize the chart to develop your answer.

   a. The Englishman lives in the red house.

   b. The Spaniard owns the dog.

   c. Coffee is drunk in the green house.

   d. The Russian drinks tea.

   e. The green house is immediately to the right of the white house.

   f. The hockey player owns hamsters.

   g. The football player lives in the yellow house.

   h. Milk is drunk in the middle house.

   i. The American lives in the first house on the left.

   j. The table tennis player lives in the house next to the man with the fox.

   k. The football player lives next to the house where the horse is kept.

   l. The basketball player drinks orange juice.

   m. The Japanese likes baseball.

   n. The American lives next to the blue house.

	HOUSE 1	HOUSE 2	HOUSE 3	HOUSE 4	HOUSE 5
Color					
Country					
Sport					
Drink					
Pet					

2. Develop a chart similar to Figure 2-3 for the following assignment: Johnson Electronics has requested your advice as to when assets need to be classified as current assets.

3. Develop a chart similar to Figure 2-3 for the following assignment: Your client, Baxter Controls, has requested your advice as to when a contingent liability should be booked (recorded) as a liability.

4. Insert the correct punctuation in the following sentences.

   a. A general ledger contains all the assets liabilities and owners equity accounts

   b. The purpose of a trial balance is to prove that debits equal credits but does not prove that all transactions have been recorded

c. The current assets section of the balance sheet contains items such as cash accounts receivable and prepaid expenses and the current liabilities section contains items such as accounts payable notes payable and short term debt

d. The auditing exam was to begin at 200 pm but the professors car broke down so we didn't begin until 230 pm

e. Did William ask How can we finish the audit tonight because Linda said We have twenty hours of work left to do

5. Rewrite the following sentences into shorter, more concise sentences, while maintaining the main points of the sentence.

a. For good reasons, the secretary may grant extensions of time in 30-day increments for filing of the lease and all required bonds, provided that additional extensions requests are submitted and approved before the expiration of the original 30 days or the previously granted extension.

b. If the State agency finds that an individual has received a payment to which the individual was not entitled, whether or not the payment was due to the individual's fault or misrepresentation, the individual shall be liable to repay to the State the total sum of the payment to which the individual was not entitled.

c. Universities differ greatly in style, with some being located on out of town campuses in parkland, others having buildings scattered about parts of city centers and others being at various points between these two extremes.

6. Rewrite the following double-negative sentence in order to eliminate the double negative.

No termination will be approved unless the administrator reviews the application and finds that it is not lacking any requisite materials.

7. Rewrite the following sentences using active voice.

a. The fraud was reported by the employee.

b. The book was enjoyed by me because the seven fraud investigation techniques were described so well by the author.

Web-Based Professional Research

LEARNING OBJECTIVES

After completing this chapter, you should understand the following:

- The role of the Internet in society.
- Uses of the Internet for the professional accountant.
- How to navigate the Internet.
- Popular search engines.
- Web sites for the professional accountant.
- Internet dangers requiring protective measures.

A researcher must gather relevant information in an effective and efficient way. The web offers exciting new tools to aid the researcher in gathering information on a timely basis. This chapter provides an overview of using the Internet for professional accounting, auditing, and tax research. Information about the Internet, how to access Internet sites and databases effectively, various computerized tools, and leading web sites are discussed. Practice with these tools by completing the in-chapter exercises and by answering the end-of-chapter questions and exercises. Two notes of caution, however: web sites often change and dangers that require protective measures exist on the Internet!

The Internet is a tool that will have an increasingly significant impact on the way people conduct business, including accountants, auditors, and tax professionals. The Internet permits an accounting professional to accomplish the following major tasks:

- **Discuss various accounting, auditing, or tax issues by participating in discussion groups.** Figure 3-1 presents a sample of discussion groups on ANet, a joint venture between Australian and American academics that provides Internet services to accountants around the world. Accountants have used newsgroups to confer with fellow experts to obtain answers to technical questions. Currently, various industry groups are on the Internet and many CPA firms, both large and small, are providing information concerning their firms via the Internet.

- **Search for accounting, auditing, or tax information.** Accountants have used the Internet to search for federal and state legislation that may have an impact on clients. Another way in which accountants use the Internet is to retrieve financial statements from SEC filings through the SEC's EDGAR (Electronic Data Gathering and Retrieval) System. Accountants and individuals can also download tax forms, or even file tax returns electronically. Figure 3-2 illustrates just one example of how the Internet can help a small CPA firm provide practical services to clients.

The Internet is changing society on a worldwide basis, including how business is conducted. An astounding amount of data is available on the Internet. The following sections will help you become more proficient in using this exciting and dynamic tool for professional research.

RESEARCH TOOLS

| Internet |
| FARS |
| LexisNexis |
| AICPA reSOURCE |
| PwC Edgarscan |
| Thomson ONE |
| RIA Checkpoint SE |
| ACL |
| i2 |

QUICK FACTS

The Internet opens a vast world of information for the professional researcher.

FIGURE 3-1 | SAMPLE OF ANET DISCUSSION GROUPS

MAILING LIST NAME	PURPOSE
AAccSys–L	Provides discussion concerning matters of accounting information systems theory and practice.
AAudit–L	Provides discussion on issues related to external and internal auditing.
AEthics–L	Provides discussion on the ethical dimensions of accounting and auditing.
AFinAcc–L	Provides discussion dealing with issues of financial accounting.
AIntSys–L	Provides discussion relating to the application of artificial intelligence and expert systems in accounting.
ATax–L	Provides discussion on all aspects of tax accounting.

THE INTERNET

The Internet is similar to a spider web of thousands of communications networks that physically cover the world. Because the Internet was created as an information exchange tool, finding relevant information on the Web is not always easy. Various navigation tools are available to help make the Internet a valuable tool for professional accountants and other business researchers.

Navigating the Internet

Searching for information on the Internet is not the challenge, but searching for high-quality information or information highly relevant to the specific research goal is. The major techniques for accessing and searching (surfing) are briefly described starting on page 43.

FIGURE 3-2 | AN EXAMPLE OF A SMALL CPA FIRM'S UTILIZING THE INTERNET

Mark Jensen, CPA, states that the Internet has become the "greatest equalizer" because it provides his small practice with many of the research tools utilized by the big international accounting firms. "It lets me offer resources and services to my clients and future clients that the big firms have to offer," says Jensen.

Mark was asked by a would-be entrepreneur to help write a business plan to open a computer software store in southern New York. Both Jensen and the client were computer literate, but neither of them knew much about the software business. So Mark accessed the Internet, and within an hour was deluged with information about software stores.

A word search for "software" yielded more than 100 articles about computer stores, including one from *The Washington Post* about a software store start-up. Jensen also gleaned information about software stores from the small business forums on the Internet. Mark and his client used the information to prepare a business plan that helped secure financing for the business.

Being online via the Internet allows Jensen to search through news sources throughout the world. Publications and news services such as *The New York Times*, Associated Press, United Press International, Reuters, *Financial Times of London*, and the Dow Jones News Service are just a few of the sources available on the Internet.

Mark also retrieves news items for clients as an effective way to maintain relationships and attract new clients. One of his clients is involved in the machine tools industry and Mark frequently notifies the client when a major industry event takes place.

Besides tracking news, Jensen uses the Internet to exchange e-mail with clients and associates. He also can access the SEC's EDGAR System and obtain recent SEC filings of major public companies, such as their 10-K, 10-Q, or other filings.

FTP. File transfer protocol (FTP) is a method of moving files from one computer to another. It is almost as easy as moving files from a disk to the hard drive of a computer. With a standard protocol system, file transfers can occur regardless of the type of computer used for the file transfers. However, FTP allows transfer of text documents only.

Vast libraries of files exist on the multitude of systems connected to the Internet. A user can obtain various documents such as recent corporate filings with the SEC, or a recent Supreme Court decision, or download software programs such as Turbotax or shareware programs. The file transfer protocol system (FTP) is the basic way of obtaining these files.

A database system automatically and regularly searches the Internet and indexes files into a single searchable database called *Archie*. This allows a user to access this database (Archie) and quickly search the index of files for the particular file needed to transfer.

USENET. News and opinions are freely disbursed on the Internet, and all types of news appear on the Internet. USENET is the tool used to access this information. Currently, USENET consists of a collection of over 10,000 bulletin-board-type discussion groups called newsgroups. The basic benefit of participating in a newsgroup is that you share ideas with others who have the same interests on a particular subject. These discussions of similar topics have resulted in the creation of thousands of newsgroups. A sample of accounting newsgroups was presented in Figure 3-1. A more comprehensive list of accounting, auditing, and tax newsgroups is at the authors' web site for this text (*http:// weirich.swlearning.com*).

RESEARCH TIPS

Utilize Internet discussion groups to obtain valuable information from professionals about various issues.

World Wide Web (Web)

The Web's structure creates a hypertext (http—hypertext transfer protocol) system for all of the data on the Internet. In a hypertext system you can link a word in a document to another document. The location of this other document can vary, ranging from the same computer to a different computer in a distant foreign country. These links allow you to search documents interactively, rather than just in a linear method.

Web Browsers. A Web browser is the software that provides the user ready access to the different Internet sites located on the Web. Two of the most popular browsing tools for the web setting are Microsoft's Internet Explorer and Netscape's Communicator. These multimedia browsers display documents, embedded graphics, video, and sound. These tools and the downloading of music from the web have become so popular that some people claim they are causing a minor traffic jam on the Internet.

URL. The Universal (or Uniform) Resource Locator (URL) is the Internet address of a web site. Each page in a web site has its own unique address or URL. This unique address has three parts. The parts for Ernst & Young's careers home page are shown below.

http: // www.ey.com / careers/default.asp

Interpretive Language: Hypertext Transfer Protocol   Site Domain   Folder and page location within site domain.

For example, the URL of Ernst & Young's web page is at *http://www.ey.com*. The http:// signifies the type of protocol the web site is using. Today, most web browsers assume that you are looking for a web site, and will automatically add the *http://* to any address you type. The only time you need to specify a protocol is if you are looking for ftp or gopher sites. The rest of the URL is the domain and location for a particular page within a site. Ernst & Young's web site has a section on careers and employment at the firm. The first page of that section is located at *http://www.ey.com/careers/default.asp*. The *www.ey.com* is the domain of Ernst & Young's web site. The career sections home page is located in the folder "careers," and "default.asp" is the name of the current page.

The most commonly utilized domain names that appear in the URL of a document are as follows:

.com	commercial
.net	gateway or host
.org	nonprofit organization
.edu	educational and research
.gov	government
.mil	military agency
.int	international, intergovernmental

As the Web continues to grow, you should expect to see additional domain names. As you explore many international sites, you will observe that countries outside the United States also have domain names.

Searching the Web

RESEARCH TIPS

Make more effective Internet searches by combining keywords and phrases with operators.

An immense wealth of information is available on the Internet. The problem is trying to find the relevant information. Conducting a keyword search can generate a list of thousands of sites, many of which may not have anything to do with the desired topic. A search on the name *Bill Gates* will bring up sites related to Microsoft's founder, gates that are found in a fence, legislative bills, bills found on a bird, and any other site with the words *bill* and/or *gates*. Performing an effective search on the Internet means choosing correct keywords, phrases, and operators, which include character and Boolean operators. The operators help to narrow and refine your searches. The following table contains common operators and their meanings.

Word/ Symbol	Meaning
+	Designates words that **must** be included in each document.
–	Designates words that **must not** be included in any document.
" "	Designates phrases that **must** be included in each document.
AND	Designates words that **must** be included in each document.
OR	Designates more than one word, either of which **may be** included.
NOT	Designates words that **must not** be included in any document.
( )	Designates groups of words using any of the above operators.

For effective use of Web sources, one needs to know how to use the search and retrieval commands for online search engines. The above listed operations (Boolean Operators) can aid you in conducting an efficient search of the Web. For example, if you were to search for college basketball scores using a search engine the following results would occur:

College scores basketball	returns 2.5 million hits
+college+scores+basketball	returns 300,000 hits
+college+scores+basketball+uconn	returns 11,000 hits

Types of Searches and Search Engines. You can conduct a search in three different ways: using search engines, directories, or search features found in some individual web sites.

Using a search engine on the Web is the most popular way to look for general information. A search engine is a software program located on a remote computer. A search engine allows you to search for documents using keywords and operators. One very popular search engine is Google. However, many different search engines exist on the Web. Each search engine conducts the searches differently. For example, some search engines search every word on a page for your keywords; others look only in the title of each document. Consequently, you should use at least two different search engines, if not three, to conduct your research on the Web. Also, search by multiple keywords, both separately and together.

Search engines can vary in how they read a string of words, utilize special characters, or use operators. Some allow you to search for words using part of the word followed by a wildcard (* or $). For example, if you want to search for amortization, but you don't know how to spell it, in some search engines you could search for amort* or amort$. Every search engine has a help or search tips page. Read it to find out what operators it uses.

Using directories is a second way to search the web. Directory sites organize their links into categories, allowing you to narrow your search as you go along. One of the best directories on the web is Yahoo!. Each directory organizes its links differently, and there are multiple routes to access each link. For example, you could search for an international accounting firm in Yahoo!'s directory by first choosing the Business & Economy category, then the directories category, then companies, then financial services, then accounting, and finally CPA firms. The path would look like this, with the carat (>) dividing each category: Home > Business and Economy > Directories> Companies> Financial Services> Accounting> CPA Firms. You could also get to this site by first clicking the regional category, then U.S., then the state, then choosing the Business & Economy link, then companies, then financial services, then accounting, and so on until you find the desired company.

Directories make looking for information on the Web logical and easy, but an individual directory usually contains only a small portion of the number of web sites that a search engine would find. Some search engines also contain directories. For example, Yahoo! is one of the most popular search engines that also has a directory. Many times it is helpful in a search to use this type of dual engine, since it also shows the category for the links. This makes it easier to find related or similar sites to the one in your search results, even if the other sites do not appear in the original search.

Search engine directories can return links only to sites and documents registered with that particular search engine. Results obtained through a search in one search engine are sometimes not found on another engine. This stresses again the necessity to search on more than one search engine. Since each search engine has a different retrieval scheme, find ones that you are comfortable using and that meet your research needs.

Using search capabilities that some web sites have built into them is a third way to conduct a search. Search capabilities let you search a web site for relevant information. These search features are often found in web sites for newspapers, companies, and other large organizations. This technique enables you to search for information that is sometimes not otherwise readily available.

For example, if you are searching for the most recent annual report (form 10K) filed by the computer company Dell, you can go to the Securities and Exchange Commission (SEC) web site and use the search capabilities of EDGAR. You must take care not to confuse the search capabilities provided on the SEC's home page. Instead, you must first click on EDGAR to locate the desired search capability. While alternative web sites to the SEC exist that make the search of SEC filings even easier, you cannot rely on search engines or directories to find the desired information. You must use the search capabilities of the SEC or other special web sites to find the desired document.

Source Credibility. The reliability of any Internet information is only as credible as its source. Anybody can publish a web site and register it with a search engine. There is generally no government regulation of web page content. Consequently, you must rely on your own judgment when evaluating the credibility of a web site. Some highly reliable sources include government sites such as the U.S. Treasury, academic institutions, and some established commercial sites. Also, if the information found on the Internet is available in other formats, such as legislative bills, that increases the credibility of the

> **RESEARCH TIPS**
>
> Use directories, search engines, and web sites with built-in search capabilities to find relevant sources on the Internet.

information. In other words, the ability to verify the information that you have found, helps to make it more credible.

The Internet is a constantly changing universe. New sites are increasingly added as more and more companies take their business online and more people post web pages. In addition, existing web sites are constantly changing and updated as needed. Many times, web sites no longer exist because they are moved to new locations or are discarded completely. As a result, the internet has many broken links—links to web sites that no longer function. Don't get frustrated or discouraged by finding broken links. There is a huge amount of valid, credible information on the Web to discover. Refine your searches and try a variety of search methods to make your web search as effective and complete as possible.

Search Engines. The following are popular search engines. You may utilize these search engines as you conduct professional research.

- **Yahoo!** (see Figure 3-3) has both a search engine and a directory. Its directory is one of the best and most comprehensive available on the Web. In addition to the previously mentioned operators, Yahoo! also allows you to conduct searches on URL and document titles only. You can do this by typing **t:** or **u:** in front of your keywords. For example, if you know that Ernst & Young's web site address contains the firm's name, but are unsure of the exact address, you can do a URL search by typing in **u: Ernst + Young**. This will return a link to Ernst & Young's web site as the first link. You will see the category path it is listed under. Doing a title search for Ernst & Young by typing in **t: + Ernst + Young** will yield the same results. Yahoo! is a great place to start your searches.

FIGURE 3-3 | YAHOO!'S HOME PAGE

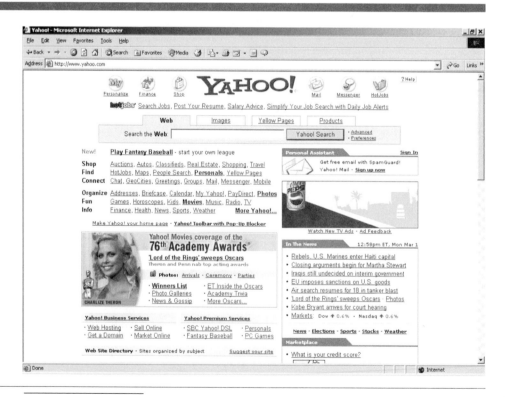

Practice Exercises   *Yahoo!*

A-1. Access Yahoo!'s web site and click on the **Advanced** search. You are attempting to find some .gov domains that contain the keywords "Financial Accounting Standards Board." Search to show results with the exact phrase in your results and search for pages written only in English. List your first three hits:

_____

_____

_____

A-2. Repeat exercise 1, but use as your keywords "International Accounting Standards." However, mark all domains for your search and again search for pages written in English. List your first three hits:

_____

_____

_____

• **Google** (see Figure 3-4) provides access to more than three billion web pages. With special features such as cached links, dictionary definitions, phone books, spell checker, and others, Google takes a snapshot of each page examined as it crawls the Web and caches (stores) these as a backup. When clicking on the "cached link" you will see the web page as it looked when it was indexed. Google has also expanded the number of non-HTML file types searched. In addition to PDF documents, Google now searches Microsoft Office, Post Script, Corel, WordPerfect, Lotus 1-2-3, and others. These additional file types provide Google users a wider view of the content available on the Web.

FIGURE 3-4 | GOOGLE'S HOME PAGE

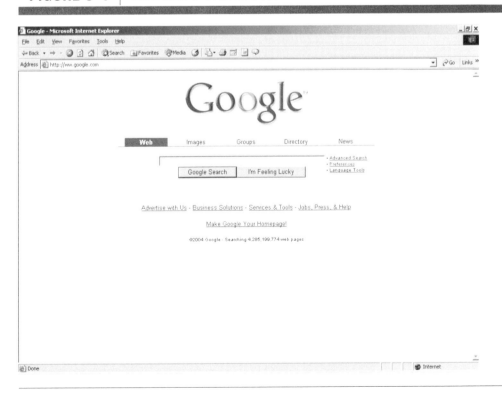

Practice Exercises   *Google*

B-1. Open the Google web site and click on the **Advanced Search**. You are attempting to prepare for a presentation on the Financial Accounting Standards Board and would like to know if there are any PowerPoint presentations about the FASB on the Web. Search for the exact phrase, and under **File Format** click on **Microsoft PowerPoint**. How many presentations did you find?

Number of FASB presentations located: _____

B-2. Your next presentation will be on International Accounting Standards. Repeat Exercise 1 and determine how many presentations exist related to International Accounting Standards.

Number of International Accounting Standards presentations located: _____

- **MetaCrawler** (see Figure 3-5) is a search engine that searches many other search engines, such as Google, Ask Jeeves, Yahoo! and Look Smart. MetaCrawler queries the other search engines, organizes the results into a uniform format, and eliminates any duplicates. It then ranks them by relevance, and returns them to the user. This means that MetaCrawler is more likely to obtain accurate results for your search query. It also helps reduce the number of returns on your search, speeding up your research. Another advantage of MetaCrawler is the standardization of query syntax, which improves the quality of your results.

FIGURE 3-5 | METACRAWLER HOME PAGE

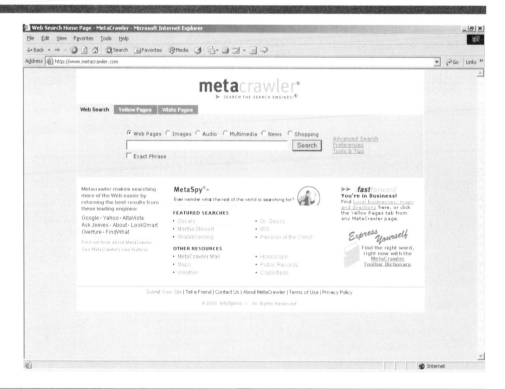

Practice Exercises   *MetaCrawler*

C-1. As indicated in the discussion on MetaCrawler, this search engine searches other search engines and indicates in the results the search engine containing the keywords. Therefore, click **Advanced Search** and use the Boolean terms to search for "Restructuring and costs." After you search click on **Refine Your Results** and click on **Accounting**. What search engines contained your keywords and how many hits were identified for each search engine?

Number of search engines identified: _____

For each search engine list the number of hits.

Search Engine	Number of Hits
_____	_____
_____	_____
_____	_____
_____	_____
_____	_____

C-2. You are attempting to determine the role of the Public Company Accounting Oversight Board (PCAOB). Open MetaCrawler and determine how many search engines listed hits, and locate a site that identifies the role of the PCAOB. _____

Number of search engines containing keywords: _____

Role of the PCAOB: _____

_____

_____

• **AltaVista** (see Figure 3-6) utilizes a ranking algorithm to determine the order in which matching documents are presented. Each document is first graded based on the number of search terms contained in the document. The Refine feature of the software dynamically sorts results into different topics, similar to a dynamic thesaurus, by giving you suggested keywords in order to refine your search. It also has a graphic version of the Refine feature.

Practice Exercises   *AltaVista*

D-1. You are attempting to determine how many filed securities fraud cases are listed by using the search engine AltaVista. Using corporate fraud as your initial key phrase, how many hits did AltaVista find?

Number of hits: _____

D-2. Refine your search using securities fraud as your key phrase, and determine how many hits exist.

Number of hits: _____

D-3. Refine your search once more and now use "filed securities fraud cases" as key words. How many hits were identified? List the first three.

Number of hits: _____

First three hits: _____

_____

_____

FIGURE 3-6 | ALTAVISTA'S HOME PAGE

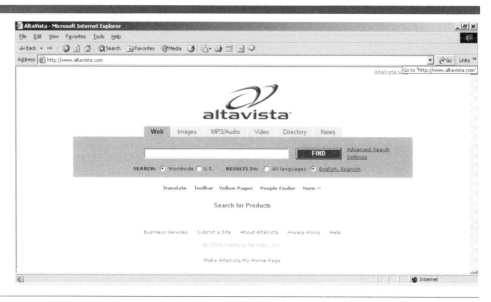

Reproduced with permission of Yahoo! Inc. © 2004 by Yahoo! Inc. YAHOO! and the YAHOO! logo are trademarks of Yahoo! Inc.

- One of the best features of **Excite** (see Figure 3-7) is that it ranks your search results by percentage, lists the best matches to your keyword(s) first, and then lists additional matches by percentage. It is fairly easy to use, and allows you to set up a personalized start page. Search results are not limited to just web pages. A search on Excite can produce results on relevant information that includes stock quotes, sports scores, weather reports, and company information useful for investigation purposes, as well as headline news.

This software not only searches documents containing the exact words you entered into the Search box, but also searches for ideas closely related to the words in your query. For example, a search on "elderly individuals" would also yield a search for "senior citizens." For advanced searches, Excite uses many of the Boolean operators presented earlier in this chapter. It does have a limited directory, but some of the categories are good resources. Excite has many useful city guides, and a very good mapping feature. This feature could benefit a fraud investigator, as discussed in Chapter 10, in attempting to find a location that supposedly contains stolen inventory belonging to the client.

Practice Exercises | *Excite*

E-1. You were given the assignment by a partner to find some information related to stock options. Access the Excite web site and search on the keywords "stock options." List the first three hits.

First three hits:

_____

_____

_____

E-2. You are planning a presentation and would like some photos related to stock options. Click on **Photos** and determine if any related photos exist for "stock options."

Number of photos you located: _____

FIGURE 3-7   EXCITE'S HOME PAGE

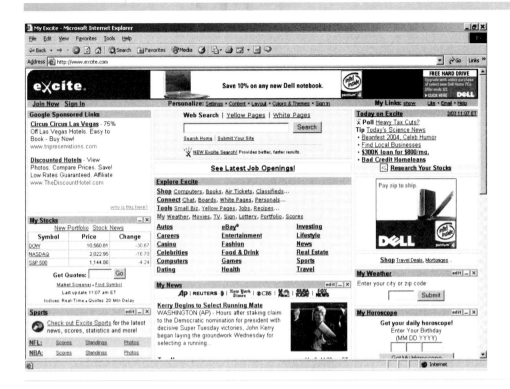

Making the Most of Search Engines

Search engines continue to improve. It seems that new search engines are developing and old search engines are constantly adding new features. Here are a few tips to advance your search skills from novice to expert!

Use the "Advanced Search" option. This feature allows you to refine the query with such terms as "and," "or," and "not." These are the Boolean operatives previously identified in this chapter. The advanced search enables the search engine to exclude common "hits" that are not related to what you are actually looking for. This feature is commonly located by following a link near the tab for regular searches and should provide more precise searching.

Control how the results are presented. Many search engines now have a feature to control how the results you see are presented. One handy customization feature is increasing the number of results that are shown on a page or single screen load. Most engines default to 20, but increasing the number to 100, as allowed by both Google (in "Preferences") and Yahoo (in "Advanced Search"), reduces the number of pages you must access to work through your results.

OTHER BUSINESS AND ACCOUNTING WEB SITES

The Internet is growing at an exponential rate as new sites are added on a daily basis. Some popular business and accounting web sites are included in the following list. Visit some of the sites to see the wealth of information available to you as a professional accounting researcher.

aicpa.org	American Institute of CPAs
businessweek.com	*BusinessWeek* Online
cfenet.com	Association of Certified Fraud Examiners
fasb.org	Financial Accounting Standard Board
ftc.gov	Federal Trade Commission
iasb.org.uk	International Accounting Standards Board
irs.gov	Internal Revenue Service
nasba.org	National Association of State Board of Accountancy
nyse.com	New York Stock Exchange
pcaobus.org	Public Company Accounting Oversight Board
sec.gov	U.S. Securities and Exchange Commission
theiia.org	The Institute of Internal Auditors

Some web sites serve as directories in a specialized field. For example, *taxsites.com* is a tax and accounting directory site that maintains updated links to numerous commercial, governmental, and professional organizational sites. Chapter 6 also provides other special-purpose commercial databases accessible through the Web. Particular focus in that chapter will be on LexisNexis®, Westlaw, Thomson One, and other research tools. Currently, the CPA exam requires one to use scaled-down versions of the FARS (Chapter 5) and AICPA reSOURCE Library (Chapter 8), as well as the RIA tax database discussed in Chapter 7.

INTERNET DANGERS REQUIRING PROTECTIVE MEASURES

One must take protective measures when using e-mail or conducting research on the Internet. Many dangers exist, including viruses, spyware, and Internet fraud. Simple precautionary steps to minimize potential danger for the researcher may include keeping confidential client data on a separate computer, not on the computer used for most Internet research. Also, always back up all critical data.

A virus is programming code that is usually disguised in an e-mail attachment, file download, or on a diskette. While some viruses are merely annoying, others are dangerous because they may include a secret malicious program called a trojan horse, to delete files, destroy a hard disk, or even open up a computer system to hackers. Thus, it is necessary for everyone to install antivirus software and regularly update it. Try to download files only from reputable Internet sites. Similarly, it is also necessary to update your operating system to add the patches that fix potential security openings for hackers. A software firewall acts as a gatekeeper between your computer and the Internet. Although a firewall is highly recommended, you should not acquire a false sense of security with it.

Spyware is a program that secretly collects data about a user and relays that information to someone else. Programs exist to identify and eliminate spyware from your computer. Similarly, if your security setting accepts cookies, it is relatively easy for web sites that you visit to collect information about your computer. Many browsers have added features to speed up performances in order to help with web surfing; however, these features potentially allow someone to see where you have been online. Clean your tracks when using Internet Explorer by going to "Tools" and then Internet Options. Click on **Delete files** to erase all the graphics and other files saved in your cache from the web pages you have visited.

As the Internet becomes increasingly used for financial transactions, such as purchasing airline tickets and books, and even accessing bank accounts, fraud on the Internet continues to multiply. Do not use public computers or wireless networks for conducting financial transactions. Make your purchases from reputable organizations. For passwords, make sure that you use complex passwords that contain various numbers, upper- and lowercase letters, and special characters. Regularly change your passwords and maintain a watchful eye in protecting your data.

SUMMARY

This chapter presented an overview of a major information technology tool (the Internet), which has an increasingly significant impact on how the professional accountant gathers information. The authors' web site for this text provides a listing of some popular web sites for the professional accountant. Subsequent chapters will provide specific usage of commercial databases and other information on the Internet and other computer tools to use for conducting accounting, auditing, and tax research.

DISCUSSION QUESTIONS

1. What is the Internet? Briefly explain ways the Internet can be utilized by the professional accountant.

2. What are the four basic ways of navigating the Internet?

3. Identify three ANet Discussion Groups available to the accountant/auditor.

4. What is a search engine?

5. When searching the Web utilizing a search engine, what would be the appropriate Boolean operator if you wanted the words *Stock Options* to be included in each document?

6. How would you configure your search if you were attempting to search for any form of the following words: *depreciate, depreciation, depreciating, depreciated*?

EXERCISES

1. Access Google's web site. Obtain the names of two companies filing IPOs (Initial Public Offerings of securities) with the SEC. Why were the companies filing the IPOs?

2. Visit the AICPA's web site (*http://www.aicpa.org*) and click on the *students* link in the left listing at the bottom. List three things included under this link.

3. Access Yahoo!'s web site. Click on the *Advanced Search* link. Obtain a listing of five hits that resulted from searching for a title that must contain the words "fraud detection" with .gov as your domain and English as the language. What is contained in these five listings?

4. Access Excite's web site. You are conducting an investigation of a family member. Click on the *White Pages* link and search for a personal relative. What did you find? If at first you do not succeed, enter the name of another relative until you get a hit.

The Environment of Accounting Research

LEARNING OBJECTIVES

After completing this chapter, you should understand:

- The SEC's role and the complex environment for accounting.
- The Financial Accounting Standards Board that sets accounting standards for the private sector.
- The Government Accounting Standards Board that sets accounting standards for state and local government accounting.
- Other organizations that influence the accounting standard setting process.
- The types of authoritative pronouncements.
- The meaning and hierarchy of GAAP.
- The current status of international accounting standards.

THE ACCOUNTING ENVIRONMENT

Research on accounting issues is conducted in a dynamic environment. New professional standards are constantly issued and existing standards updated or deleted. In researching accounting issues, one needs to use the most recent authoritative pronouncements.

The development of accounting standards is influenced by a variety of factors, including:

1. The requirements of the federal government and other regulatory bodies.
2. The influence of various tax laws on the financial reporting process.
3. The practices of certain specialized industries, such as the motion picture industry.
4. Inconsistencies in practice.
5. Disagreements among accountants, business executives, and others as to the objectives of financial statements.
6. The influence of professional organizations.
7. International differences among countries in setting international accounting standards.
8. Increasing litigation concerns.
9. The public's confidence in financial reporting.

Accounting research has a complex environment, as illustrated in Figure 4-1. The acronyms shown for the various organizations influencing accounting are explained later in this and subsequent chapters. Within this environment are numerous accounting standards, rules, and recommended practices. Yet, with so many directions in which to turn

RESEARCH TIPS

Acquire a comprehensive understanding of the dynamic accounting environment to add depth of understanding to your research.

for guidance and with the need to solve the dilemma efficiently, the accountant must have a basic understanding of when the organization's standards apply.

This chapter concentrates on the standard-setting process in accounting, including the process conducted by the private sector (Financial Accounting Standards Board—FASB) and its predecessors, the public sector for state and local government accounting (Governmental Accounting Standards Board—GASB), and selected other standard-setting bodies in the United States and internationally. Besides the Securities and Exchange Commission (SEC), the Internal Revenue Service (IRS), and the Cost Accounting Standards Board (CASB), many other professional organizations have also set or influenced certain accounting standards for entities in their domains.

SEC AND THE STANDARD-SETTING ENVIRONMENT

The Securities and Exchange Commission (SEC) in the United States was established by the Securities and Exchange Act of 1934. The law charged the SEC with the duty of insuring full and fair disclosures of all material facts relating to publicly traded securities. Public companies, those with more than $10 million in assets whose securities are held by more than 500 owners, must comply with U.S. securities laws, such as filing annual and periodic reports with the SEC. Congress empowered the SEC to specify the documents that public companies must file with the Commission and prescribe the accounting principles used in generating the financial data.

The SEC has the statutory authority to issue rules and regulations to administer the securities statutes. Those rules and regulations are formal SEC policy, as approved by the five SEC commissioners. All other SEC employees are staff, which consists of professionals that includes accountants, lawyers, economists, and securities analysts. The SEC staff are assigned to the four Divisions in the SEC: Division of Corporation Finance, Division of Market Regulation, Division of Enforcement, and Division of Investment Management.

FIGURE 4-1 | ACCOUNTING RESEARCH ENVIRONMENT

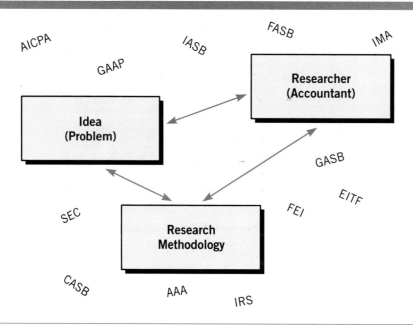

The SEC term "rules and regulations" refers to all rules and regulations adopted by the Commission, including the forms and instructions that are used to file registration statements and periodic reports. Some rules provide definitions of terms in certain statutes or regulations and are called general rules. Other rules are found in regulations, which are a compilation of rules related to a specific subject (e.g., Regulation 14A on solicitation of proxies). Still other rules relate to procedural matters, such as the steps to be followed in proceedings before the Commission, where to file documents, and what type size to use in materials filed with the SEC. Additional discussion of SEC issuances is provided in a subsequent chapter on accounting research. The SEC has delegated the major responsibility for accounting standard setting to the FASB but has retained an oversight function. The SEC recognizes use of these principles as acceptable for use in filings with the Commission. In monitoring the FASB's activities, the SEC has from time to time overruled the FASB or its predecessor the AICPA's Accounting Principles Board (APB), as in the issues of accounting for the investment tax credit, accounting for inflation, and accounting for oil and gas exploration.

Over time, accounting standards have emerged to meet the needs of financial statement users. The number of users of financial statements—primarily investors, lenders, and governmental entities—has increased enormously over the past 80 years, and the complexity of the business enterprise has increased with it. It has resulted in a greater demand by users for more uniformity in accounting procedures to make easier comparison of financial statements. Government agencies, legislative bodies, and professional organizations have gradually responded to this demand.

Currently, the Financial Accounting Standards Board (FASB) is responsible for setting accounting standards in the private sector, just as the Governmental Accounting Standards Board (GASB) is for the public sector. Before 1973, the American Institute of Certified Public Accountants (AICPA) set standards for both sectors. Following is a discussion of these accounting standard-setting bodies and their processes.

> **QUICK FACTS**
> The SEC retains an oversight function for accounting standards for public companies.

FINANCIAL ACCOUNTING STANDARDS BOARD

The role of the FASB in today's capital markets is to develop high quality financial reporting standards that result in credible and transparent financial information in order to service the investing public. The FASB's financial accounting standard-setting process actually involves several entities: the Financial Accounting Foundation (FAF), the board itself, the FASB staff, and the Emerging Issues Task Force, as noted in Figure 4-2. The GASB, which is also under the umbrella of the FAF, is discussed later in this chapter.

The FASB Board represents a broad spectrum of the financial community. It typically consists of partners from large and small CPA firms, corporate executives, financial analysts, and an academic. The FASB pursues its investigative activities with a full-time research staff of approximately 40 professionals from various backgrounds. The FASB acquires advice from the Financial Accounting Standards Advisory Council (FASAC) on the priorities of its current and proposed projects, on selecting and organizing task forces, and on any other matters that the FASB requests. In addition to the regular FASB staff, the Board has several formal channels for gathering information in the standard setting process, including various advisory councils and project resource groups. These information channels aid the Board when considering the appropriateness of current standards or conducting research for creating new accounting standards.

> **QUICK FACTS**
> The FASB is responsible for setting accounting standards in the private sector.

FASB Authorities

The FASB's most authoritative pronouncements are labeled *Statements of Financial Accounting Standards* (SFASs). The FASB also issues *Interpretations of Financial*

FIGURE 4-2   ORGANIZATION OF FAF, FASB, AND GASB

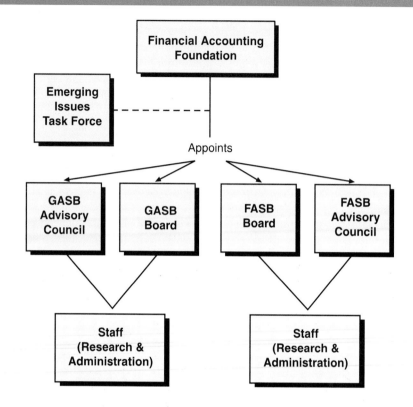

Accounting Standards, which interpret the FASB's own *Statements*, as well as predecessor authorities from the AICPA entitled *Accounting Research Bulletins* and *APB Opinions*. Most SFASs contain:

a.   A summary.

b.   A table of contents.

c.   Introduction and other narrative.

d.   The actual standard.

e.   A list of the FASB members actually voting.

f.   The basis for a qualifying or dissenting vote of an FASB member.

g.   Appendices containing background information, a glossary of terms, numerical and other examples of applying the standard, and other ancillary information.

To help practitioners and their clients implement the provisions of FASB Standards, the FASB's staff periodically issues *Technical Bulletins* to provide timely guidance on implementation issues. These *Technical Bulletins* allow conformity with FASB pronouncements without the need for the entire FASB Board to issue a new authoritative statement.

The Emerging Issues Task Force (EITF) was established in 1984 to help answer questions by financial statement preparers and users about issues not "clearly" covered by an existing set of authoritative pronouncements. Chaired by the FASB's Director of Research and Technical Activities, the EITF consists of individuals in a position to be aware of issues before they become widespread and before divergent practices regarding them become entrenched. The EITF normally addresses industry-specific issues, rather

RESEARCH TIPS

Use FASB's *Statements of Financial Accounting Standards* (SFASs) for the strongest authoritative support.

than those encompassing accounting and financial reporting as a whole. For example, EITF No. 03-5, "Applicability of AICPA Statement of Position 97-2 *Software Revenue Recognition*, to Non-Software Deliverables in an Arrangement Containing More-Than-Incidental Software" applies primarily to the software industry. Similarly, EITF No. 03-8, "Accounting for Claims-Made Insurance and Retroactive Insurance Contracts by the Insured Entity" applies to the insurance industry.

If the EITF is unable to reach a consensus on an issue under consideration and it decides that the "problem" merits further action, it will forward the file to the FASB Board for further deliberation. Conversely, if the Task Force can reach a consensus on an issue, the FASB can usually infer that no Board action is necessary. Thus, EITF's consensus positions are included in the hierarchy of GAAP for financial and state and local government reporting, as detailed in a subsequent section of this chapter.

The FASB staff often receives questions regarding the appropriate application of FASB literature. The FASB staff issues application guidance through FASB *Staff Positions* (FSP) in order to more quickly and consistently respond to practitioners' and users' needs. After receiving approval from FASB Board members, a 30-day exposure period exists for interested parties to comment on a proposed FSP. The FSPs are posted on the FASB web site (*http://www.fasb.org*) and remain there until they are incorporated into printed FASB literature. Prior to 2003, the FASB issued *Staff Implementation Guides* in response to such issues.

FASB Due Process

Given the importance of FASB standards, the Board uses an extensive due process, so much so that it has spent over eleven years deliberating on certain standards. The standard-setting process followed by the Board appears in Figure 4-3. Briefly, the FASB is held to a fixed procedure; before issuing a Statement of Financial Accounting Standards (SFAS), it must take the following steps:

1. Identify the problem or issue and take into account legal or SEC pressures.

2. Decide whether to consider the issue. At this point, the board generally seeks opinion from the FASAC, advisory councils, project resource groups, and such professional organizations as the Financial Executives International (FEI), the Institute of Management Accountants (IMA), and the Risk Management Association.

3. Establish a task force to study the problem; usually about 15 people are chosen.

4. Have its research staff investigate the issues.

5. Issue a discussion memo to interested parties.

6. Hold public hearings and request written comments on the issue. Several hundred responses are usually received.

7. Analyze the results of the investigation, communicate responses, and conduct public hearings.

8. If action is appropriate, issue an exposure draft, a preliminary SFAS. The normal exposure period is at least 60 days.

9. Request additional comments on the exposure draft and hold further public hearings.

10. After analyzing the public response, issue a final Statement of Financial Accounting Standards (SFAS).

Having gone through this due process procedure, the FASB's final pronouncement is placed in the highest level of authoritative support in the GAAP hierarchy. SFASs are issued in a standard format and are now located at the FASB's web site

FIGURE 4-3 | FASB STANDARD-SETTING PROCESS

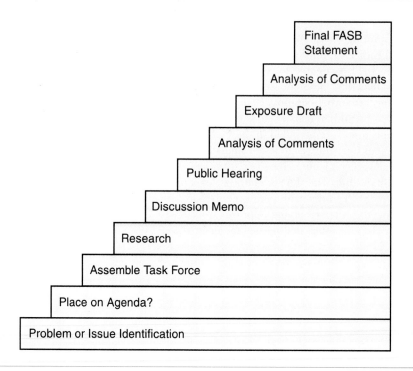

(*http://www.fasb.org*), reprinted in the *Official Release* section of the *Journal of Accountancy*, and available in the Financial Accounting Research System database discussed in a subsequent chapter.

FASB's Conceptual Framework Project

In certain situations, an accounting issue may arise for which no precedent exists and no authoritative pronouncement has been issued. In such cases, the researcher must develop a theoretically justifiable conclusion. A number of organizations and individuals have directed their efforts toward the development of accounting theory in order to provide a framework for resolving issues in a theoretically consistent manner.

The American Accounting Association (AAA)—an international professional organization primarily consisting of accounting professors—sponsors and conducts extensive research of a theoretical or conceptual nature. The AICPA also promotes research in accounting theory and has published a series of *Accounting Research Monographs* and has also issued four conceptual statements.

Despite these and other efforts, however, a widely accepted theoretical framework of accounting has not been fully developed. Recognizing the need for such a framework, the FASB has undertaken a comprehensive, long-range project called the Conceptual Framework Project. This project encompasses a series of pronouncements entitled *Statements of Financial Accounting Concepts* (SFACs), which describe concepts and relationships that underlie financial accounting standards. These pronouncements have addressed or will address such issues as elements of financial statements and their recognition, measurement, and display; capital maintenance; unit of measure; criteria for distinguishing information to be included in financial statements from that which should be provided by other means of financial reporting; and criteria for evaluating and selecting accounting information (qualitative characteristics).

Statements of Financial Accounting Concepts Nos. 1–7

The conceptual framework seeks to establish objectives and concepts for the development of accounting standards and in the preparation of financial statements, especially where no published standards exist. The project's focus is to produce a constitution for accounting, resulting in a coherent set of accounting standards. However, since the FASB did not use full due process in this project, the SFACs are not authoritative; as with FASB Statements, CPAs need not justify departures from their guidance. However, the researcher normally utilizes these pronouncements when no authoritative pronouncement is directly on point to the issue under consideration. In such cases, the researcher needs to develop a theoretical foundation for the solution to the problem.

The first seven Concept Statements issued under the Conceptual Framework Project are as follows:

1. "Objectives of Financial Reporting of Business Enterprises." SFAC No. 1 sets forth the objectives of general purpose external financial reporting by business enterprises. For example, it states that financial reports should help society better allocate scarce economic resources.

2. "Qualitative Characteristics of Accounting Information." SFAC No. 2 examines the characteristics of accounting information that make the information useful.

3. SFAC No. 3 was superseded by SFAC No. 6.

4. "Objectives of Financial Reporting of Nonbusiness Organizations." SFAC No. 4 establishes the objectives of general purpose external financial reporting by nonbusiness organizations.

5. "Recognition and Measurement in Financial Statements." SFAC No. 5 establishes recognition criteria and guidance regarding what information should be incorporated into financial statements. SFAC No. 5 also describes and defines the concept of earnings and what should be included in a full set of an entity's financial statements.

6. "Elements of Financial Statements." SFAC No. 6 redefines the ten interrelated elements of financial statements: assets, liabilities, equity, investment by owners, distributions to owners, comprehensive income, revenues, expenses, gains, and losses. It also defines three classes of net assets for not-for-profit organizations as well as accrual accounting and other related concepts. Besides amending portions of SFAC No. 2, SFAC No. 6 also supersedes SFAC No. 3.

7. "Using Cash Flow Information and Present Value in Accounting Measurements." SFAC No. 7 provides a framework for using future cash flows as the basis for accounting measurements and for the interest method of amortization. It also provides general principles that govern the use of present value.

> **RESEARCH TIPS**
>
> When specific authority does not exist, use FASB concepts to develop a solution.

Rules-Based versus Principles-Based Accounting Standards

The SEC recently studied the approach by which accounting standards are established, in response to the Sarbanes-Oxley Act of 2002, which sought to improve the U.S. system of financial reporting. The study concluded that imperfections exist when standards are created either on a principles-only or a rules-only basis. Rules-only standards provide detailed and structured technical guidance; however, often the *intention* of the standard is overlooked. Conversely, principles-only standards may state a goal or objective while providing little technical guidance or structure for complying with the standard. Based on its study, the SEC recommends a more consistent and efficient system of "principles-based" or "objective-oriented" standards with guidance for operational sufficiency. Such standards would provide a more useful conceptual framework and more timely information to the practitioner or user of financial statements. These objective oriented standards should have the following characteristics:

- Arise from an improved and consistently applied conceptual framework.

- Clearly state the accounting objective of the standard.

- Provide sufficient detail and structure so that the standard can be operationalized and applied on a consistent basis.

- Minimize exceptions from the standard.

- Avoid use of percentage tests ("bright-lines") that allow financial engineers to achieve technical compliance with the standard while evading the intent of the standard.

As the accounting standard setting moves forward, the issue of principles-based or objectives-based standards should characterize the FASB's standard setting process.

FASB Strives to Simplify Standards

In response to the growing number of increasingly complex accounting standards, the FASB has realized the need for simplification of its standards. The term "standards overload" is often used to describe the profession's concern as to the number and complexity of accounting rules and required disclosures, and the difficulty of finding all the accounting rules on any given subject. This new framework emphasizes issuing standards that focus more on objectives (substance) rather than detailed rules (form).

Additionally, another project aimed at simplifying the FASB standards focuses on improving the quality of the cost-benefit analysis performed on proposed standards. Through this project, the FASB strives to reduce the costs of issuing a new standard (e.g., development time, learning time, monetary expense, etc.) without decreasing its benefits to financial reporting. Overall, the FASB's goal is to make accounting standards that are easier to understand and apply, and financial statements that are more useful to and utilizable by ordinary investors.

AMERICAN INSTITUTE OF CERTIFIED PUBLIC ACCOUNTANTS

Before the establishment of the FASB in 1973, the AICPA was the recognized standard-setting body for the private sector. The AICPA's Committee on Accounting Procedures published 51 Accounting Research Bulletins (ARBs) from 1939 to 1959, dealing with a wide spectrum of accounting issues. Because of the FASB's approval and clearance, some of these ARBs from the AICPA still apply. However, FASB Statements have superceded some ARB pronouncements and modified the application of others.

In 1959, the Accounting Principles Board (APB) began. The APB has issued 31 APB Opinions, now binding on all CPAs. Since 1984, the AICPA has required disclosure of departures from APB Opinions (APBOs) either in the notes to financial statements or in the audit reports. CPAs could not give their approval to financial statements that deviated from APB Opinions unless they wanted to assume the considerable personal risk and the burden of proof of defending the "unauthorized practices." Since few business enterprises or auditors were anxious to assume the burden of defending financial statements that differed from APB Opinions, this action gave new strength and authority to the APB Opinions. The APB has also issued four nonauthoritative Statements (which address broad concepts rather than specific accounting principles) and several unofficial interpretations.

Following the formation of the FASB, the AICPA created an Accounting Standards Division to influence the development of accounting standards. The Accounting

Standards Executive Committee (AcSEC) of the Accounting Standards Division became the spokesperson for the AICPA on financial accounting matters. AcSEC responds to FASB and SEC accounting pronouncements by issuing *Comment Letters* and prepares *Issues Papers* to develop financial accounting and reporting issues that the FASB should consider. AcSEC also often publishes brief notes and news releases in the AICPA's biweekly publication, *The CPA Letter*, which reaches more than 340,000 members.

In the past, AcSEC also issued Statements of Position (SOPs) to propose revisions of AICPA-published Industry Audit and Accounting Guides. However, due to recent changes in the profession, authority for issuing SOPs will reside with the FASB. Prior SOPs do not establish enforceable accounting standards; however, members of the AICPA must justify departures from practices recommended in the SOPs.

Various committees of the AICPA also publish *Accounting Research Monographs*, *Accounting Trends and Techniques*, and other publications, which are discussed in Chapter 6. The annual *Accounting Trends and Techniques* publication summarizes current accounting practices of over 600 publicly owned companies. It presents tabulations of the numbers of surveyed companies that use particular practices; it also presents excerpts of actual reports issued by the surveyed companies.

GOVERNMENTAL ACCOUNTING STANDARDS BOARD

Financial reports of local and state units of government for many years have varied in quality and lacked uniformity due to an absence of clearly defined principles. A body of generally accepted accounting principles (GAAP) for local units of government has slowly evolved. However, given the large value of assets that governmental entities "manage," as well as infamous financial crises in municipal units such as New York, Cleveland, and Orange County in California, the financial community has paid increasing attention to governmental units' financial statements.

Public sector (governmental) accounting is only now reaching the plateau of responsibility and credibility inhabited by private sector (proprietary) accounting. The Governmental Accounting Standards Board (GASB) has developed in a fashion similar to that of the Financial Accounting Standards Board (FASB). GASB received authoritative status for its standards under Rule 203 of the AICPA's Rules of Conduct and legislation in the various states.

GASB's role is to set financial accounting and reporting standards for the public sector (i.e., state and local governmental entities) as the FASB does for all private entities. The GASB was established in 1984 by the Financial Accounting Foundation (FAF). This caused the addition of two government organizations (the Government Finance Officers Association [GFOA] and the National Association of State Auditors, Comptrollers, and Treasurers) to the list of FAF sponsors. Both organizations continue to focus primarily on GASB standards for the public sector.

The GASB consists of seven members who are required to have knowledge of governmental accounting and finance and a concern for the public interest in matters of financial accounting and reporting. The GASB's professional staff works directly with the Board and its task forces, conducts research, participates in public hearings, analyzes oral and written comments received from the public on documents, and prepares drafts of documents for consideration by the Board.

GASB uses the following due process for major projects:

- Research the subject to define the issues and to determine the scope of the projects.

- Appoint a task force to advise the Board on the issues and to aid in developing alternative solutions prior to the issuance of a discussion document.

- Issue a discussion memorandum or invitation to comment, which will set forth the definition of the problem, scope of the project, and the issues involved; discuss relevant research; and include alternative solutions to the issues identified.

- Hold a public hearing, at which concerned individuals will be encouraged to state their views on the issues contained in the discussion document.

- Issue an exposure draft of a proposed Statement for public comment, prior to adoption of a final Statement.

- Issue a final Statement. A majority vote of the Board members is needed to issue a Statement.

During these steps, the Board deliberates the issues in meetings open to the public. The Board may issue a Statement in an expedited process following exposure for public comment if, in the judgment of its members, the Board can make an informed decision based on available information. GASB pronouncements serve as a beginning reference for the researcher in addressing an issue associated with state or local governmental accounting. Because GASB uses a due process procedure, its pronouncements are among the highest level of governmental GAAP.

Similar to its FASB counterpart, the GASB has an advisory council. The Governmental Accounting Standards Advisory Council (GASAC) is responsible for consulting with the GASB as to major policy questions, technical issues on the Board's agenda, project priorities, matters likely to require the attention of the GASB, selection and organization of task forces, and such other matters as may be requested by the GASB or its chairperson. The GASAC also is responsible for helping develop the GASB's annual budget.

State and local government accounting first developed in 1968 with the publication of *Government Accounting, Auditing, and Financial Reporting*, known by the acronym GAAFR or simply as "The Blue Book." GAAFR brought together different governmental accounting practices and provided an authoritative source for such accounting; it became the basis for many state laws for uniform municipal accounting. In an attempt to eliminate the accounting differences and to update, clarify, amplify, and reorder the principles of GAAFR, the National Council on Governmental Accounting (NCGA) in 1979 issued *Statement 1, Governmental Accounting and Financial Reporting Principles*. Statement 1 contained significant modifications to the basic fund accounting and financial reporting philosophy of GAAFR.

Three major primary research publications exist in the governmental arena. First, the *GASB Codification of Government Accounting & Financial Reporting Studies* contains all GASB Statements, Interpretations, Technical Bulletins, and Concept Statements. It also codifies the National Council on Government Accounting's Statements and Interpretations, as well as the AICPA's Audit Guides of State and Local Governments and Statements of Position. The *GASB Codification* corresponds to the private sector's *FASB Accounting Standards*.

Second, the U.S. Comptroller General's "Yellow Book" contains a codification of audit standards for government organizations, programs, activities, and functions. This text operates much the same as the AICPA *Professional Standards*.

Finally, the U.S. Congress's "Single Audit Act of 1984" requires all state and local government units receiving at least $300,000 of federal assistance per fiscal year to have an audit made in conformity with the standards of this Act. These audits contain both financial and compliance components and are subject to oversight by federal agencies designated by the United States Office of Management and Budget.

RESEARCH TIPS

Use the "Blue Book" for state and local government accounting; while the "Yellow Book" is for government auditing standards.

OTHER ORGANIZATIONS INFLUENCING STANDARD SETTING

The Cost Accounting Standards Board (CASB) is an independent board within the Office of Management and Budget's Office of Federal Procurement Policy. The CASB has increased the uniformity of cost allocations among companies holding large government contracts. It has exclusive authority to issue cost accounting standards that govern the measurement, assignment, and allocation of costs on federal government contracts over $500,000. The CASB was created by Congress in 1971, discontinued in 1980, and recreated in 1989, but is currently inactive and without staff. Yet, the CASB continues to serve as an important source of authoritative guidance.

Income tax laws have significantly influenced the development and implementation of GAAP because of the willingness of the accounting profession to accept tax accounting requirements as GAAP. In order to save the expenses of maintaining two sets of books, many smaller businesses use tax-basis statements as their external financial statements. CPAs must recognize certain reporting problems when the two statements are not identical. The Internal Revenue Code, IRS Regulations, Revenue Rulings, and other tax accounting pronouncements also affect accounting practice. Researching a tax issue is discussed in Chapter 7.

Many other professional organizations influence directly or indirectly the setting of accounting standards:

- The Securities Industry Associates (SIA), which represents investment bankers and manages the portfolios of large institutional investors, and the Financial Analysts Federation are typical of the kind of organizations that influence the setting of standards and the shaping of GAAP. They help select members of the Financial Accounting Foundation (FAF), which in turn selects the members of the FASB and the GASB. These groups represent users of financial statements and usually favor standards providing for additional disclosures.

- The National Association of State Auditors, Controllers, and Treasurers is an information clearinghouse and research base for state financial officials. Although it publishes no journal, the Association performs financial management projects for state fiscal officers, and it also appoints members to the FAF.

- The Financial Executives International (FEI) influences accounting standards development by having an active committee make recommendations on discussion memoranda issued by the FASB. The FEI also conducts its own research on important issues through the Financial Executives Research Foundation.

- The Institute of Management Accountants (IMA), also has a committee providing formal input to the FASB.

- The American Accounting Association (AAA) emphasizes the need for a theoretical foundation for accounting; the AAA influences standard setting through research and analysis of accounting concepts presented in committee reports and in its quarterly journal, *The Accounting Review*, and other publications.

Figure 4-4 summarizes the constituencies and the missions of organizations affecting standard setting and the shaping of GAAP.

FIGURE 4-4	THE ROLE OF PROFESSIONAL ACCOUNTING ORGANIZATIONS IN DEVELOPING GAAP

Organization	Principal Membership	Principal Mission	Professional Journal
* 1. American Accounting Association (AAA)	Accounting professors	Helps develop a logical, theoretical basis for accounting. Promotes research and education in accounting.	*Accounting Horizons*
http://www.aaahg.org			
* 2. American Institute of Certified Public Accountants (AICPA)	Certified Public Accountants	Its various committees have issued authoritative pronouncements on accounting principles and auditing standards. Conducts programs of research and education, surveys practice, and communicates concerns of members.	*Journal of Accountancy*
http://www.aicpa.org			
* 3. Association of Government Accountants (AGA)	Federal, state, and local government accountants	Professional society of accountants, auditors, comptrollers, and budget officers employed by federal, state, and local governments in management and administrative positions. Monitors the activities of and often provides input to the Government Accounting Standards Board (GASB).	*The Journal of Government Financial Management*
http://www.agacgfm.org			
* 4. Association for Investment Management and Research	Financial analysts and Chartered Financial Analysts	Promotes the development of improved standards of investment research and portfolio management. An organization of primary users of accounting information, it represents those who analyze information and provide professional advice on investment matters.	*Financial Analysts Journal*
http://www.aimr.com			
* 5. Financial Executives International (FEI)	Corporate financial executives	Professional organization of financial and management executives performing duties of a controller, treasurer, or VP-finance, primarily from large corporations. Sponsors research activities through its affiliated Financial Executives Research Foundation.	*Financial Executive*
http://www.fei.org			
* 6. Governmental Finance Officers Association (GFOA)	State and local public finance officials	Provides technical service center and technical inquiry service for public finance officials. Monitors the activities of and often provides input to the GASB.	*Governmental Finance Review*
http://www.gfoa.org			
* 7. Institute of Internal Auditors (IIA)	Internal auditors and Certified Internal Auditors	Cultivates, promotes, and disseminates knowledge concerning internal auditors. Sponsors research on the internal auditor's role in promoting more reliable financial information.	*The Internal Auditor*
http://www.theiia.org			

RESEARCH TOOLS

Internet
FARS
LexisNexis
AICPA reSOURCE
PwC Edgarscan
Thomson ONE
RIA Checkpoint SE
ACL
i2

(continued)

FIGURE 4-4 | THE ROLE OF PROFESSIONAL ACCOUNTING ORGANIZATIONS IN DEVELOPING GAAP (CONTINUED)

Organization	Principal Membership	Principal Mission	Professional Journal
* 8. Institute of Management Accountants (IMA)	Corporate controllers and financial officers and Certified Management Accountants	Conducts research primarily on management accounting methods and procedures, and has recently increased its role in the development of financial accounting standards.	*Strategic Finance*
http://www.imanet.org			
* 9. National Association of State Auditors, Controllers, and Treasurers	State financial officials	Serves as an information clearinghouse and research base for state financial officials.	
http://www.nasact.org			
10. Risk Management Association	Bank officers	Promotes studies on comparative industry practices to provide benchmarks against which to judge corporate performance.	*The RMA Journal*
http://www.rmahq.org			
11. Securities Industry Association (SIA)	Broker dealers in securities	Monitors and provides input to stockbrokers regarding SEC, stock exchanges (e.g., NYSE and AMEX), and congressional actions.	*Securities Industry Trends*
http://www.sia.com			

* Also appoints members to the Financial Accounting Foundation.

Practice Exercises — *Exercises Related to Standard Setters*

1. Access the FASB's web site (*http://www.fasb.org*) and answer the following:
   a. List the titles of the two most recently issued FASB Statements.

   _____

   _____

   b. What is the primary function of the Financial Accounting Standards Advisory Council (FASAC)?

   _____

   _____

2. Access the SEC's web site (*http://www.sec.gov*) and answer the following.
   a. List the two most recently issued proposed rules.

   _____

   _____

   b. Locate and briefly describe the SEC's Internet Enforcement Program located under the Enforcement Division.

   _____

   _____

GENERALLY ACCEPTED ACCOUNTING PRINCIPLES

GAAP is "a technical accounting term which encompasses the conventions, rules, and procedures necessary to define accepted accounting practice at a particular time," according to APB Statement No. 4. This definition implies two truths:

1. GAAP is not a static, well-defined set of accounting principles, but a fluid set of principles based on current accounting thought and practice. GAAP changes in response to changes in the business environment. Therefore, the researcher must review the most current authoritative support, recognizing that recent pronouncements sometimes supercede or modify older pronouncements.

2. GAAP is not composed of mutually exclusive accounting principles. Alternative principles for similar transactions sometimes may be considered equally acceptable. The researcher must not quit when one acceptable principle is found.

GAAP performs two major functions:

1. **Measurement.** GAAP requires recognizing or matching revenues of a given period with all expenses that were incurred to generate those revenues (e.g., depreciating fixed assets and recognizing stock options and pension liabilities). Besides attempting to measure periodic income objectively, the measurement principle focuses on the valuation of financial statement accounts (e.g., reporting inventories at the lower of cost or market valuations).

2. **Disclosure.** GAAP provides information necessary for the users' decision models (e.g., methods to group accounts and descriptive terminology, as in reporting lease obligations in the footnotes). However, GAAP does not require disclosure of certain macroeconomic factors (e.g., interest rates and unemployment rates) that may interest the entity, bankers, and other financial statement users.

CPAs may not express an opinion that the financial statements are presented in conformity with GAAP if the statements depart materially from an accounting principle promulgated by an "authoritative body" designated by the AICPA Council, such as the FASB and the AICPA's APB. While opinions from these bodies provide the "substantial authoritative support" necessary to create GAAP, other sources of GAAP are available. Most notable are standard industry practices either when a practice addresses a principle that does not otherwise exist in GAAP or when a practice seems to conflict with GAAP. In either case, management must justify the practice, and the CPA must evaluate the case to ascertain whether the practice violates established GAAP. In addition, if "unusual circumstances" would make it misleading to follow the normal procedure, management must disclose departures from the authoritative guidelines and justify the alternative principle.

The FASB arrives at GAAP considering three objectives of financial reporting set out in Statement of Financial Accounting Concepts No. 1. Financial reporting should provide information that:

1. Is useful to present and potential investors and creditors and other users in making rational investment, credit, and similar decisions. The information should be comprehensible to those who have a reasonable understanding of business and economic activities and are willing to study the information with reasonable diligence.

2. Helps present potential investors, creditors, and other users in assessing the amounts, timing, and uncertainty of prospective cash receipts from dividends or interest, as well as the proceeds from the sale, redemption, or maturity of securities or loans. Since investors' and creditors' cash flows are related to enterprise cash flows, financial reporting should provide information to help investors, creditors, and others assess the amounts, timing, and uncertainty of prospective net cash inflows to the related enterprise.

3. Clarifies the economic resources of an enterprise, the claims to those resources (obligations of the enterprise to transfer resources to other entities and owners' equity), and the effects of transactions, events, and circumstances that change its resources and claims to those resources.

The Hierarchy of GAAP[1]

RESEARCH TIPS

Know the distinction between the levels of GAAP, and attempt to utilize the highest level in your research.

Accountants in general agree that a body of generally accepted accounting principles exists. A hierarchy exists for the components of GAAP. This hierarchy shows the researcher where to begin in a search for a solution to the problem or issue under review. Figures 4-5 and 4-6 present the basic components of the hierarchy for Financial Statement GAAP and Government GAAP, respectively, as five different levels. Those in level one have the highest level of authority.

The foundation for this hierarchy contains the basic assumption or concepts of financial or government accounting. This foundation includes basic assumptions and principles underlying financial reporting: e.g., the going-concern assumption, substance over form, neutrality, the accrual basis, conservatism, materiality, objectivity, consistency, and full disclosure.

Levels one through four contain the components of four groups of reference sources containing established accounting principles. Level five provides other accounting literature in the absence of an established authoritative accounting principle as authorized by the AICPA's Rule 203 of the Code of Professional Conduct.

The following additional information about the levels of Financial Statement GAAP should enhance the reader's understanding of the items within each level.

Level 1 This level includes pronouncements of an authoritative body designated by the AICPA that officially establish GAAP, including:

a. FASB Statements of Financial Accounting Standards (SFASs) and Interpretations.

b. Thirty-one Opinions of the AICPA's Accounting Principles Board (APBOs).

c. Fifty-one Accounting Research Bulletins (ARBs), which were issued by the Committee on Accounting Procedures (CAP) of the AICPA.

d. Rules and Interpretative Releases issued by the Securities and Exchange Commission. Since the SEC has the ultimate authority to establish GAAP for publicly listed entities, these pronouncements have the highest level of authority that applies specifically to SEC registrants.

In short, FASB statements supersede some APB opinions, which, in turn, supersede some ARB statements, but those unsuperseded APB opinions and ARB statements are still effective. More recently issued standards supersede earlier ones. An FASB interpretation clarifies, explains, or elaborates on prior FASB, APB, and ARB statements, and has the same authority they do.

---

[1] Statement on Auditing Standards No. 69, "The Meaning of Present Fairly in Conformity with Generally Accepted Accounting Principles in the Independent Auditor's Report," AICPA, 1991 as amended by SASs No. 91 and 93.

FIGURE 4-5 | BASIC PRINCIPLES AND ASSUMPTIONS UNDERLYING FINANCIAL REPORTING

Level	Components
1	Pronouncements of an authoritative Body designated by the AICPA Council in Rule 203 of the Code of Professional Conduct. a. FASB Statements and Interpretations b. APB Opinions c. AICPA Accounting Research Bulletins d. Rules and Interpretative Releases of the SEC for SEC registrants
2	Pronouncements of bodies composed of expert accountants who follow a due process procedure; such pronouncements have been cleared by a body referred to in Level 1. a. Cleared AICPA Industry Audit and Accounting Guides b. Cleared AICPA Statements of Position (SOPs) c. FASB Technical Bulletins
3	Pronouncements of bodies organized by the FASB or AICPA but that do not necessarily go through due process procedures. a. AcSEC Practice Bulletins cleared by the FASB b. Consensus Positions of the FASB Emerging Issues Task Force
4	Practices or pronouncements that are widely recognized as being generally accepted because they represent prevalent practice in a particular industry, or the knowledgeable application to specific circumstances of pronouncements that are generally accepted. a. AICPA Accounting Interpretations b. Implementation Guides by the FASB Staff, now referred to as FASB Staff Positions (FSPs). c. Notable Industry Practices d. Uncleared SOPs, and audit and accounting guides
5	Other Accounting Literature a. APB Statements b. AICPA Issues Papers c. FASB Concepts Statements d. International Accounting Standards Committee Statements e. AICPA Technical Practice Aids f. Textbooks g. Journal articles and monographs

Level 2 This level includes pronouncements of bodies of expert accountants who follow a "due process" of deliberating and issuing accounting statements.

   a. FASB (and previously, AICPA) Statements of Position (SOPs), which have been reviewed and cleared.

   b. FASB Technical Bulletins, which provide guidance in applying authoritative pronouncements.

   c. AICPA Industry Audit and Accounting Guides, which normally are reviewed by the AICPA's Accounting Standards Executive Committee (AcSEC) and cleared by the FASB.

Level 3 This level includes AcSEC Practice Bulletins that have been cleared by the FASB, and also includes consensus positions of the FASB Emerging Issues Task Force (EITF).

FIGURE 4-6 | BASIC PRINCIPLES AND ASSUMPTIONS UNDERLYING STATE AND LOCAL GOVERNMENT REPORTING

NOTE: For Federal Governmental Entities, the first four levels would also include pronouncements issued by the Federal Accounting Standards Advisory Board (FASAB).

Level	Components
1	**Pronouncements of an Authoritative Body** a. FASB Pronouncements acknowledged by the GASB b. NCGA Pronouncements acknowledged by the GASB c. GASB and AICPA Pronouncements NOTE: If the accounting treatment of a transaction or event is not specified by a pronouncement of either 1a or 1b, then 1c is presumed to apply.
2	**Pronouncements of bodies composed of expert accountants who follow a due process procedure.** a. GASB Technical Bulletins b. Cleared AICPA Industry Audit and Accounting Guides, such as: Audits of State and Local Governmental Units Audits of Certain Nonprofit Organizations Audits of Colleges and Universities c. Cleared AICPA Statements of Position
3	Consensus positions of the GASB, EITF, and cleared AcSEC practice bulletins for state and local government.
4	**Practices or pronouncements that are widely recognized as being generally accepted because they represent prevalent practice in a particular industry, or the knowledgeable application to specific circumstances of pronouncements that are generally accepted.** a. Uncleared SOPs and Audit and Accounting Guides b. Questions and Answers issued by GASB staff c. Industry practice
5	**Other Accounting Literature** a. GASB Statements of Financial Accounting Concepts b. Elements of the Financial Statement Hierarchy c. Textbooks d. Journal articles

Level 4 Included in this level are the AICPA Interpretations as well as implementation guides (referred to as "Questions and Answers") issued by the FASB staff. Also included in this level are the uncleared FASB (and previously, AICPA) Statements of Position and uncleared audit and accounting guides (cleared SOPs and guides appear in Level 3) and practices widely recognized in a particular industry.

Level 5 This level provides other accounting literature that the researcher could reference in the absence of a higher-level authority.

While reference to an authoritative pronouncement usually provides adequate support for an accounting decision, accountants forced to rely on lower levels of support must often build a case involving multiple references. Figure 4-7 provides a division between primary, self-supporting references and secondary, non-self-supporting references.

In researching an issue, this question often arises: Where does the researcher start and when can he or she stop the research process? To begin, the researcher would focus on the primary authoritative support, which has the highest level of authority according to the hierarchy of GAAP. If no primary sources are cited, the researcher would then drop down and review the secondary support.

RESEARCH TIPS

When using lower levels of support, attempt to reference multiple authorities.

FIGURE 4-7 | ACCOUNTING AUTHORITATIVE SUPPORT

Primary Authoritative Support

Sources that provide sufficient authoritative support for including a particular accounting principle within GAAP.
  A. General Application to the Field of Accounting
     1. FASB, FASAB, and GASB Statements of Financial and Governmental Accounting Standards
     2. FASB, FASAB, and GASB Interpretations
     3. Opinions of the AICPA's Accounting Principles Board
     4. Accounting Research Bulletins of the Committee on Accounting Procedures
     5. Consensus Positions of EITF of the FASB
  B. Special Application to Certain Entities
     1. Regulations of the Securities and Exchange Commission
     2. AICPA Industry Accounting Guides
     3. AICPA Statements of Position
     4. Statements of the Cost Accounting Standards Board
     5. Interpretations of the Cost Accounting Standards Board

Secondary Authoritative Support

Sources that support inclusion of particular accounting principles within GAAP, but individually are not sufficient authoritative support.
  A. Official Publications of Authoritative Bodies
     1. FASB Statements of Financial Accounting Concepts
     2. GASB Concept Statements
     3. FASB Technical Bulletins
     4. APB Statements of the AICPA
     5. Interpretations of APB Opinions
  B. Other Sources of Information
     1. Pronouncements of industry regulatory authorities
     2. Substantive industry practices
     3. Published research studies of authoritative professional and industrial societies
     4. Publications of recognized industry associations
     5. Accounting research monographs of the AICPA
     6. SEC Staff Accounting Bulletins
     7. Pronouncements of the IFAC and other international accounting bodies
     8. Accounting textbooks and reference books authored by recognized authorities in the field

RESEARCH TIPS

If possible, start your research with primary support and the highest level of authority.

If the researcher determines that the answer to the question is located in a primary authoritative support, he or she can stop the research process since these sources are sufficient for a conclusion. However, if the researcher cited secondary support, additional research is needed since any secondary source individually is insufficient authority. The researcher must recognize that many research questions will not have clear cut answers and, therefore, professional judgment is a key element in deciding when to stop the research process.

Using Authoritative Support

Accountants rely heavily on the GAAP authorities in supporting their positions. CPAs may not attest to the validity of financial statements (i.e., they may not express an opinion that the statements are presented in conformity with GAAP) if the statements depart materially from an accounting principle promulgated by an authoritative body (i.e., a senior technical committee) designated by the AICPA Council, such as the FASB, the GASB, or the AICPA's APB. Sometimes an accountant attempts to discover a consensus among users of financial information to document industry practices.

A CPA may sometimes justify using an alternative principle to GAAP if unusual circumstances would make it misleading to follow the normal GAAP principles. That is, under Rule 203 of the AICPA's Code of Professional Conduct, if the entity's management believes the circumstances do not warrant compliance with the accounting standard, an exception is permitted. Under these circumstances, however, the auditor's report must clearly disclose the nature of the exception and the reason for it in the financial statements.

READING AN AUTHORITATIVE PRONOUNCEMENT

In researching an issue, the researcher may need to read a specific FASB Statement, GASB Statement, or APB Opinion. In such a case, the researcher should be aware that there is a basic format that is followed in these pronouncements. Depending upon the complexity of the pronouncement, the following elements may be included: an introduction to the accounting issues addressed by the pronouncement, the background of the business event and accounting issues, the basis of the Board's conclusions, the actual opinion or statement of accounting standard, the effective date to implement the standard, illustrations of application, and the disclosures required. These basic elements are not necessarily presented as separate sections of all Opinions or Statements. Those that are relatively short may combine the introduction and background information and eliminate the illustration of applications section if it is not a complicated principle. However, there is always a separate section designated as the Opinion or Standard of Accounting.

The *introductory section* defines the accounting issue that necessitated an authoritative pronouncement. This section gives the scope of the pronouncement; that is, it defines the type of entity affected. It can also limit the application of the pronouncement to companies of specific size (e.g., sales exceeding $250 million). The introduction also gives the effects of the new pronouncement on previously issued standards. It specifies which pronouncements or sections of prior pronouncements are superseded by the new standard. Generally, within the introduction, there is a summary of the standard so that the researcher sees quickly if the standard applies to the specific situation being investigated.

The *background information* section describes in more detail the business events and related accounting treatments presented in the pronouncement. This section develops the various arguments supporting alternative approaches to resolving the issue. The underlying assumptions for these alternatives are defined, and the different interpretations of the economic impact of the business event are presented. This section follows the introduction in the APB Opinions, while the FASB generally places the background information in an appendix to the official pronouncement.

The *basis for conclusion* of the authoritative standard is described in the Opinions and Statements. This section explains the rationale for the accounting principles prescribed in the pronouncement, indicating which arguments were accepted and which were rejected. (Generally, the APB incorporates the basis of conclusion within the Opinion section of the pronouncement. The FASB incorporates dissenting viewpoints at the end of its main section, Standards of Financial Accounting and Reporting, and positions the Basis for Conclusion in a separate appendix.) The background information and basis for conclusion provide the researcher with a description of the business events and transactions covered by the pronouncement. These sections can be helpful in determining if the pronouncement

RESEARCH TIPS

Use the organization of a pronouncement to find the most relevant parts within the authority.

addresses the specific issue under investigation. If the researcher is in the early stages of investigation, these sections can be helpful in defining the business transactions, determining their economic impact, and relating them to the proper reporting format.

The *opinion or standard section* prescribes the accounting principles that must be applied to the business transactions described in the pronouncement. The length of this section will depend upon the complexity of the business events involved.

This standard section represents the heart of the official pronouncement and must be followed when the researcher concludes that the standard applies to the business transactions under investigation. The section can be very short, as in the case of FASB Statement No. 129, "Disclosure of Information about Capital Structure," which basically establishes standards for disclosing information about an entity's capital structure, or it can be very long and complicated, as in FASB Statement No. 142, "Goodwill and Other Intangible Assets." In Statement No. 142, the board established specialized terminology; eliminated the amortization of goodwill; and established accounting, reporting, impairment considerations and disclosure requirements for intangible assets. All of these items are within the standard section.

The *effective date section* states when the new pronouncement goes into effect. It also identifies any transition period that might be used by a company to implement a new standard. For example, FASB Statement No. 13, "Accounting for Leases," had a four-year transition period to permit companies to gather data for retroactive application of this complicated pronouncement on lease transactions. Some standards may take effect retroactively, while others take effect shortly after their issuance. If the board prescribes the method of implementation, retroactive restatement, cumulative effect, or prospective application, the method will be indicated in this section of the pronouncement.

Accounting Choices Have Economic Consequences

Selecting an accounting alternative often affects economic decisions within a business. For example, debates as to the proper accounting for stock options and the use of market values for derivatives have resulted in major economic implications for many companies. When alternatives within GAAP exist, accountants should consider the probable economic impact in selecting various accounting principles.

The development of financial accounting standards can affect economic behavior and wealth distribution in three ways, according to Rappaport.[2] The standards can influence intended external users (e.g., competitors and stockholders), unintended external users (e.g., competitors, labor unions, and special interest groups) and internal users (e.g., corporate management). For example, assume that the research suggests the future value of equipment is impaired so as to immediately expense it, rather than continuing to capitalize it over several years. This reduction in income could adversely impact the company's earnings per share and stock price; it could reduce the union members' profit sharing payouts or make their competitors' financial statements look relatively stronger, enabling them to attract new investors; and it could reduce the bonuses available to corporate management, thereby causing them to relocate to their competitors' organizations.

The previous example demonstrates the "Law of Unintended Consequences," which often generates many unexpected ramifications from the decisions. Nonetheless, accountants are ethically bound to follow GAAP to help report accurate financial information—regardless of future economic consequences. Legally, various civil and criminal penalties exist after Sarbanes-Oxley for defrauding shareholders of public companies,

---

[2] Rappaport, Alfred, "Economic Impact of Accounting Standards—Implications for the FASB," *The Journal of Accountancy*, Vol. 2 (May 1977): 89–97.

altering documents, improper certification of financial reports, and engaging in other improper conduct.

INTERNATIONAL ACCOUNTING

International competition has forced many firms to look to new markets and investors to finance the expansion or modernization needed to remain competitive in world markets. Increasingly internationalized capital markets result in a need for internationally comparable financial statements and accounting standards. Accounting principles and reporting practices are forms of communication which, in theory, should move across national boundaries as freely as the business practices they are intended to reflect. In truth, however, these accounting principles mirror the disparate economic and social environments of their respective nations and regions. As businesses and trade barriers between nations become less restrictive (e.g., under the influence of the North American Free Trade Agreement), differences among national accounting and auditing standards become more troubling.

International accounting is still characterized largely by a collection of authoritative pronouncements of each individual country. This makes the task of comparing companies across national boundaries cumbersome and potentially confusing. Moreover, the growth of international joint ventures, American subsidiaries abroad, and foreign investments requires greater mastery of international accounting standards.

Efforts have increased in recent years to move toward international standards. The movement toward harmonization has included the work of individual scholars as well as the activities of supranational groups. Included in the latter category are the International Federation of Accountants (IFAC), the International Accounting Standards Board (IASB), the Organization for Economic Cooperation and Development (OECD), and the European Union (EU).

The International Accounting Standards Board (IASB), through a due process procedure, has issued a number of International Financial Reporting Standards (IFRSs) that incorporate the previously issued International Accounting Standards (IASs) by the International Accounting Standards Committee (IACS). The IASB has a board comprised of representatives of various accounting backgrounds from nine countries. Its standards are used for the following purposes:

1. As a basis for national accounting requirements in many countries.

2. As international benchmarks by countries that develop their own requirements.

3. By stock exchanges and regulatory authorities that allow financial statements to be presented in accordance with IASs.

4. By supranational bodies, such as the European Union, to produce results that meet the needs of capital markets.

5. By companies themselves.[3]

While the IASB works closely with the IFAC and membership in one automatically includes membership in the other, the IASB independently issues standards for presenting audited financial information. IASB has received support from the International Organization of Securities Commissions (IOSCO) and the World Trade Organization to create acceptable accounting standards for multinational securities and other international offerings.

> **QUICK FACTS**
>
> Increased internationalization of the capital markets increase the need for international accounting researchers.

> **QUICK FACTS**
>
> The International Accounting Standards Board's International Financial Reporting Standards are increasingly used around the world.

---

[3] *AICPA Professional Standards*, International Volume, June 1, 2003.

The IASB and IOSCO agreed to a list of necessary accounting issues to address in a "core" set of international accounting standards for use in cross-border offerings and multiple listings. Ideally, establishing a core set of international accounting standards should reduce the costs of doing business and raising capital across borders, streamline internal accounting and auditing functions for multinationals, increase the efficiency of market regulations, and decrease the costs of international financial statement analysis and investment. However, the SEC has offered three conditions for accepting international accounting standards:

1. IASB standards should include a core set of accounting pronouncements that constitute a comprehensive, generally accepted basis of accounting.

2. IASB standards should be of high quality; they must result in comparability and transparency, and they must provide for full disclosure.

3. IASB standards should be rigorously interpreted and applied.

Since local regulations govern the preparation and issuance of financial statements in most countries, differences of form and content persist among countries. One objective of IASB is to harmonize this diversity. Although the IASB does not have the authority to require compliance with International Accounting Standards, the success of international accounting harmonization will depend upon the recognition and support of interested groups. The IASB web site is accessible at *http://www.iasb.org*.

Practice Exercises — *Exercises Related to Professional Organizations*

1. Access the FEI's web site (*http://www.fei.org*) and locate and list the three most recently issued comment letters to the FASB.

    a. _____

    b. _____

    c. _____

2. Access the AICPA's web site (*http://www.aicpa.org*) and under "Accounting Standards" locate and list the three most recently issued exposure drafts of the Accounting Standards Executive Committee.

    a. _____

    b. _____

    c. _____

3. Access the IASB's web site (*http://www.iasb.org.*) and list three of its active projects.

    a. _____

    b. _____

    c. _____

SUMMARY

This chapter has presented an overview of the bodies that set standards in accounting, the process of standard setting, the types of authoritative pronouncements, the meaning and hierarchy of GAAP, and the current status of international accounting. Since GAAP is not a static, well-defined set of accounting principles, but is a fluid set of principles based on current accounting thought and practice, accountants must research changes in pronouncements. Given that GAAP is not composed of mutually exclusive accounting principles, research in accounting does not consist of searching for a single acceptable principle but often for alternative principles that one must carefully examine.

DISCUSSION QUESTIONS

1. Discuss the environmental factors that influence the standard-setting process.
2. Identify the most authoritative accounting pronouncements of the FASB, AICPA, and GASB.
3. What is an underlying reason for the establishment of accounting standards?
4. Describe the rule-making or due-process procedures of the FASB in the establishment of a standard.
5. What is the FASB's Conceptual Framework Project? Explain the benefit of this Project to the practitioner.
6. Discuss the authority of the Statements of Financial Accounting Concepts.
7. Identify the authoritative publications of the AICPA.
8. What is the purpose of the GASB? Why should the public have an interest in governmental financial reporting?
9. What constitutes generally accepted accounting principles?
10. What are the implications of GAAP and authoritative support to the researcher?
11. To conduct efficient research, where should one start in reviewing the accounting literature in search of a solution to a problem?
12. How can the promulgation of an accounting standard impact economic behavior? Discuss a specific example.
13. Distinguish between primary authoritative support and secondary authoritative support.
14. What two governmental organizations were added to the list of sponsoring organizations of the Financial Accounting Foundation (FAF) due to the establishment of the GASB's authoritative status?
15. Discuss how the FASB is addressing the "standards overload" issue.
16. What standards did the IASB develop?

EXERCISES

1. Utilizing Figure 2-3 (Eight Elements of Reasoning), develop the eight elements for the following issue: Daimler Auto Parts, Inc., headquartered in Munich, Germany, is attempting to register with the SEC in order to list its stock on the New York Stock Exchange. Daimler currently is capitalizing most of its research and development (R&D) costs. Management of Daimler has requested your advice in regards to the proper accounting for R&D as to conformity with U.S. GAAP and/or International Accounting Standards.

2. Access the FASB's web site (*http://www.fasb.org*) and click on the "FASB Facts" link and name the current FASB Board members.

3. Access the FASB's web site (*http://www.fasb.org*) and identify the three most recent exposure drafts issued by the FASB.

4. Access the GASB's web site (*http://www.gasb.org*) and list and summarize the GASB Concept Statements.

5. Access the GASB's web site (*http://www.gasb.org*) and identify the two most recent exposure drafts issued by the GASB.

Major Accounting Research Tools

LEARNING OBJECTIVES

After completing this chapter, you should understand:

- The challenges that accounting research presents.
- The contents of the Financial Accounting Research System (FARS).
- The research process.
- Using FARS and other databases to locate GAAP authorities.
- Examples of using FARS effectively and efficiently.
- The contents of the Governmental Accounting Research System (GARS).
- Other accounting databases or standards accessible on the Web.
- Cases that assist in practicing accounting research.

This chapter focuses primarily on the FASB's Accounting Standards and the Online Financial Accounting Research System (FARS Online). The chapter also includes discussion on SEC accounting pronouncements as well as the GASB's Governmental Accounting Research System (GARS). Finally, to test your financial research skills, the appendix to the chapter includes two examples of simulations that appear on the Financial Accounting and Reporting section of the CPA exam.

Due to the recent increase in accounting and auditing pronouncements and the increase in financial reporting in general, more and more organizations use an electronic database to gain rapid access to key accounting authorities for decision making. Even if the FASB simplifies U.S. financial accounting research by following a proposal to codify (logically reorder) existing accounting sources from various sources, research skills are increasingly needed for the future accounting professional.

Professional accounting research is challenging because of the volume of accounting rules, their level of complexity, the extensive detail and length of accounting standards, and the difficulty in finding all relevant accounting rules on a particular topic. Also, there is a lack of a centralized source of authority. Recall that while financial accounting looks to the FASB, state and local government accounting looks to the Governmental Accounting Standards Board (GASB), U.S. federal accounting looks to the Federal Accounting Standards Advisory Board (FASAB), international accounting looks primarily to the International Accounting Standards Board (ISAB), and various other accounting sources exist, such as the Securities and Exchange Commission (SEC) for accounting by public companies. The databases and their content, as well as web sources of information are discussed for each of these accounting standard setting bodies.

RESEARCH TOOLS
Internet
FARS
LexisNexis
AICPA reSOURCE
PwC Edgarscan
Thomson ONE
RIA Checkpoint SE
ACL
i2

RESEARCH TIPS

Utilize the Financial Accounting Research System for issues in the private sector.

COMPUTERIZED RESEARCH DATABASES AND TOOLS

Database systems are designed to retrieve relevant documents from a vast library or collection of data. Compared to free Internet sources, commercial databases have several advantages. They generally provide a more comprehensive document retrieval system. Commercial databases usually have better search capabilities and make an effort to seek out reliable sources of information. They are used extensively in many professions and have become essential in the accounting profession. Such retrieval systems help the researcher search quickly through large amounts of data for words or phrases that are pertinent to the research inquiry, which, in turn, refer to authoritative pronouncements or other topical sources of information.

Searches in a database may occur through (1) keyword searches, (2) use of an index, (3) a citation, or (4) walking through a table of contents. A keyword search looks for those documents that contain a specified pattern of words, phrases, or numbers. An index system helps particularly when the index is comprehensive and the precise terminology may vary. A citation relies on a citation to find a particular relevant source. Similar to using an index, walking through a table of contents by progressing from the big concept to more detailed refinements may help the researcher if the structure of the authority is clear.

To perform a keyword search more effectively avoid using terms that routinely appear, such as articles (an, the, ...), personal pronouns (his, her, ...) or prepositions (of, for, ...). Some databases enable expansion of the keywords to check for derivative words, different spellings of compound words, and sometimes even synonyms. Use of a date restriction also helps to screen research results for more relevant information. Specialized searches are often possible, such as retrieving a document by its citation.

Several helpful tools exist within many online databases. One memory tool is the display of one's precise location in the database. Usually this happens either on the top or left side of a search to enable the researcher to remember the location in the database. Another common tool is the database's ability to remember what prior searches were made. This enables one to return more easily to one's previous research.

When case law is researched, as in tax research (Chapter 7), databases usually provide a "citator" which enables the researcher to trace the full history of a case, as well as learn what subsequent cases have referred to that case. Various citators have different abilities in explaining what aspect of the case was referenced and in what context, such as following the other court's decision.

Examples of common applications of databases by accountants or auditors include the following:

- Using analytical procedures to compare a client to other companies in its industry.

- Obtaining a more in-depth understanding of current developments in the client's industry.

- Inquiring into the executive backgrounds of potential new clients.

- Acquiring timely notice regarding any pending changes to the tax laws, regulations, or forms.

Challenges in electronic researching include finding all relevant authoritative sources, even if a document does not include the exact words specified in the search request. Thus, carefully select the word patterns for the search inquiry. Sometimes the researcher needs to expand or reduce the word pattern when using a particular database.

By understanding the electronic research costs, you can avoid creating a negative impression of your research skills. Basic pricing structures can vary as to how your employer pays for its electronic databases. While universities generally provide unlimited access to student searches, some firms may pay on a search basis or document printing basis. It also helps to understand the billing system that your firm uses, to appreciate the client's perspective that your electronic research is not only effective, but efficient in saving money for the client. If the client sees a separate charge for your research, it's especially important to document your research activities and review them to ensure that your time spent and any database costs passed on to the client are properly chargeable.

RESEARCH TIPS

In your searches, use keywords, an index, a citation, or scan the table of contents to find relevant authorities.

RESEARCH TIPS

Always understand the cost structure for your electronic research.

USING A DATABASE

A research strategy suggested for using most databases is as follows:

1. Define the specific information needed.

2. Determine the sources to search.

3. Develop a search inquiry using keywords and sometimes connectors and limitations.

4. Select how to view the search results, such as full-text or just the citations.

5. Print or download the relevant documents.

In considering the specific information desired, conducting cost-effective electronic research is a necessary skill for the researcher to develop. The researcher should have a basic understanding of the pricing plan for the electronic database. Some parts of a database may have lower costs than other parts of a database. Many clients are not willing to pay unlimited research costs. Restricting a search to a particular field search, such as a head-note, can make the search more efficient and save the researcher time. Retrieving a document by using a citation to the document is the most efficient way to access that document.

In defining the search inquiry, the researcher should take advantage of powerful search tools within the database in order to conduct effective and efficient specialized searches. The search results are often more efficient using specialized searches with date limitations. Use "connector" terms to search within the same sentence, paragraph, or other nearby region. Often one can specify the order of the search terms.

In determining the sources to search, use segment searching based on the headlines, topic, or country. For example, a database may provide Dunn & Bradstreet and similar sources for evaluating U.S. companies. A search in this part of the database may require first finding the appropriate "North American Industry Classification" (NAICS) or its predecessor "Standard Industrial Classification" (SIC) Code.

Massive legal databases such as Westlaw® and LexisNexis® also provide access to many news sources and extensive public records. A researcher is more effective and efficient when specifically identifying the source of interest, such as Tax Assessor Deed Transfer and Mortgage Records, State Judgments and Lien Filings, Business Locator, Asset Locator, sources listing professional licenses, or other sources of information.

One chooses the appropriate database by reviewing a database directory that provides a description of each part of the database. Then one should select the smallest database containing the relevant documents. Some databases combine different sources of related information to assist the researcher. For example, federal tax materials often include a library combining all primary legal tax authorities, as discussed more fully in the chapter on tax research.

Many traditional databases now available on the web have recently divided into many alternative products, marketed for different target audiences. Country-specific products of a database often exist for Canada, the United Kingdom, and most industrialized countries. For the university community, both Westlaw and LexisNexis market specialized versions called Westlaw Campus and LexisNexis Academic, as explained in more detail in Chapter 6. Westlaw is also providing new means to access its information, such as a wireless version, so that a personal digital assistant (PDA) with Web capabilities can access the information.

The researcher can usually view the search results in various forms, such as full text or just the citations. To enable the researcher to consider the information more carefully at a later time, print or download the relevant documents. However, university subscriptions of some databases will probably permit only screen printing in order to manage the database expenses.

RESEARCH TIPS

Use powerful search tools in databases to research more effectively and efficiently.

RESEARCH TIPS

Carefully select the relevant parts of a database to search.

FASB'S FINANCIAL ACCOUNTING RESEARCH SYSTEM (FARS)

The Financial Accounting Standards Board's (FASB Online) Financial Accounting Research System (FARS) enables comprehensive, but not complete, research on accounting issues for the private sector. **A demo of FARS highlighting the functionality of the system is available at ResearchLink at** *http://weirich.swlearning.com.* Currently, at the FASB's web site, the FASB has released many of its pronouncements in nonsearchable format. It is suggested that you **access** and **review this demo** before proceeding with this chapter.

The FARS opening screen information is shown in Figure 5-1. The FARS database is structured similar to the manual research materials by the FASB. FARS contains several major infobases including: Original Pronouncements, Current Text, Emerging Issues Task Force (EITF) Abstracts, Staff Implementation Guides (replaced in 2003 by FASB Staff Positions), and a Table of Contents. Each of those sources is now explained in more detail.

1. **Original Pronouncements** (FASB-OP) contains various standards in chronological order in full text view. These include original source documents standards from the FASB (including FASB *Statements, Interpretations, Implementation Guides, Technical Bulletins, Concepts Statements,* and *Appendices*), AICPA (*Accounting Pronouncements, Interpretations, (Accounting Research Bulletins* and *Accounting Terminology Bulletins*), and the AICPA's Accounting Principles Board (*APB Statements and Opinions*). Similar to the presentation in the hardbound volumes, materials that are superseded or amended are presented with a gray background to remind the reader that such materials are outdated and one should not rely upon them.

2. **Current Text** (FASB-CT) integrates currently effective accounting and reporting standards in a condensed version of the most authoritative Original Pronouncements.

FIGURE 5-1 | **FASB'S ONLINE FINANCIAL ACCOUNTING RESEARCH SYSTEM (FARS ONLINE)**

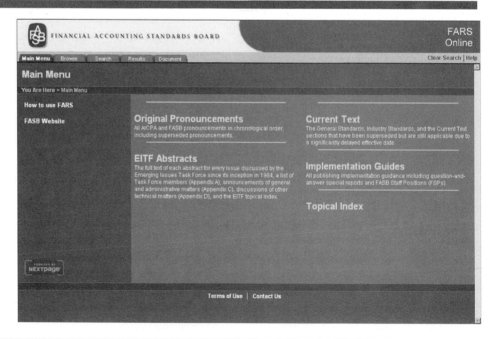

The Current Text summarizes primarily from GAAP Level 1 (*SFAS Statements, FASB Interpretations, APB Opinions,* and *AICPA Accounting Research Bulletins*). The Current Text does not include some materials in the Original Pronouncements, such as FASB Staff Implementation Guide and FASB Statements of Financial Accounting Concepts.

The Current Text reproduces the hardbound volumes of the FASB's Current Text of Accounting Standards. Thus, the Current Text is divided into a discussion of "General Standards" and "Industry Standards." While the General Standards are those that are applicable to all enterprises, the Industry Standards apply to not-for-profit organizations or enterprises in specific industries, such as broadcasting, banking, cable television, computer software, contractor accounting, development stage enterprises, finance companies, franchising, insurance, investment companies, mortgage banking, motion pictures, the music industry, oil and gas, pension funds, real estate, and regulated operations.

The topics listed in the Current Text are provided in Figure 5-2. For each listed topic, the Current Text section references the authoritative sources (e.g., APB Opinion numbers) and provides a listing of not-yet-implemented pronouncements and superseded authorities. Also included is an appendix listing relevant AICPA materials, cleared by the FASB: Practice Bulletins, Accounting and Audit Guides, and Statements of Position. The sources on this appendix list are AICPA materials not provided in the FARS database.

3. **Emerging Issues Task Force (EITF) Statements** contains EITF Abstracts (including the accounting issue considered, date discussed, related authoritative citations, and the issue's current status), general and administrative matters, a topical index, a table of contents, and more. Recall that EITF Statements provide early identification of emerging issues and are part of GAAP Level 3.

FIGURE 5-2 | SUMMARY OF GENERAL STANDARD TOPICS IN THE CURRENT TEXT

Accounting Changes	Contribution Debt (Convertible Debt, Restructuring)	Lending Activities
Accounting Policies	Depreciation	Liabilities Extinguishments
Additional Paid-in Capital	Derivatives and Hedging	Nonmonetary Transactions
Adjustments for Prior Periods	Disposal of Long-Lived Assets	Pension Costs
Asset Retirement Obligations	Earnings per Share	Postemployment Benefits
Balance Sheet	Employee Stock Ownership Plan	Post Retirement Benefits
Business Combination	Impairment	Quasi Reorganization
Capital Stock (Dividends-in-kind, Options, Preferred Stock)	Income Statement Presentation	Real Estate
Capital Structure	Income Taxes	Related Parties
Cash Flow Statements	Insurance Cost	Research & Development
Changing Prices	Intangible Assets	Retained Earnings
Commitments (Long Term)	Interest (Capitalization, Imputation	Revenue Recognition
Compensation (Deferred Comp., Stock, Paid Absences)	Interim Financial Reporting	Segment Disclosure
Comprehensive Income	Inventory	Taxes (Property)
Consolidation	Investments (Debt & Equity Securities, Equity Method)	Valuation
Contingencies	Leases	

QUICK FACTS

Major infobases in FARS include Original Pronouncements, Current Text, Emerging Issues, Task Force Abstracts, and a Topical Index.

4. **Implementation Guides** (FASB-Q&A) by the FASB Staff consists of Questions and Answers for certain Statements from the FASB. (For example, one discusses whether a company should voluntarily apply the provisions of *Statement of Financial Accounting Standard* (SFAS) No. 80 to future contracts on foreign currencies). These Implementation Guides started to apply to SFAS No. 80 and selected ones thereafter until 2003. Now the FASB issues FASB Staff Positions. This infobase is part of GAAP Level 4.

5. **Table of Contents** (FASINDEX) provides an alphabetical listing of all topics. The Topical Index is identical to the index found in Volume III (hardcopy edition) of the *Current Text of Accounting Standards*.

The AICPA has published an even more comprehensive index entitled "Index to Accounting and Auditing Technical Pronouncements." The AICPA's Index is designed to provide a cumulative index of authoritative pronouncements from a variety of sources, including the FASB, GASB, SEC, AICPA, and others.

Practice Exercises   *FARS Online*

1. Use the Topical Index in FARS to answer the following.

   a. Identify the first three subdivisions of the general topic of depreciation:

   _____

   _____

   b. Company X-Co has a $10,000,000 gain from exercising stock options. What are the key words for the researcher to use in discovering the relevant authority to resolve the issue?

   _____

   _____

2. Use the Current Text in FARS to answer the following.

   a. How does the discussion of depreciation in the General Standards compare to the discussion of Depreciation in SFAS No. 93?

   _____

   _____

   b. Summarize one industry accounting issue related to the motion picture industry.

   _____

   _____

THE RESEARCH PROCESS

The FARS database enables researchers to obtain authoritative evidence to help solve their research questions more efficiently than researchers could using manual tools. In researching an issue, often the following questions arise:

- Where does one start the research?

- What are the possible search strategies?

- How does one move around in the database?

- When can one stop the research?

To begin the research, one sometimes goes to a secondary source first to acquire an overview of a topic and a greater understanding of the basic terminology. Then one selects a search process to find relevant accounting authorities.

Search processes in FARS include using the Topical Index, the Table of Contents, and Search inquiries. The Table of Contents is useful for browsing an infobase by providing a listing in outline form of the infobase's records. Select a heading of interest to proceed directly to that section. One can perform a query on a term or document title, or use some custom query templates. If the search results produce an overwhelming number of search hits, use boolean operators (i.e., and, or), proximity conditions, and wildcards (i.e., "%," the percent sign) to narrow the search results. One can also limit the search request by date or to a specific infobase.

Understanding the organization of the database views helps one move around in the database. Most views in FARS contain a document pane that displays the body of the infobase—the text, objects, links, highlighters, and other data stored in the infobase, the Contents pane, which displays a dynamic table of contents for the infobase; the Hits pane, which shows search results after a query is performed; and the Reference Window pane, which is connected to the top of the Document pane.

To move around in FARS, one can double-click on a heading in the Contents view to proceed to the desired section in the Document view. Similarly, double-clicking on a reference in the Hits List takes one to the appropriate source in the Document view.

Within topics, reference sources are displayed in three columns. The first column shows any relevant keywords, the second column shows the reference to any relevant Original Pronouncements. The third column shows the Current Text references. If a particular record is useful, either copy and paste the materials into your own document or export it to a file.

In deciding when to stop the research, consider the distinction between primary and secondary authorities in accounting. Primary authorities in accounting are considered self supporting; by themselves they individually support a particular accounting principle within GAAP. Secondary authorities in accounting are not sufficient by themselves to support a particular accounting principle, but the researcher should use them in combination with other supporting authorities. A listing of primary and secondary authoritative support was provided in Chapter 4 in Figure 4-7. Essentially when one must rely upon GAAP Levels 4 or 5, the researcher should support the position with multiple sources. Thus, the researcher must perform more extensive research when struggling with an issue not answered with the highest levels of GAAP authorities.

The decision to stop the research process is much easier if the results generate primary authoritative support for a definitive conclusion. However, if the researcher cited secondary support, additional research is needed since any secondary source individually is insufficient authority. The researcher must recognize that many research questions lack clear-cut answers and, therefore, professional judgment is a key element in deciding when sufficient support exists to stop the research process.

USING FARS TO LOCATE GAAP AUTHORITIES

FARS is the major source for finding essential GAAP authorities. Because most of GAAP authorities arise from the FASB, many authorities beyond GAAP Level 1 are available exclusively on FARS. Use the Original Pronouncements infobase to find GAAP Level 1 authorities (*FASB Statements* and *Interpretations*, and the predecessor AICPA's *Accounting Research Bulletins* and *Accounting Principles Board Opinions*). To find part of GAAP Level 2 authorities (FASB *Technical Bulletins* and AICPA *Statements of Position* that are cleared by the FASB), also use the Original Pronouncements.

Use the FARS EITF infobase to find part of GAAP Level 3 (Abstracts of *Emerging Issue Task Force Statements*). Use the FARS *Staff Implementation Guides* (FASB Staff Position) infobase to locate part of GAAP Level 4. The only component of GAAP Level 5 available in FARS are the *FASB Concepts* located in the Original Pronouncements infobase.

GAAP authorities that are not provided in FARS usually require accessing the AICPA reSOURCE Online Library database (highlighted in Chapter 8) after reviewing the FARS Current Text infobase list of AICPA authorities cleared by the FASB. Thus, other GAAP Level 2 authorities (the *AICPA Industry and Audit Guides* and the AICPA *Statements of Position*) are available from the AICPA reSOURCE database. These guides are more fully discussed in the text with the auditing authorities. Similarly, for the AICPA Practice Bulletins, the remaining GAAP Level 3 authority, use the AICPA reSOURCE database to access them. The remaining parts of GAAP Level 4 are more difficult to find. Industry practices that are widely recognized and prevalent in the industry are left to the individual accountant's analysis, which one should document by using some of the accounting and business databases described in the next chapter.

GAAP Level 5 authorities, which one uses only in the absence of another source of established accounting principles, can come from a wide variety of locations. For example, GAAP Level 5 includes *AICPA Technical Practice Aids*, accessible from the AICPA reSOURCE database. The AICPA provides other electronically formatted publications and software as aids for the practitioner that qualify as part of GAAP Level 5 authorities. For example, many of the AICPA self-study programs are now available in a CD-ROM format. The AICPA has also established an online service for members called the *Accountants' Forum*. This service allows members to have electronic access to the AICPA's professional literature, exposure drafts, legislative alerts, newsletters, and other information sources. Through the AICPA Accountants' Forum, members can discuss GAAP authorities with each other on the electronic bulletin boards.

Other GAAP Level 5 authorities include relevant journals and treatises available in the legal, accounting, and business databases discussed in the next chapter. These secondary sources on GAAP are often helpful to the researcher in quickly understanding the authority in an area of accounting. For example, the researcher may use LexisNexis to locate the *Miller GAAP Guide* (located under business and accounting). This guide is organized alphabetically by topic under GAAP and by accounting principles and specialized industry accounting concerns.

RESEARCH TIPS

FARS provides the most important GAAP authorities, but does not ensure comprehensive GAAP research.

RESEARCH TIPS

To find GAAP Level 5 authorities, use FARS for FASB Concept Statements, and various other databases for other sources.

Practice Exercises   *GAAP Authorities*

1. Use the Original Pronouncements infobase in FARS to find the list of Accounting Principles Board Opinions. Select APB No. 6.

    a. What is the title of APB No. 6?

    _____

    b. Identify the most recent ARB amended by APB No. 6.

    _____

    c. Identify the most recent SFAS amending APB No. 6.

    _____

2. Use the Current Text in FARS Online to answer the following.

    a. What authorities are referenced in the Current Text under section L10?

    _____

    _____

Practice Exercises   *GAAP Authorities (continued)*

b. What authorities are referenced in the current text under section R50.114?

_____

_____

_____

EXAMPLES FOR USING FARS ONLINE

The following provides a brief tutorial with screen shots of using FARS Online for a research project on lease costs. You should also go to the text's web site (http://weirich.swlearning.com) for a link to the FASB's FARS Online tutorial for further details of this very useful database. Assume the researcher wants to determine whether certain costs qualify as lease costs, and, if so, whether to capitalize them or to write them off. The researcher should first select the Table of Contents on the FARS opening screen, as previously shown in Figure 5-1. This results in the Table of Contents overview as shown in Figure 5-3.

To research lease costs, select the diamond next to the "L" and scroll down to "Classifying Leases (Other Than Leveraged Leases)," as shown in Figure 5-4. The hyperlinks in the database enable one to check the accounting authority for classifying leases. The strongest authority refers to FASB Statement No. 13 (paragraphs 6–7) in the Original Pronouncements. Figure 5-5 shows part of FASB Statement No. 13, paragraph 7. A researcher should check for further authoritative information on leases and select FASB's Current Text—Section L10-102, as previously shown next to FAS 13, paragraphs 6–7 in Figure 5-4. The number starting with "L" simply designates the location within FASB's Current Text for the discussion on leases.

FIGURE 5-3   FARS TABLE OF CONTENTS

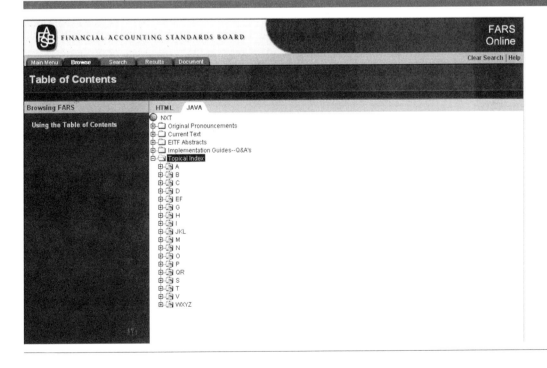

FIGURE 5-4 | FARS TABLE OF CONTENTS ON LEASES

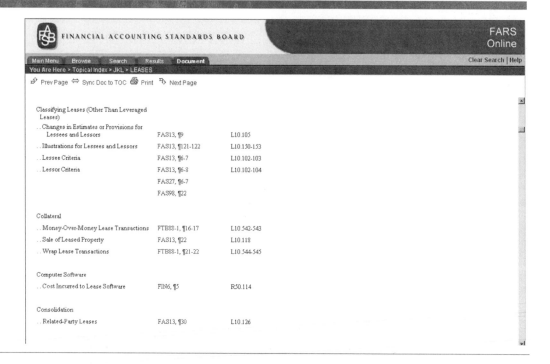

Figure 5-6 lists the FASB authorities on leases. When checking the remaining levels of GAAP the researcher will discover EITF No. 84–37 which discusses "Sale-Leaseback Transaction with Repurchase Option," as shown in Figure 5-7. The researcher will discover that no official consensus exists on whether an acquiring company should capitalize or expense the initial lease costs.

Assume that the researcher has confirmed the lease as an operating lease, and wants to know if the company can defer some initial costs such as the broker's fee for finding the lessee. Using the FARS database, the researcher then checks GAAP Level 4 to see if any *Staff Implementation Guide* provides guidance. *Staff Implementation Guides* provide a link to "A Guide to Implementation of Statement 91 on Accounting for Nonrefundable Fees and Costs Associated with . . . Initial Direct Costs of Leases" (see Figure 5-8). Thus, the company as a lessor should defer the initial direct lease costs and allocate them over the lease term in proportion to the recognized rental income, as one would find in reading this Guide (Figure 5-9).

SEC ACCOUNTING FOR PUBLIC COMPANIES

RESEARCH TIPS

SEC sources in a database are usually in a different location than the accounting sources.

In many databases, SEC accounting sources are located in a different part of a database from FASB sources. SEC accounting is not the same as GAAP accounting. SEC sources follow the traditional legal hierarchy explained in more detail when discussing tax authorities in Chapter 7.

Securities laws generally appear under title 15 of the United States Code (U.S.C.). Since there are relatively few major securities laws, these are more commonly cited by the name of the particular Law, such as the Securities Exchange Act of 1934. These laws are available on the Web and in legal databases such as Westlaw and LexisNexis, described in the next chapter.

FIGURE 5-5   FASB STATEMENT ON ACCOUNTING FOR LEASES

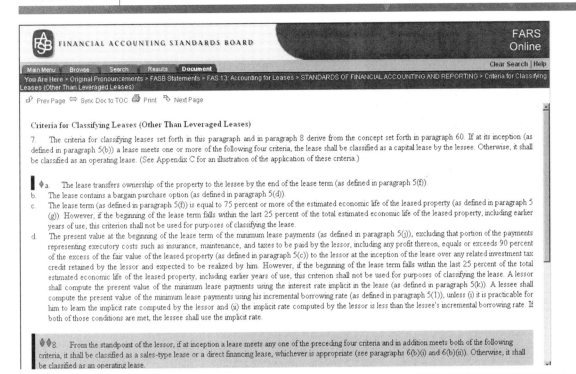

FIGURE 5-6   FASB AUTHORITIES ON LEASES

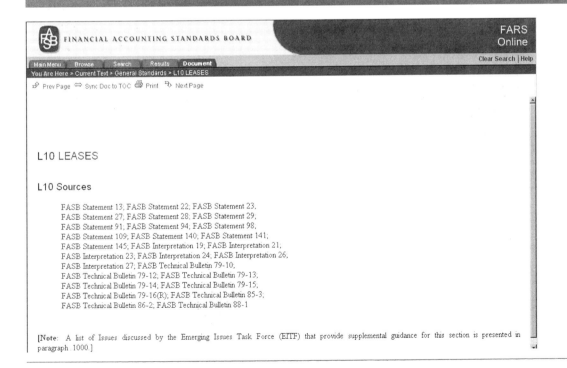

FIGURE 5-7 | EIFT EXAMPLE ON SALE-LEASEBACK TRANSACTIONS

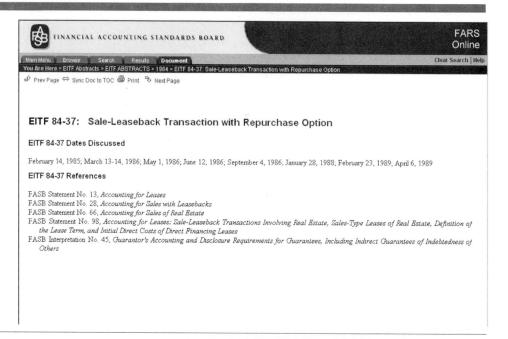

The SEC has the statutory authority to establish accounting rules and regulations for public companies. For example, it requires companies to make and keep books, records, and accounts, which, in reasonable detail, accurately and fairly reflect its transactions and the disposition of its assets. Issuers must devise and maintain internal controls sufficient

FIGURE 5-8 | IMPLEMENTATION GUIDE INTRODUCTORY EXAMPLE

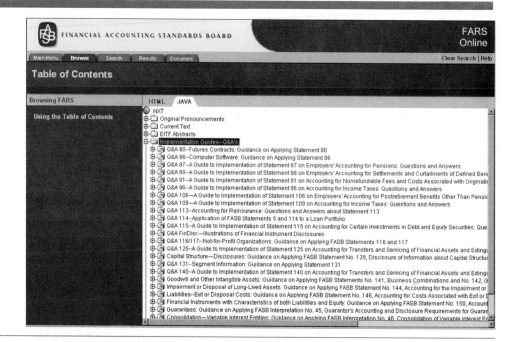

FIGURE 5-9   IMPLEMENTATION GUIDE DETAILED EXAMPLE

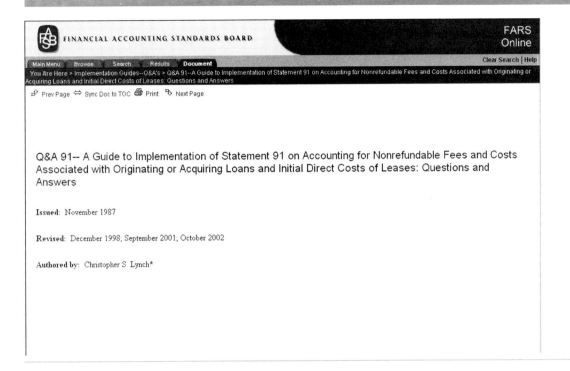

to allow the preparation of financial statements in conformity with GAAP and to maintain the accountability of assets. Such corporations must file an annual Form 10-K report, quarterly Form 10-Q reports, and Form 8-K when significant accounting matters arise (e.g., a change in auditors).

Practice Exercises   *GAAP Authorities Beyond Level 1*

1. Find and read *FASB Technical Bulletin 86-2*, one of the authorities listed on leases.

   a. What aspect of leases does this authority discuss?

   _____

   _____

   b. Does *FASB Technical Bulletin 86-2* reference any SFAS? If yes, what is it?

   _____

   _____

2. Find and read the *Staff Implementation Guide* entitled "A Guide to Implementation of Statement 91 on Accounting for Nonrefundable Fees and Costs Associated with . . . Initial Direct Costs of Leases."

   a. What was the precise question asked in that authority regarding leases?

   _____

   _____

   b. What authoritative accounting sources did that *Staff Implementation Guide* discuss?

   _____

SEC REGULATIONS AND BEYOND

Regulations interpreting the statutory securities laws are codified in the Codification of Federal Regulations (CFR). Securities regulations issued by the SEC are placed in a different title number than the corresponding statutory law, CFR title 17. Securities Regulations include:

1. **Regulation S-X, Form and Content of Financial Statements**, which describes the types of reports that public companies must file and the forms to use.

2. **Regulation S-K, Integrated Disclosure Rules**, which prescribes the requirements for information presented outside the financial statements required under Regulation S-X.

The Commission's Published Views and Interpretations. Beyond regulations, the SEC's administrative interpretations includes various types of Releases, which include the following.

1. **Financial Reporting Releases (FRRs)** prescribe the accounting principles that public companies must follow. FRRs update the SEC's Codification of Financial Reporting Policies and Regulations S-K and S-X. A typical SEC Financial Reporting Release contains the following types of information:

    • The background of the topic.

    • An evaluation of the comments received on the proposed rules.

    • A discussion of the final rules.

    • A discussion of transition provisions.

    • The text of new rules.

2. **Accounting and Auditing Enforcement Releases (AAERs)** announce enforcement actions of the SEC's reporting and disclosure requirements. AAERs generally include a summary of the enforcement action, a discussion of the facts, the Commission's conclusions, and any orders issued (e.g., an order to restrict practice before the SEC by the accountant involved for a specific time period).

3. **Accounting Series Releases (ASRs)**, predecessor to the development of FFRs and AAERs. They were issued from 1937 to 1982. The SEC has codified nonenforcement-related ASRs that are still in effect. The SEC has published a topical index to enforcement-related ASRs.

    All releases are identified with "release numbers": a prefix indicating the applicable statute or special type of release and a sequential number that is assigned in the order of issuance. Some common prefixes and their applicable statute or special type of release are shown below.

Prefix	Applicable Statute or Special Type of Release
33	Securities Act of 1933
34	Securities Exchange Act of 1934
AS	Accounting Series Release
FR	Financial Reporting Release
ER	Accounting and Auditing Enforcement Release

    Some reference sources, however, replace the prefix with the applicable statute or special type of release. A release often has several release numbers because it applies to more than one statute. For example, Release Nos. 33-6483, 34-20186, and FR-14 represent the same release on an accounting matter that affects filings under the 1933 and 1934 Acts.

The Codification of Financial Reporting (CFR) Policies is a compendium of the SEC's current published views and interpretations relating to financial reporting. It supplements the rules in regulations S-K and S-X by providing background and rationale for certain of those rules. Generally the Codification of Financial Reporting Policies are updated only for the discussion of final rules. While that information is generally adequate in that it provides the important views of the SEC, accountants occasionally refer to the original release for more detailed background information.

SEC Staff Policy. This source is not approved formally by the commissioners; therefore, it cannot be considered as part of the official rules or interpretations of the Commission. SEC staff policy is published in no-action and interpretative letters, *Staff Accounting Bulletins* (SABs), correspondence about accountants' independence, and 1933 and 1934 Act Industry Guides.

No-action and interpretative letters are published SEC staff responses to inquiries for interpretations of the application of statutes or rules and regulations to a particular transaction contemplated by a registrant or to make a general interpretation of the statutes. The response may indicate that the staff will not recommend that the Commission take any action regarding the proposed transaction or that certain procedures must be followed regarding the transaction.

The SEC also publishes a series of *Staff Accounting Bulletins* (SABs), which are unofficial interpretations of the SEC's prescribed accounting principles. SABs represent interpretations and practices followed by the SEC's staff in the Chief Accountant's Office and the Division of Corporate Finance in administering the disclosure requirements of the Federal Securities laws. SABs are analogous to the FASB Technical Bulletins. SABs relate to accounting and disclosure practices under the rules and regulations. The SEC has maintained a codification of SABs to make the SABs more useful to users.

Given this extensive literature regarding SEC pronouncements, Figure 5-10 summarizes the hierarchy of the major SEC Authoritative Pronouncements and Publications.[1] Many of the previously discussed SEC administrative materials are available on its web site at *http://www.sec.gov*. The SEC's web page on information for accountants is helpful, as shown in Figure 5-11.

QUICK FACTS
SEC authorities affecting accounting include securities laws, regulations, various releases, and Staff Accounting Bulletins.

RESEARCH TOOLS
Internet
FARS
LexisNexis
AICPA reSOURCE
PwC Edgarscan
Thomson ONE
RIA Checkpoint SE
ACL
i2

FIGURE 5-10 HIERARCHY OF SEC AUTHORITIES AND PUBLICATIONS

Level 1: **Statutes**
i.e., 1933 Securities Act
1934 Securities Exchange Act

Level 2: **Regulations and Forms**
i.e., Regulation S–X
Regulation S–K

Level 3: **Commission Releases**
i.e., Financial Reporting Releases
Accounting and Auditing Enforcement Releases
Securities Releases
Exchange Act Releases

Level 4: **Staff Advice**
i.e., No-Action Letters
Staff Accounting Bulletins

[1] Miller, Paul B. W., and Jack Robertson. "A Guide to SEC Regulations and Publications: Mastering the Maze," *Research in Accounting Regulation*, Vol. 3 (July–August 1989): 239–249.

FIGURE 5-11 | SEC WEB PAGE ON INFORMATION FOR ACCOUNTANTS

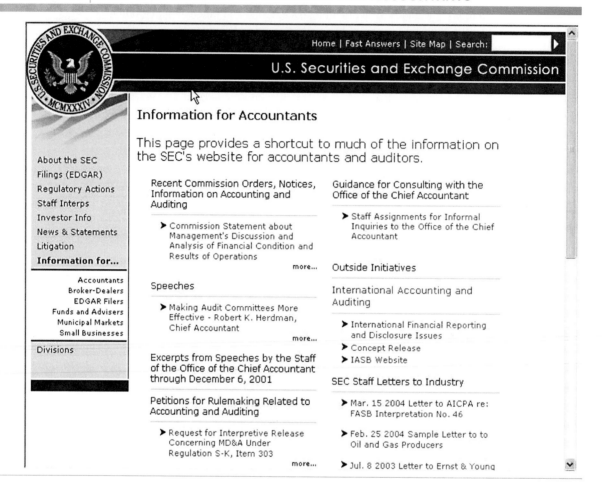

Often it helps to use a securities law service, such as the Commerce Clearing House, Inc. (CCH) Federal Securities Law Reporter, which reprints the statutes, regulations, abstracts of selective administrative authorities, case abstracts, and helpful practice aids, such as forms used in practice to communicate with the SEC. Such services are found in some commercial databases. For example, the Research Institute of America (RIA) Checkpoint® database has an SEC reference library. The next chapter explains several other databases that make searching SEC authorities more user friendly.

The SEC influences accounting standards set by the FASB and actions within the profession. In December 2001, the SEC sought to remind professionals that "the selection and application of the company's accounting policies must be appropriately reasoned… [E]ven a technically accurate application of GAAP may nonetheless fail to communicate important information if it is not accompanied by appropriate and clear analytical disclosures to facilitate an investor's understanding… " This release suggested, as the U.S. courts have repeatedly stated, that compliance with the technical professional standards in GAAP are not enough. A professional must comply with the underlying intentions of the law and regulations for financial information.

Practice Exercises *SEC and Its Authorities*

1. Use either the SEC's web site or a database described in the next chapter and locate the following SEC sources.

   a. What does Rule 10(b)(5) discuss? (*Hint*: It interprets Sec. 10(b)(5) of the Securities Act of 1934.)

   _____

   b. What does SAB 99 discuss?

   _____

2. Use the Internet to acquire further understanding for explaining SEC actions to officers in a public company who ask you the following questions.

   a. What does the Chief Accountant for the SEC do?

   _____

   b. How should you prepare a client to handle an SEC investigation?

   _____

GASB'S GOVERNMENTAL ACCOUNTING RESEARCH SYSTEM (GARS)

For researching accounting issues for state and local governments, use the GASB's Governmental Accounting Research System (GARS) for comprehensive, but not complete, research. The GARS database is available for subscription. A GARS database demonstration is available for downloading from *http://www.GASB.org* (under Publications). Alternatively, individual standards are generally available for downloading from the Web at a nominal cost per standard. A summary of the GASB standards are freely available on the Web.

The GARS opening screen from the demonstration is shown in Figure 5-12. The GARS database is structured similarly to the FARS database. It contains several major infobases, including Original Pronouncements, Current Text, EITF Abstracts, Staff Implementation Guides by the GASB staff, and a Topical Index.

RESEARCH TIPS

Utilize GARS to find authorities governing state and local governmental accounting.

FIGURE 5-12 | GARS REFERENCE GUIDE (FROM THE DEMONSTRATION)

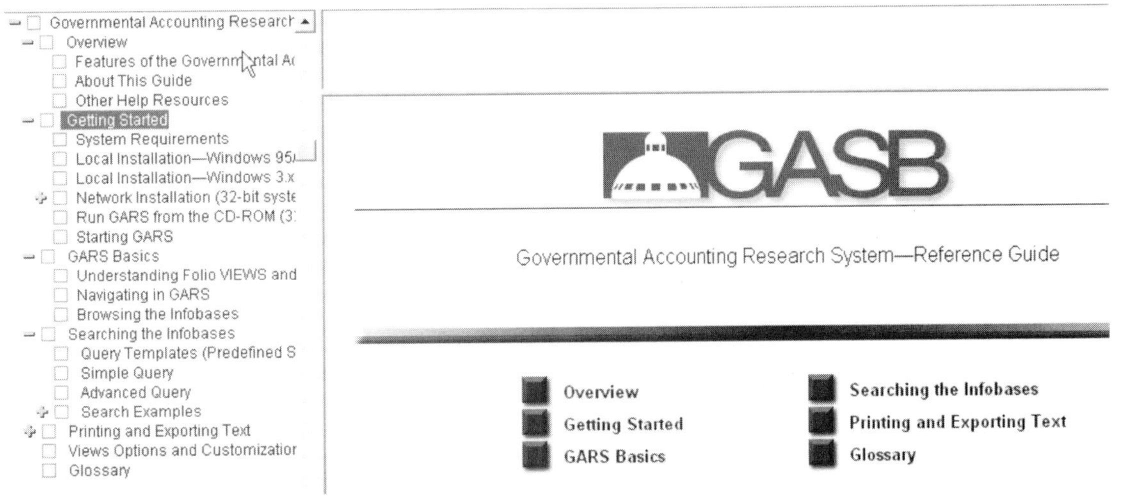

A demonstration of GARS that is available on the Web illustrates the GASB's organization of the original pronouncements for state and local accounting research, as shown in Figure 5-13. GASB's codification of accounting standards in the Current Text is displayed in Figure 5-14.

Recall that Governmental Accounting GAAP uses a hierarchy of sources that is similar to financial accounting, except that the clearance of non-GASB authorities must arise from the GASB, not the FASB.

Practice Exercises   *GARS*

1. Use the GASB web site (*http://www.gasb.org*) and look under the Technical Issues.
   a. Determine how many Statements of Government Accounting Standards Board exist.

   _____

   b. Summarize GASB Statement No. 33

   _____

   _____

   _____

OTHER SOURCES OF ACCOUNTING AUTHORITIES

RESEARCH TIPS

When doing Federal GAAP research, use FASAB's authorities provided on its web site, FARS, and AICPA reSOURCE databases.

Recall that the Federal Accounting Standards Advisory Board (FASAB) establishes accounting principles for federal entities. The FASAB for federal accounting has codified its sources of concepts, standards, interpretations, and technical releases, and made them freely available on its web site at *http://www.fasab.gov*, in nonsearchable text documents, as illustrated in Figure 5-15.

FASAB's discussion of authorities first presents Concepts to guide the FASAB as it deliberates on specific issues for its Standards. FASAB Interpretations clarify the original meaning of its standards, add definitions, or provide other guidance for its standards. The Interpretations are generally narrow in scope. These FASAB authorities are organized similarly to the FARS and GARS, with Original Pronouncements, Current Text, and other information, such as exposure drafts.

Federal GAAP research can find Level 1 authorities *FASAB Statements* and *Interpretations* from the FASAB's web site. Use the FARS database to access FASB and AICPA pronouncements specifically made applicable to federal entities by the FASAB. Research Federal GAAP Level 2 authorities using the FASAB's web site for *FASAB Technical Bulletins* and the AICPA reSOURCE database to access *AICPA Statement of Positions* and *AICPA Industry Audit and Accounting Guides* that are made specifically applicable to the federal government and accepted by the FASAB. Federal GAAP Level 3 authorities are acquired from the FASAB's web site for the *Technical Releases* created by the Accounting and Auditing Policy Committee and from the AICPA reSOURCE database for the approved materials from the *AcSEC Practice Bulletins*. Finally, Federal GAAP Level 4 research consists of all other accounting literature on Federal GAAP from a variety of sources.

RESEARCH TOOLS

Internet
FARS
LexisNexis
AICPA reSOURCE
PwC Edgarscan
Thomson ONE
RIA Checkpoint SE
ACL
i2

Recall that most countries create their own accounting standards. Use *http://www.taxsites. com* to find the name and web location of these authoritative bodies. Particularly important outside of the United States is the International Accounting Standards Board (IASB) which creates International Financial Reporting Standards (IFRS). For example, the European Union is committed to adopting their international standards. The IASB's web site at *http://www.iasb.org.uk* offers an online database, available for subscription. It also offers free downloading of various materials and has a nominal charge for other selected materials.

FIGURE 5-13 GARS ORIGINAL PRONOUNCEMENTS (DEMONSTRATION VERSION)

Original Pronouncements

I DEMONSTRATION VERSION

Copyright 2000 Governmental Accounting Standards Board

To search the entire infobase, click the **Query** button 🔍 on the **Toolbar** or to search using a predefined query template, choose from the list under Query Template in the **Search** menu. To access a segment of the infobase, click on any link token (♦) in the menu below.

♦Foreword

♦Statements of the Governmental Accounting Standards Board (GASBS)

♦Interpretations of the Governmental Accounting Standards Board (GASBI)

♦Technical Bulletins of the Governmental Accounting Standards Board (GASBTB)

♦Concepts Statements of the Governmental Accounting Standards Board (GASBCS)

♦Statements of the National Council on Governmental Accounting (NCGAS)

♦Interpretations of the National Council on Governmental Accounting (NCGAI)

♦Concepts Statement of the National Council on Governmental Accounting (NCGACS)

♦Industry Audit Guide (ASLGU) and Statements of Position (SOP) of the American Institute of Certified Public Accountants

FIGURE 5-14 GARS CURRENT TEXT (DEMONSTRATION VERSION)

Codification

I DEMONSTRATION VERSION

Copyright 2000 Governmental Accounting Standards Board

To search the entire infobase, click the **Query** button 🔍 on the **Toolbar** or to search using a predefined query template, To directly access a segment of the infobase, click on any link token (♦) in the menu

♦Front Matter

♦General Principles (1100-1900)

♦Financial Reporting (2100-2900)

♦Specific Balance Sheet and Operating Statement Items (B50-U50)

♦Stand-Alone Reporting—Specialized Units and Activities (Co5-Ut5)

♦Appendixes

FIGURE 5-15 | FASAB'S WEB SITE PROVIDING FREE ACCESS TO ITS AUTHORITIES

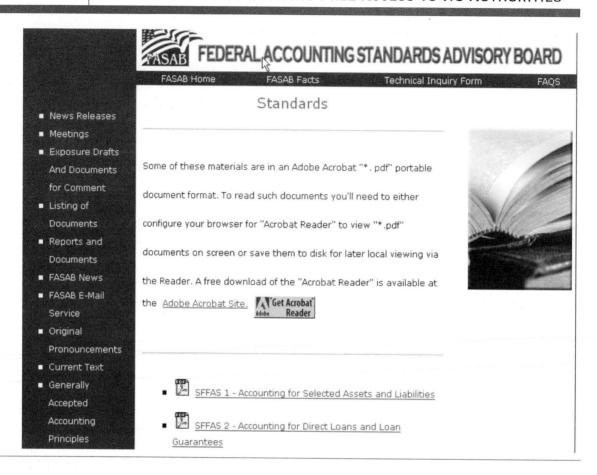

Practice Exercises   *Federal GAAP*

1. Go to the FASAB web site at *http://www.fasab.gov*. What is the primary financial statement defining a "current asset"?

    _____

2. Access *http://www.taxsites.com.*

    a. Identify the rule-making body for the United Kingdom's accounting standards.

    _____

    b. Identify the strongest sources of accounting authority in the United Kingdom.

    _____

    c. Identify the rule-making body for Australia's accounting standards.

    _____

    d. Identify the strongest sources of accounting authority in Australia.

    _____

CASES TO PRACTICE ACCOUNTING RESEARCH

Recall that leading academics have advocated learning from cases, particularly from real companies (see *Accounting Education: Charting the Course through a Perilous Future* by W. Steve Albrecht and Robert J. Sack, available at *http://www.aicpa.org/edu/accteduc.htm*). In the process of studying a case, one develops further analytical skills, enhances technological writing, and refines extemporaneous oral communication skills, particularly if a role-playing simulation is created. Case studies often enable the student to become more familiar with recent events in the profession.

Many cases exist that raise questions about the accounting or auditing practices. The primary sources of these cases are the Deloitte Trueblood Accounting & Auditing Cases (Trueblood Cases), the AICPA, and cases in publications such as *Issues in Accounting Education*.

Each year Deloitte publishes 10 new Trueblood Cases of one to four pages that present difficult intellectual and practical challenges that require a broad array of skills and knowledge to solve. These cases are now available (without the solutions) for viewing and downloading from Deloitte Foundation's web site: *http://www.deloitte.com/*. Conduct a search for the Deloitte "foundation" and review the Trueblood Case Study Series. The cases are indexed among over 20 topics. That web site also explains how professors can acquire access to the case solutions from the separate, password-protected part of the web site. These solutions include more background information, a detailed discussion of the issues involved, and suggested solutions to the questions presented in each case study.

Every year the AICPA has a case competition and publishes numerous cases. Information about these cases are found under the educational materials of the AICPA's web site. *The cases tend to require lengthier analysis than the Deloitte cases.*

Issues in Accounting Education is the educational journal of the American Accounting Association (AAA), the leading professional organization for accounting professors. Usually every issue of the journal presents a few cases that professors could use in their accounting, tax, or auditing classes. The PriceWaterhouse/American Accounting

RESEARCH TOOLS
Internet
FARS
LexisNexis
AICPA reSOURCE
PwC Edgarscan
Thomson ONE
RIA Checkpoint SE
ACL
i2

QUICK FACTS

Using case studies can help develop research and analytical skills.

Practice Exercises — *Finding Cases*

1. Go to the Deloitte Foundation web site at *http://www.deloitte.com* and download a TrueBlood Case involving a Joint Venture or Partnership.

   a. Write a sentence summarizing the issue in the case.
   _____

   b. Use the FARS database to find the authorities providing the answer to the issue presented. Identify those authorities.
   _____

2. Access the AICPA web site at *http://www.aicpa.org* and click on the link for the Antifraud Resource Center.

   a. List the title of two fraud cases.
   _____
   _____

   b. Read one case and summarize the abstract of the case.
   _____
   _____
   _____

Association case notebook—*Auditing/Accounting Teaching Cases and Exercises*—is freely available on the Web as a source of materials for assignment to students. However, the web version omits the elements of each case that might compromise the usefulness of the case in the classroom. Faculty may purchase a suggested solutions manual based on the professional standards that were in effect when the cases were created.

Because of the rapid changes in tax laws, tax cases are more likely to become quickly out-dated. Thus, one should use extra caution when considering a tax case since the age of the case increases the probability that some authority in the answer has changed. It is always advisable to reperform the research of any suggested solution, rather than entirely trusting the source.

SUMMARY

Accounting research is challenging. GAAP has five levels of hierarchy and many sources. One needs to use FARS and the AICPA's reSOURCE databases to find relevant authorities. Thus, one must understand how the databases are structured and their contents, as well as search techniques. Sometimes one needs to research SEC accounting rules and regulations for public companies and use other databases and web sites to acquire those authorities. Researching governmental accounting GAAP poses similar challenges to financial accounting GAAP. Although the Web offers an increasing amount of sources, one must use commercial databases to acquire access to all necessary professional authorities. Thus, one must practice developing research and analytical skills to meet the standards of the accounting profession and the public's expectations.

DISCUSSION QUESTIONS

1. What are the advantages of commercial databases, compared to free Internet sources?
2. What are some tools to help in using a database?
3. What is the typical search process in a database?
4. What are the challenges to accounting research?
5. What are the major infobases comprising the FASB's Financial Accounting Research System (FARS Online)?
6. Which FARS infobase contains:
    a. FASB Concepts Statements?
    b. AICPA Practice Bulletins?
7. What Original Pronouncements are integrated into the Current Text?
8. Does the Current Text provide complete GAAP research? Explain.
9. How are secondary sources on GAAP used to help the researcher?
10. Where does the researcher find:
    a. GAAP Level 1 sources?
    b. GAAP Level 2 sources?
    c. GAAP Level 3 sources?
    d. GAAP Level 4 sources?
    e. GAAP Level 5 sources?

11. What are the SEC accounting authorities and where are they located?

12. What does the GARS database contain?

13. What authorities are provided on the Web by the FASAB?

EXERCISES

1. Use FARS Online to identify the strongest accounting authority governing each of the following:
   a. The accounting for prepaid advertising
   b. The accounting for negative loan amortization
   c. The accounting for accelerated depreciation
   d. The accounting for the range of an estimated loss contingency
   e. The accounting for a reporting period
   f. The accounting for factoring of trade receivables with recourse

2. Rank the authorities found in the previous problem from strongest to weakest in their GAAP levels.

3. Use FARS Online to identify the strongest accounting authority governing each of the following:
   a. The accounting for goodwill
   b. The accounting for start-up costs, sometimes referred to as organizational costs
   c. The accounting for installment receivable
   d. The accounting for subordinated debt
   e. The accounting for imputed interest
   f. The accounting for loss from operations

4. Rank the authorities found in the previous problem from strongest to weakest in their GAAP levels.

5. Using FARS Online, find Accounting Terminology Bulletin 4.
   a. What does it discuss?
   b. How did you find that authority?
   c. Using that authority, how is an expense defined in its broadest sense?
   d. Precisely where in that authority did you find that definition?

6. Using FARS Online, find FASB Interpretation 36.
   a. What does it discuss?
   b. How did you find that authority?
   c. What industry does that authority affect?
   d. What are the major organizational parts of that authority (placed in bold)?

7. Using FARS Online to search GAAP Level 1 authorities, which expenditure qualifies as a Research & Development cost to expense?
   a. The salaries of the research staff designing new products
   b. The commissions paid to sales staff marketing new products

8. Use FARS Online to search GAAP Level 2 authorities and answer the following.
   a. What is a "contingency"?
   b. Precisely where in the authority did you find that definition?
   c. Under what circumstances are contingent losses recorded?
   d. Precisely where in the authority did you find the rule?

9. The FASB Statement No. 106 establishes the accounting standard for post-retirement benefits other than pensions. One can recognize the obligation immediately or amortize it over 20 years. Using the FARS database, review each relevant EITF authority and explain what, if anything, was agreed upon this issue. Provide citations for each conclusion.

10. Use the Topical Index in FARS to research the disclosure requirements for the postretirement benefits other than pensions.

    a. Explain these requirements.

    b. How many levels of GAAP authorities exist on the topic? Explain.

11. In some cases, preferred stock has some characteristics of a debt instrument.

    a. How should the accountant classify such debt in the financial statement?

    b. Reference relevant authorities from FARS to support your answer.

12. Go to the SEC web site at *http://www.sec.gov*.

    a. Access the "information for accountant" folder, and then go to the financial reporting information center. Determine how many accounting and auditing releases were issued in the current year.

    b. SFAS No.115 establishes the accounting standard for investment securities. Search the relevant accounting interpretation and guidance for SFAS No. 115. What conflicts did the SEC resolve under SFAS No. 115?

APPENDIX

CPA Exam—Financial Accounting Simulations

Following are examples of two simulations similar to those appearing on the CPA exam. Review the opening screens and utilize the FARS database to answer the research question segment for the two simulations.

FIGURE A5-1 SIMULATION SCREEN FOR FINANCIAL ACCOUNTING AND REPORTING

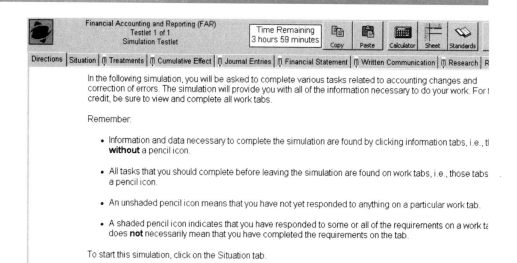

FIGURE A5-2

OPENING SCREEN AFTER CLICKING ON THE
"STANDARDS" ICON IN FIGURE A5-1

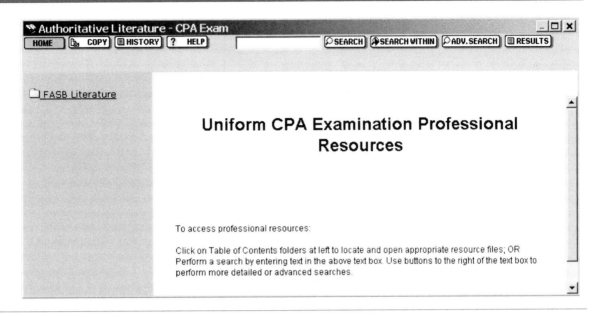

OPENING SCREEN AFTER CLICKING ON THE
"FASB LITERATURE" LINK IN FIGURE A5-2

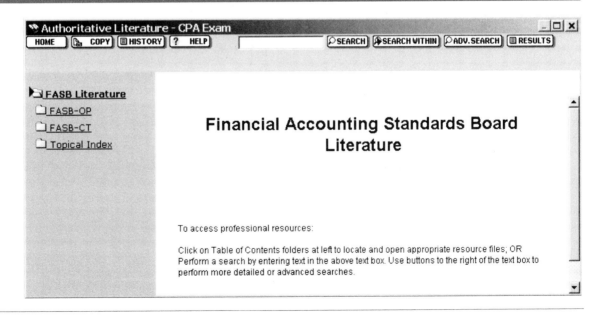

FIGURE A5-4 SIMULATION 1

DIRECTIONS	The **Directions** tab informs the candidate as to the instructions or question requirements for this particular case simulation. Directions will vary depending on the type of simulation/case presented; e.g., "In the following simulation, you will be asked various questions regarding. . . ."
SITUATION	The CFO and controller of Damen Enterprises has asked for your assistance in the preparation of the year-end financial statements for the current year. The President and CFO have had detailed discussion as to contingent liabilities and have come to disagree on the issue, and now have turned to you for advice as to when contingent liabilities need to be booked (recorded) by an entity. Refer to the Research tab for instructions.
RESOURCES	The **Resources** tab provides various resources (tools) that the candidate will utilize in completing the simulation. Here the candidate might find the on-screen calculator, financial statements, performance measures, or various audit schedules or working papers.
ANALYSIS	Clicking on this tab provides the candidate with detailed information for analysis or completion. This could include the completion of a depreciation or bond amortization schedule, completion of a tax return, or the execution of selected audit procedures. Here is where the candidate will input data into drop-down boxes or into Excel spreadsheets.
COMMUNICATION	Written communication is still an integral part of the CPA exam. Under this tab, the candidate will be required to prepare (type) some form of written communication (i.e., to the client or audit partner) to discuss various accounting, auditing, or tax issues related to the facts presented under the Situation tab.
RESEARCH	Here is where the candidate will be required to research relevant databases. Candidates will perform keyword searches utilizing the FASB Literature database.

Simulation 1

Required: For the above given situation, utilize the FASB Literature and perform a keyword search. Locate the appropriate authoritative literature that addresses the issue in the above Situation tab. Cut and paste the appropriate authoritative literature paragraph(s) that address the situation under discussion.

FIGURE A5-5 | SIMULATION 2

| **DIRECTIONS** | The **Directions** tab informs the candidate as to the instructions or question requirements for this particular case simulation. Directions will vary depending on the type of simulation/case presented; e.g., "In the following simulation, you will be asked various questions regarding. . . . " |

| **SITUATION** | You are the assistant controller of Gordon Inc. Your company has incurred an extraordinary item that needs to be reported in the financial statements. Since you do not remember the proper handling of such items, you plan to conduct some research to determine the appropriate handling of extraordinary items. |

| **RESOURCES** | The **Resources** tab provides various resources (tools) that the candidate will utilize in completing the simulation. Here the candidate might find the on-screen calculator, financial statements, performance measures, or various audit schedules or working papers. |

| **ANALYSIS** | Clicking on this tab provides the candidate with detailed information for analysis or completion. This could include the completion of a depreciation or bond amortization schedule, completion of a tax return, or the execution of selected audit procedures. Here is where the candidate will input data into drop-down boxes or into Excel spreadsheets. |

| **COMMUNICATION** | Written communication is still an integral part of the CPA exam. Under this tab, the candidate will be required to prepare (type) some form of written communication (i.e., to the client or audit partner) to discuss various accounting, auditing, or tax issues related to the facts presented under the Situation tab. |

| **RESEARCH** | Here is where the candidate will be required to research relevant databases. Candidates will perform keyword searches utilizing the FASB Literature database. |

Simulation 2

Required: For the above given situation, utilize the FASB Literature and perform a keyword search. Locate the appropriate authoritative literature that addresses the issue in the above Situation tab. Cut and paste the appropriate authoritative literature paragraph(s) that address the situation under discussion.

Other Research Databases and Tools

LEARNING OBJECTIVES

After completing this chapter, you should understand:

- The contents of major legal databases: Westlaw and LexisNexis.

- The contents of major business research databases: Thomson ONE and Thomson Research.

- An overview of other selected databases of use to accountants.

- How to evaluate the potential reliability and usefulness of databases.

- An overview of miscellaneous accounting and general business research tools.

The previous chapters have presented practical guidance for conducting accounting and auditing research. Chapter 5 specifically focused on the search for authoritative accounting support through the use of FARS and other major accounting databases. This chapter presents other research tools currently available to the researcher.

WESTLAW

Westlaw is a comprehensive legal database that includes some nonlegal materials. Westlaw provides access to over 16,700 sources of information. It is the best database for case law research with its long history of making editorial enhancements to cases and developing tools that assist the researcher. Examples of common searches by accountants in Westlaw include the following:

- Locating securities and tax law sources of information.

- Finding background information on the president of a new client or the company itself.

- Monitoring important world issues, such as the Mideast crisis and any resulting financial impact on oil prices that materially impact a client.

Search query terms are powerful in Westlaw because of various tools. Westlaw automatically searches for plurals and possessive when the singular search query is used. Similarly, given an acronym with periods (e.g., P.C.A.O.B.), Westlaw automatically searches for alternatives without the periods and with different spacing. Searches in Westlaw can use universal characters such as an asterisk (*) to serve as a placeholder for any variable character. If one searches in Westlaw without using quotes, Westlaw automatically connects the terms with an "and."

Westlaw offers various other search aids, such as its Table of Contents, hyperlinks, and a powerful citator called "KeyCite." Westlaw's Table of Contents enables the researcher to browse the web site's organization to drill down to relevant chapters and specific sections. Westlaw hyperlinks primary and secondary sources, as well as the citator service. Thus, after retrieving one relevant document, the researcher can easily jump to other

RESEARCH TIPS

Use Westlaw to access extensive editorial enhancements to cases, such as headnotes.

RESEARCH TOOLS

Internet
FARS
LexisNexis
AICPA reSOURCE
PwC Edgarscan
Thomson ONE
RIA Checkpoint SE
ACL
i2
Westlaw

related sources that were cited in the document. Westlaw includes technology that offers additional information related to one's search of a statute or case. The suggested materials are accessible via hyperlinks located to the right of the search results.

Westlaw's powerful special citator research service, KeyCite, determines whether a statute, regulation, case, or administrative source remains valid. KeyCite enables the researcher to determine what subsequent similar authorities have referenced that authority. KeyCite history uses color-coded flags to indicate the status. Red flags suggest stopping because the statutory law was amended or repealed, or the case is no longer valid law for at least one of its points. A yellow flag indicates caution because pending legislation exists affecting the statute, or the statute was renumbered, or the case has some negative history. KeyCite is an option provided on the Westlaw toolbar.

Several other helpful tools exist in Westlaw. For example, the "Most Cited Cases" link enables the researcher to more easily find the strongest cases to support an argument. "Westclip" is a tool that delivers up-to-date news on a desired search query on a regular basis. For business and professional news, Westlaw includes many sources, including various newspapers, magazines, and wire services. "My Westlaw" enables selecting customized tabs, such as company information, banking and finance, estate planning, e-commerce, securities, and tax. The keysearch path is displayed on the top of the Westlaw page to assist the researcher in keeping track of how this document was located.

Editorial enhancements by Westlaw to cases and statutes include (1) a synopsis, (2) headnotes, and (3) key numbers. A synopsis for a case summarizes the procedural history of the case, the court's holding, and the major legal points of law discussed. Headnotes provide paragraph summaries of a single part of law central to the case. Headnotes are written by attorney-editors with consistent and current legal terminology, as well as descriptive terms, such as "tenant," rather than proper names, such as "Mr. Tanaka." Usually a case has several headnotes. Key numbers assign a headnote to a particular legal topic and in the process enhance the power of Westlaw's index and its usefulness for the researcher.

For federal securities law research in Westlaw, the researcher might select the combined material database (fsec-all) or target the search in the SEC's releases (fsec-rel) or examine cases on securities laws (fsec-cs) or use various other potential parts of the database. The "Disposition Tables" feature in Westlaw enables the researcher to more easily find securities laws in their codified locations. For example, to find the Securities Act of 1933 section 10, the disposition table provides the reference to the codified location (15 USC sec. 77j).

For tax accounting, Westlaw offers a tax page that assists the researcher in more easily extracting relevant tax information. For example, the tax page displays templates to assist in retrieving a document by citator. For example, the template will identify an authority such as a Revenue Ruling issued by the Internal Revenue Service, so that the researcher merely needs to input the Revenue Ruling number to access the document. Westlaw has an additional citator for tax authorities: RIA Federal Tax Citator. The advantage of the RIA Citator is that it indicates how the subsequent case has used some aspect of the cited case, such as whether it distinguished the point of law, merely explained it, or agreed to follow it. State tax statutes, regulations, state appellate courts, and administrative decisions by many state agencies also benefit from Westlaw's editorial enhancements.

Westlaw includes various secondary sources that are helpful for the researcher. In tax, Westlaw has databases from RIA, BNA, and Warren Gorham & Lamont that assist the researcher, such as tax services and leading treatises. For internal audit, Warren Gorham & Lamont also has various internal auditing materials accessible on Westlaw. For business concerns, the researcher can access leading sources of business information such as Dunn & Bradstreet, which contains over 62 million companies in over 200 countries, or Dialog, Dow Jones Interactive, and Thomson Financial. For example, in Thomson Financial, one can obtain a company profile by the Gale Group to acquire a comprehensive overview of a company and its operations.

RESEARCH TIPS ●

Use a citator to determine the current validity of authority.

RESEARCH TIPS ●

To assist you in research, the Westlaw editorial enhancements include a synopsis, headnotes, and key numbers for indexing topics.

FIGURE 6-1 | WESTLAW CAMPUS OPENING SCREEN

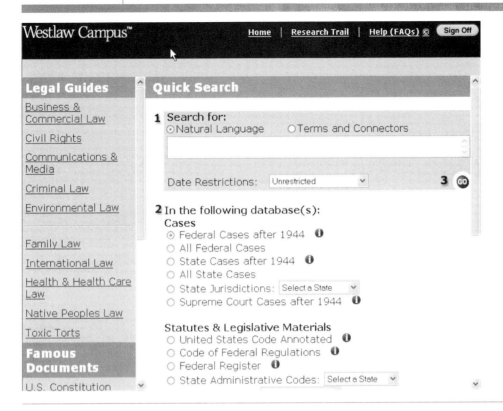

One can save the search results in Westlaw for viewing in more detail at a later time. Often one can also e-mail the search results.

Westlaw Campus

The academic version of Westlaw marketed to universities is called "Westlaw Campus," as shown in Figure 6-1. The product is geared towards business law classes that acquire a basic orientation in finding statutory law, regulations, and cases, and use unique secondary sources. Thus, Westlaw Campus provides the complete United States Code Annotated, the Code of Federal Regulations, cases, a comprehensive legal encyclopedia (*American Law Reports and American Jurisprudence* 2d), and hundreds of law reviews and journals.

Westlaw Campus is not geared towards the sophisticated needs of accounting students, but it is an introduction to the full power of Westlaw. This text does not include access to Campus, but instructors may order the textbook bundled with Campus. If you wish to visit Westlaw Campus and your business law textbook or library does not offer a subscription, go to *http://www.westlaw.com* to access an online demo and to learn more about this limited version of Westlaw.

> **RESEARCH TIPS**
>
> Use electronic databases to obtain an overview of a company and its operations.

LEXISNEXIS

LexisNexis also enables one to find authoritative legal sources, news, business information, public records, and various information on over 35 million global companies. Like Westlaw, LexisNexis is an immense database—over 3.5 billion public records.

LexisNexis has expanded from its legal research origins to include many subjects and cover information from many parts of the world. LexisNexis leads in having the largest amount of materials outside of primary legal sources.

Examples of common searches by accountants in LexisNexis include the following:

- Acquiring earnings reports and industry market share for a particular company.

- Determining which public companies have recently gone through reorganization.

- Understanding a company's organization with subsidiaries, divisions, and branches.

Legal sources of interest for the accountant perusing LexisNexis include securities and tax laws as well as various public records. For business and professional news, LexisNexis also includes many sources, including various newspapers, magazines, and wire services. Professional accounting journals, law reviews providing more detailed analysis of a topic, and shorter articles in other specialized and industry-specific business journals and newsletters are also included in LexisNexis.

LexisNexis lists over 32,000 database sources. Often a source consists of one publication over a period of time, such as *The New York Times* (NYT includes all articles since June 1980). A source may also include multiple sources for related topics, such as trade and business magazines in the source "MAGS." A list of sources in LexisNexis is available online in a "Searchable Directory of Online Sources" provided by LexisNexis Customer Service Center's web site. The list of online sources also explains the contents of theses sources.

The "Folders" in LexisNexis group related sources. For example, *Accounting, Tax & Financial Library* (ACCTG) is an important folder in LexisNexis. The ACCTG folder contains extensive case law, regulatory and other administrative materials such as private letter rulings from the Internal Revenue Service; thousands of corporate annual reports; federal tax, bankruptcy, securities laws, regulations, and relevant court rulings; and pronouncements from the SEC, PCAOB (Public Company Accounting Oversight Board), FASB, AICPA, Cost Accounting Standards Board, International Accounting Standards Committee (IASC), and others. Secondary source materials in ACCTG are from leading professional publishers such as Thomson Publishing, Harcourt Brace, Matthew Bender, Faulkner and Gray, and Warren Gorham & Lamont.

Searching under the "Company and Financial" folder in LexisNexis locates SEC filings, wire service stories, and mergers and acquisitions. One can narrow the search for mergers and acquisitions using a segment search based on the type of offer or deal, as well as the industry. Corporate filings in the SEC database include the 10-K for the annual corporate report, 10-Q for the quarterly report, and proxy filings for new stock issuances, and are available in the ACCTG folder. Corporate annual reports of public companies from 1973–1995 are located in the NAARS (National Automated Accounting Research System) folders. NAARS was the first database to provide segmental access to the financial statements, footnotes, and auditors' reports, as well as selected proxy statement information.

The "LexisNexis Company Dossier" product provides an information report on a company that includes overview information, financial statements, executive information, explanation of subsidiaries, and identification of the company's legal counsel, auditors, and others.

LexisNexis Academic

LexisNexis Academic is marketed just to universities. It provides access to only a small part of the information found on LexisNexis. A demo of the capabilities of this database is located at this text's web site (*http://weirich.swlearning.com*). **It is suggested that you review the demo at this time before proceeding further.** Five general areas on LexisNexis Academic are news, business, legal research, medical, and reference, as shown on the left side of the opening screen for LexisNexis Academic, as reproduced in Figure 6-2. A trick in using LexisNexis Academic effectively is to avoid using the search engine until

---

RESEARCH TOOLS

Internet
FARS
LexisNexis
AICPA reSOURCE
PwC Edgarscan
Thomson ONE
RIA Checkpoint SE
ACL
i2

QUICK FACTS

LexisNexis is a legal database providing news, business information, public records, and other information.

FIGURE 6-2 | LexisNexis Academic Main Menu

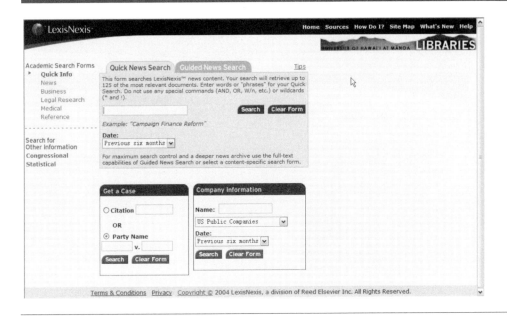

Reprinted with permission of LexisNexis Academic & Library Solutions.

you have accessed the particular area of interest. Thus, the search engine on the opening screen is only for searching in news.

Select the "Business" folder to acquire access to the accounting information. LexisNexis Academic's weakness is mixing sources by organizing them alphabetically, rather than logically by strength of authority. Thus, the Accounting folder includes several SEC sources, some AICPA materials, several secondary sources, and the Office of Management and Budget for cost accounting standards. Thus, the database provides little guidance for the researcher in distinguishing between primary authorities for accounting and well-respected secondary materials, such as treatises like *Miller's GAAP Guide* and journals like the ***AICPA's*** *Journal of Accountancy*.

Before using the search engine in LexisNexis Academic, use the drop-down box to first enter the particular source of interest, such as the SEC's "Accounting and Auditing Enforcement Releases." The LexisNexis Academic search engine is limited to a particular part of the database. Also, the search engine does not always display the results in the most helpful manner to the researcher trying to assess the relevant authorities.

Consider the example of researching the disclosure requirements for leasing activities. First, select the "Business" folder to access the "Accounting" section (Figure 6-3). Use "lease" as the keyword. Further refine the search by using "disclosure" to narrow the research results. Choose Miller GAAP Guide as the source, as shown as Figure 6-4. The research results are provided in Figure 6-5. Select "Chapter 29. Leases. Accounting and Reporting by Lessors" in the research results to obtain the relevant information on the disclosure requirements for leasing activities by the lessor, as shown in the Miller GAAP Guide in Figure 6-6.

Consider the example of reviewing the 2003 financial statements for Martha Stewart Living Omnimedia Inc. First, select the business folder and go to the company profile section, as shown in Figure 6-7. See the results of different sources of company information, as shown as Figure 6-8. You would then be able to acquire the 2003 financial statements shown as in Figure 6-9.

RESEARCH TIPS

In LexisNexis Academic, you must select the particular source before using a keyword search.

FIGURE 6-3 | LEXISNEXIS ACADEMIC BUSINESS FOLDER

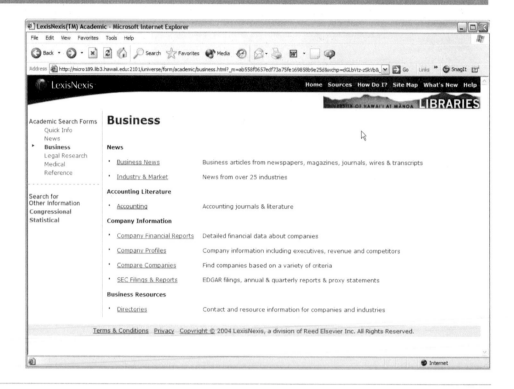

Reprinted with permission of LexisNexis Academic & Library Solutions.

FIGURE 6-4 | LEXISNEXIS ACADEMIC ACCOUNTING LITERATURE SECTION

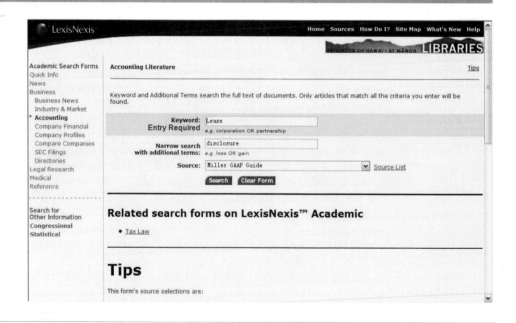

Reprinted with permission of LexisNexis Academic & Library Solutions.

FIGURE 6-5 | LEXISNEXIS ACADEMIC RESEARCH RESULTS

Reprinted with permission of LexisNexis Academic & Library Solutions.

FIGURE 6-6 | LEXISNEXIS ACADEMIC MILLER GAAP RESULTS

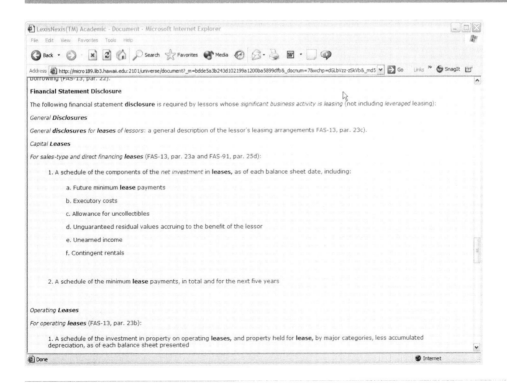

Reprinted with permission of LexisNexis Academic & Library Solutions.

FIGURE 6-7 | LEXISNEXIS ACADEMIC COMPANY PROFILES FOLDER

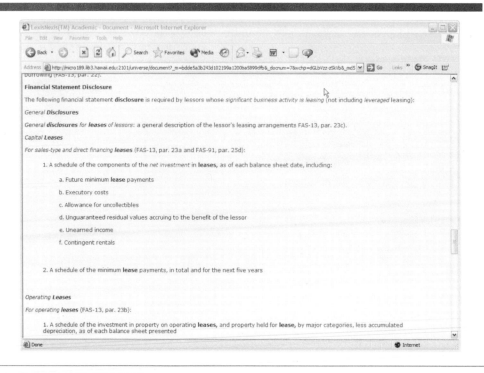

Reprinted with permission of LexisNexis Academic & Library Solutions.

FIGURE 6-8 | LEXISNEXIS ACADEMIC EXAMPLE ACCESS TO FINANCIAL STATEMENTS

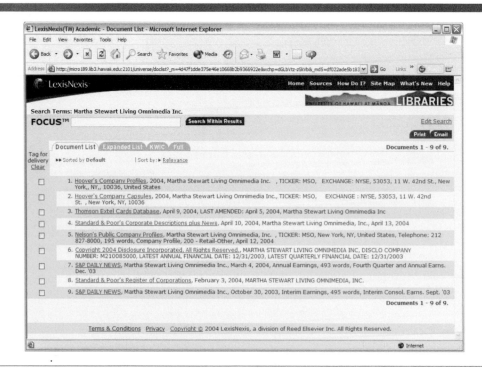

Reprinted with permission of LexisNexis Academic & Library Solutions.

FIGURE 6-9 | RESEARCH RESULTS

THOMSON ONE BANKER

Thomson ONE Banker provides comprehensive financial data and various source documents on more than 65,000 domestic and global companies. The database integrates company financial data from Worldscope, daily pricing data and indexes from Datastream, earnings estimates, press releases, company filings, and other information from various sources. Thomson ONE Banker provides access to real-time global market data, news, and authoritative information from industry-leading sources. Thomson ONE Banker offers access to stock quotes, earnings estimates, financial fundamentals, market moving news, transaction data, corporate filings, ownership profiles, and research from industry-leading sources.

Thomson ONE Banker has several powerful functions. Search across multiple databases simultaneously to identify companies that meet specific criteria for analysis. Select from hundreds of database reports and charts. Make comparisons within the industry by choosing from various comparative reports. Research fundamentals and statistics for the companies in a portfolio. Create "Public Information Books" to customize the content desired in a report.

To locate a company, go to the upper-left side of the screen and select Financial Intelligence. Insert the company's name, stock ticker symbols, or other identifier. The company overview appears on the main part of your screen. Thomson ONE Banker provides an overview of a company in various data formats, such as the financial picture or general information. Use online help to learn more about reporting, charting for comparisons to major indices, or other actions. Use the glossary to look up definitions of database items.

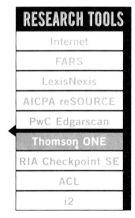

RESEARCH TOOLS

Internet

FARS

LexisNexis

AICPA reSOURCE

PwC Edgarscan

Thomson ONE

RIA Checkpoint SE

ACL

i2

Typical applications of Thomson ONE Banker includes investigating the following types of concerns:

• Creating an investment portfolio.

• Making an analytic procedure comparison.

For example, determine Microsoft Corporation's stock price high and low for the current day, which in the example is April 13, 2004. Using Thomson ONE Banker, select the overview folder, and insert the company's name—"Microsoft Corp." or "MSFT"—on the left side column. This enables you to acquire Microsoft Corp.'s most recent quarterly financial overview and stock quotes, as of April 13, 2004, as shown in Figure 6-10. By reviewing the data in the financial overview, you learn that 56,985,201 shares of stock were exchanged on April 13, 2004. The highest price was $25.77 and the lowest price was $25.41.

THOMSON RESEARCH

Thomson Research uses over a dozen leading databases to provide access to more than 6,000,000 source documents. The database covers about 90 percent of the world's stock market value and includes records for more than 17,000 active companies representing over 50 countries. Some private companies from the United States and other countries are also included in Thomson Research. The content profile for a company generally includes financial data, all the SEC filings, the auditor's report, accounting practices, product and geographic segment data, financial ratios, news, overview reports from Extel Company, Worldscope, Dun & Bradstreet, and more. An example of a company content profile from Thomson Research is shown in Figure 6-11.

Thomson Research includes Predicast's overview of markets and technology, including information on emerging technologies, joint ventures, licensing agreements, personnel changes, product announcements, and more. The database offers such time-saving functions as spreadsheet ready financial information, project tracking, and full-text keyword searching of SEC filings in EDGAR.

Use business databases, such as Thomson Research, to identify business threats and opportunities arising from patents, competitive trademarks, or upcoming mergers or acquisitions. Other typical applications of business databases include investigating the following concerns:

• The consolidation policies used to account for less-than-100-percent-owned subsidiaries.

• The balance sheet presentation of unfunded pension liabilities.

• The CPA firm that audited a company.

• Examples of dual-dated audit reports.

• The *Fortune* 500 ranking of a company.

• Pending government investigations against a company.

This text provides access to Thomson ONE Business School Edition, which contains some Thomson Research components. More information is available at *http://research. thomsonib.com*. Note that this web address does not use *www*.

OTHER DATABASES OF INTEREST TO ACCOUNTANTS

Various other databases and specialized research tools within these databases exist to help the researcher in different circumstances. Some of the popular accounting or

FIGURE 6-10 | THOMSON ONE BANKER EXAMPLE OF A COMPANY OVERVIEW

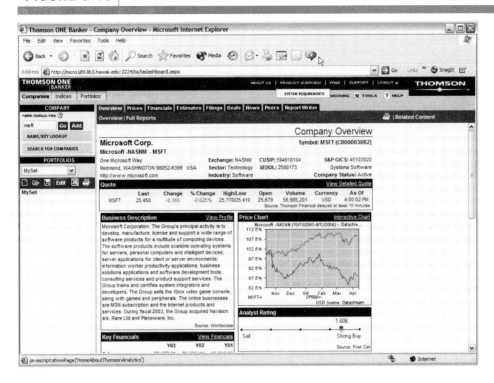

FIGURE 6-11 | THOMSON RESEARCH—EXAMPLE OF THE CONTENT PROFILE

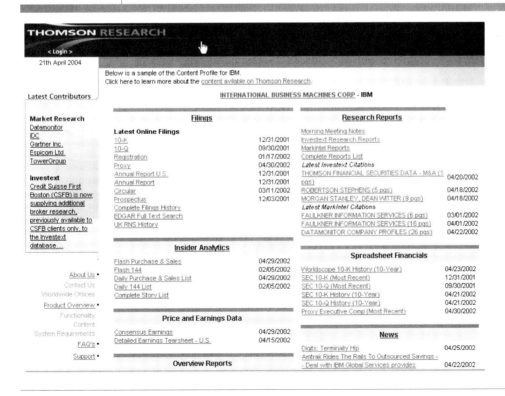

Accounting and Auditing Research
Weirich/Pearson/Reinstein

RESEARCH TIPS

Use more than one database to research a problem because each database has certain strengths and weaknesses.

business databases include CCH Business Research Network, Factiva, ABI/INFORM, Business and Company Research Center, Hoovers Online, Stat-USA, Business Source Premier, and ABI/Inform Global. A word of caution: The information content database industry continues to rapidly evolve with new products, technological enhancements, and increased utility. Thus, remain vigilant to using new or additional databases in the future.

CCH Business Research Network

This database provides access to federal securities laws, banking information, consumer credit, and other information. The securities part of the database includes the "SEC Accountants" module to view selected FASB and GASB materials, which are mostly limited to part of Level 1 authorities for GAAP. The *Capital Changes Report* includes "Corporate Capital Histories" that list a chronology of events such as incorporation, mergers, and stock dividends. *CCH Business Research Network* includes the full text of CCH publications dealing with securities, banking, capital changes, trade regulation, government contracts, public utilities, and information technology. If your library does not offer a subscription to CCH Business Research Network, go to *http://www.cch.com* and select the CCH Tax and Accounting web site to learn more about CCH materials and databases.

Factiva

This database provides a wealth of business and financial information. The database is a joint venture between Dow Jones (publisher of *The Wall Street Journal*) and Reuters (a leading financial news provider in Europe). The "Company & Industry" database provides a quick company overview with comparison reports. The "Historical Market Data Center" provides 25 years' worth of pricing on stocks, bonds, mutual funds, and global market indices. Factiva's Publications Library provides information from about 8,000 newspapers and other sources from over 100 countries and 20 languages, many of which are available in full text. In Factiva, use parentheses for search terms with two or more words. If your library does not offer a subscription to Factiva, go to *http://www.factiva.com* to learn more about the database.

Business and Company Resource Center

RESEARCH TIPS

In searching for financial information, utilize one of the following databases: Thomson ONE Banker, Thomson Research, Factiva, Business and Company Resource Center, and Hoover's Online.

This database provides Thomson Financial content used globally by financial investment banks and institutions. The database offers access to business journal news and analysis, insider buying and selling activity, consumer marketing data, corporate chronologies and histories, emerging technology reports, and more. The Business and Company Resource Center contains listings for 465,000 U.S. and international companies, extensive essays for 1,000 industrial categories, industry statistics, market share reports and company rankings. About 3,000 company histories and 1,500 company chronologies are available for more prominent global businesses. If your library does not offer a subscription to the Business and Company Resource Center, go to *http://www.galegroup.com* and the product fact sheet will list Business and Company Resource Center with a link to a promotional brochure about this database.

Hoover's Online

This database provides comprehensive company, industry, and market intelligence that drives business growth. Hoover's Online provides sales, marketing business development, and recruiting professionals with the global business intelligence they need to prospect and prepare for client meetings, sales presentations, vendor and partner negotiations, and other business opportunities. The database attempts to provide objective information by not relying on what a company's corporate staff might issue. If your library does not offer

Practice Exercises *Electronic Databases*

1. Use Thomson Research (select business and then industry and market).
   Find the industry ranking in the music business. Who are the three largest companies in the music industry?
   _____
   _____

2. Use Business Source Premier.
   a. Use the index for authors and identify the most recent publications of your professors.
   _____
   _____

   b. Access the overview of Realnetworks, Inc. Use the information to explain the significance of its RealPlayer line of web products. Specifically, how many registered users exist for the RealPlayer line of products?
   _____
   _____

3. Utilize LexisNexis and locate the accounting literature section.
   a. List the title of two articles from the *Journal of Accountancy* that discuss the term "money laundering":
   _____
   _____

   b. Locate and name two Accounting and Auditing Enforcement Releases that deal with the issue of "Revenue Recognition":
   _____
   _____

4. Utilize Thomson Research. Enter "Dow Chemical" in the Quick Company Search box and locate the most recent 10-K to answer the following:
   a. What is the date of the recent 10-K? _____
   b. Who is the auditing firm for Dow? _____
   c. What is Dow's president's name? _____

a subscription to Hoover's Online, go to *http://www.hoovers.com* to see the free version and learn more about the additional information available for different subscriptions.

Stat-USA

This database provides current and historical data on business, international trade, and the economy from the U.S. Department of Commerce. This service is especially useful in preparing for strategic business decisions. "Global Business Opportunities" (GLOBUS) offers daily trade leads from the Trade Opportunities Program, as well as the Department of Agriculture. The "National Trade Data Bank" (NTDB) provides the U.S. government's most comprehensive source of international information, including commercial guides for different countries, market research reports, and other documents. The "International Trade Library" provides over 40,000 documents related to international trade. If your library does not offer a subscription to Stat-USA, go to *http://www.stat-usa.gov* and its site map to learn more about this database.

Business Source Premier

This database by EBSCO Publishing is designed for business schools and libraries. As of July 2004, Business Source Premier contains full text for over 8,500 periodicals and other sources, including 1,103 peer-reviewed journals, 2,364 trade journals and general business magazines, and other monographs and economic and research reports. Business Source Premier also provides company profiles. The opening screen for Business Source Premier is provided in Figure 6-12. If your library does not offer a subscription to Business Source premier, go to *http://www.ebsco.com* to learn more about the electronic resources offered.

ABI/INFORM Global

This business and management database by Proquest indexes about 1,800 international professional publications, academic journals, and trade magazines. It includes full-text articles for about half of them. ABI/INFORM Global includes information on more than 60,000 companies. Find research on accounting, taxation, computers, and business topics in general, particularly advertising, banking, finance, insurance, international trade, management, marketing, and real estate. If your library does not offer a subscription to ABI/INFORM Global, go to *http://www.proquest.com* to learn more about their business products, which includes this database.

FIGURE 6-12 | BUSINESS SOURCE PREMIER OPENING SCREEN

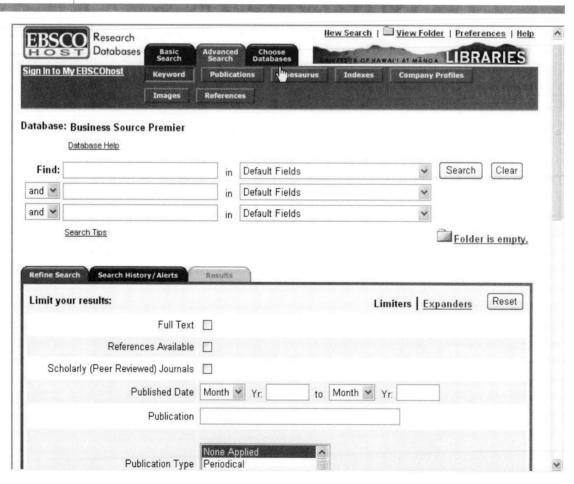

EVALUATING OTHER DATABASES AND INFORMATION

As information continues to explode, the researcher will confront new databases to use and sources of information to evaluate. To assess the database, the researcher must consider the publisher or author of the material, assess the reliability of the information presented, evaluate the current relevance of the material, and determine the likely success in finding the needed information.

The publisher or author of the material helps to determine the authority. Is the source part of a government, university, or private vendor? In assessing the source of the data, is the material in English a full-text translation or an abstract?

Ask various questions to assess the reliability of the information for accuracy and insight. Are there obvious errors or omissions? Is the quality of the information consistent? How often are the resources updated? Are the source documents timely?

MISCELLANEOUS ACCOUNTING RESEARCH TOOLS

In addition to those discussed in Chapter 5, other frequently used accounting research tools include the *Accounting and Tax Index*; the AICPA's *Accounting Trends & Techniques*, *Financial Report Surveys*, and the *Audit and Accounting Manual*; research files of public accounting firms; and public files of the accounting and auditing authoritative bodies.

Accounting and Tax Index

The index, which is arranged in a dictionary format with full citations, covers virtually every English-language publication on accounting or accounting-related and taxation-related subjects. It also incorporates accounting firms, state and national legislation, compensation plans, consulting services, and corporate financial management. The index scans more than 1,000 publications for relevant citations. It is published in three quarterly issues, and a cumulative year-end volume provides quick access to a number of books, articles, pamphlets, speeches, and government documents.

Accounting Trends and Techniques

For over 50 years, the AICPA has published an annual survey of accounting practices in *Accounting Trends & Techniques*. This publication provides comprehensive up-to-date excerpts of financial reporting practices and developments for about 600 publicly held companies. The findings illustrate the current reporting practices of such selected companies and chart significant trends in reporting practices. Approximately 90 percent of the surveyed companies are listed on the New York or American Stock Exchanges.

The survey enables the practitioner to determine how various-size companies in a wide range of industries have complied with professional standards for financial reporting. It also alerts the practitioner to emerging trends in reporting practices. Specific reporting requirements set forth in pronouncements of the APB, FASB, and SEC are cited wherever applicable. This survey is an appropriate source for the researcher to review in an attempt to determine current practice for a particular issue under investigation.

Each company surveyed in *Accounting Trends & Techniques* is assigned a reference number. As companies are removed from the survey because of an acquisition or merger, the identification number is retired. The appendix of this publication lists the companies in their reference number order. The survey contains a table of contents listing specific reporting and disclosure examples by the general categories of Balance Sheet, Income Statement, Stockholders Equity, Statement of Cash Flows, and Auditor's Report. A topical index is included at the end of the survey.

Financial Report Surveys

The AICPA's *Financial Report Surveys*, which supplement the overview that *Accounting Trends & Techniques* provides, are a continuing series of studies, which show in detail how companies in a wide range of industries disclose specific accounting and reporting questions in their financial reports. The surveys also include the complete texts of official pronouncements and other pertinent material wherever applicable. For example, Survey No. 54 presents examples on how corporate financial statements present certain provisions of FASB Statement No. 112, *Employers' Accounting for Postemployment Benefits*.

Audit and Accounting Manual

The *Audit and Accounting Manual*, prepared by the staff of the AICPA, provides a nonauthoritative guide for practitioners in the conduct of an audit. The manual explains and illustrates the actual procedures involved in major aspects of an audit engagement. Extensive examples of such items as engagement letters, audit programs, working papers, and various other forms and documents are provided. The contents of the manual include the following:

- Introduction
- Compilation and Review
- Engagement Planning and Administration
- Internal Control Structure
- Audit Approach and Programs
- Working Papers
- Correspondence, Confirmations, and Representations
- Audit Risk Alerts
- Supervision, Review, and Report Processing
- Accountants' Reports
- Quality Control Forms and Aids

Examples and exhibits in the manual are presented for illustrative purposes only. Many sections, however, provide references to authoritative pronouncements in the AICPA *Professional Standards*. The *Audit and Accounting Manual* is available in an annual paperback edition or as a looseleaf subscription service.

Research Files of Public Accounting Firms

Many public accounting firms maintain research files on various accounting and auditing issues documented from the firm's own practice. The primary purpose of such files is to provide firm personnel with access to previously researched issues and the firm's conclusions. The research file's design can be as simple or advanced as necessary to meet the firm's needs.

When confronted with a research issue, the practitioner searches the file index to determine if the issue has been previously researched and, if so, where to locate the details of the research. The index is typically an alphanumeric listing by subject matter of topics that are stored in the research files. The details of the research are often filed electronically for easy retrieval.

FASB, ACSEC, AND EITF FILES

The public files of the FASB, AcSEC, and EITF contain useful information for the researcher. The public files include all exposure drafts, letters of comment in response to the drafts, minutes of meetings, agenda items, and other correspondence related to the development of professional standards and other pronouncements, such as interpretations. The information contained in these files provides valuable insight in determining the rationale of the various boards or committees in developing standards.

GENERAL BUSINESS RESEARCH TOOLS

Some of the major business research tools that are available to the researcher in gathering business or statistical information include those listed in the following paragraphs.

Trade Directories

A trade directory often contains important information about an individual business and the products it makes, buys, or sells. Many comprehensive directories are indispensable in general business research. The main directories include *The Million Dollar Directory*, which provides a listing of U.S. companies; *Thomas Register of American Manufacturers*; and *America's Corporate Families* and *Who Owns Whom*, which provide information on linkages between parent companies and their subsidiaries.

Government Publications

The U.S. government is the world's largest publisher. Similarly, many state and local governments publish information useful in business research. A sample of the major publications of this type includes *Census of Retail Trade*, *Census of Manufacturers*, *Census of Services Industries*, *Census of Transportation*, *Survey of Current Business*, and the *Federal Reserve Bulletin*.

Statistical Sources

To help the researcher collect statistical information, the U.S. government developed the Standard Industrial Classification (SIC) code. This classification system consists of a four-digit code for all manufacturers and nonmanufacturing industries. Some of the major statistical sources that use this SIC code system are the *Handbook of Basic Economic Statistics*, the *Statistical Abstract of the United States*, and *Standard and Poor's Statistical Service*.

Business Services

Many private organizations provide business services that supply summarized financial information on all major American companies. *Moody's Investors Service*, one of the better known services, publishes a weekly *Manual* in each of six business areas: transportation, industrials, OTC (over-the-counter) industrials, public relations, banks and finance, and municipals and governments. Other business services include Corporate Records, published by Standard and Poor's Corporation, along with their services *Value Line* and *Investment Service*.

International Services

Information for the international business researcher is available in a number of sources. *Principal International Businesses* lists basic information on major companies located around the world. For statistical information, one can use such services as the *Index to International Statistics*, *Statistical Yearbook*, or *Worldcasts*.

SUMMARY

Many research tools are available in conducting practical accounting professional research. Extensive information on companies is available in legal databases (such as Westlaw and LexisNexis) as well as more newly developed business databases. The explosion of business information has made it a necessity to use computerized databases such as Westlaw, LexisNexis, Thomson ONE Banker, Thomson Research, and others offering value to accountants. Regardless of the abundance of data, there is no one definitive way to conduct business research on a particular company. The approach that one takes depends on the importance of the issue, the type and amount of information one has to start with, as well as the desired end product, and sometimes management of the cost of electronic research.

DISCUSSION QUESTIONS

1. What are the advantages in using Westlaw?
2. What type of authoritative information is available on LexisNexis?
3. Identify two newspapers, magazines, or wire services available on LexisNexis.
4. Identify a publication in LexisNexis that contains corporate earnings.
5. Where can one find information on the sources in LexisNexis?
6. How does a specialized search vary from the common research strategy?
7. What is included in a LexisNexis Company Dossier?
8. What are the general areas of LexisNexis Academic?
9. How does the LexisNexis Academic database compare to the LexisNexis database?
10. What does the Thomson Research database cover?
11. What is the major type of information in the Westlaw database?
12. When would one use the Factiva database?
13. What type of information is available in the CCH Business Research Network?
14. What insight is offered by the Business and Company Resource Center database?
15. How is Hoover's Online distinguishable from other databases providing corporate information?
16. What is the major source of information in Stat-USA?
17. When would a researcher use Business Source Premier?
18. What does ABI/INFORM Global include?

EXERCISES

1. Access LexisNexis Academic. Select Business and then the Accounting link. In the drop-down box, select *Miller's GAAP Guide* and search using the keyword "derivatives." What documents were displayed?
2. Access LexisNexis Academic. Select Business and then the Accounting link. In the drop-down box, select AICPA and Auditing Publications and search using the keyword "derivatives." Give the citation for the two most recent journal articles on this topic and summarize each article in a paragraph.

3. Access LexisNexis Academic. Select the business section and see how many possible choices are available to find information about a company that you may be interested in researching. As an example, make a search for "IBM 2002" using those resources and discuss the different results obtained based on the different sections used. Did you find any advantages or disadvantages from using any of the search options? Please discuss.

4. Access LexisNexis Academic. Go to the tax law section, and conduct research on the new dividend tax treatment after the 2003 tax reform. What journals were displayed?

5. Access Thomson ONE Banker. Review Microsoft Corp.'s five-year financial reports and ratio reports and discuss what the company's financial situation looks like.

6. Access CCH Business Research Network. Determine the major GAAP's provisions affecting the financial statement's presentation of unfunded pension liability.

7. Access CCH Business Research Network. Conduct a search to find out the federal laws and regulations concerning the environmental liability disclosure requirements on a public company.

8. Access Stat-USA. Conduct research to find out how much steel the United States traded internationally in Year 2003.

9. Use Business Source Premier or Factiva to find Alexander & Baldwin. Write a one-sentence explanation describing Alexander & Baldwin's business. Use the full company profile to identify the company's top competitors.

10. Access ABI/INFORM Global. Conduct research to find out what effects the Sarbanes-Oxley Act has had since it was passed in 2002.

11. Access ABI/INFORM Global. Using the topic guide, conduct research on Google Inc.'s new Gmail system and find out what is the most controversial issue of the new system.

12. What other accounting and business databases does your library provide? Select one database and provide four PowerPoint® slides explaining it.

Tax Research for Compliance and Tax Planning

LEARNING OBJECTIVES

After completing this chapter, you should understand:

- Tax research goals.
- Tax research challenges.
- Tax research databases, such as RIA Checkpoint.
- Primary tax authorities, particularly the code, treasury regulations, and cases.
- Evaluating different tax authorities.
- An overview of the tax research process.
- AICPA's Statements on Standards for Tax Services.

Many taxpayers use tax software or seek professional help in completing their tax returns. Complexity in tax rules and their application have made skill in tax research a marketable expertise. The purpose of this chapter is to present more information and guidance in conducting tax research for compliance and tax planning. The tax research methodology is similar to accounting and auditing research.

TAX RESEARCH GOALS

The objective of tax research is not necessarily to produce the lowest possible tax liability for the taxpayer. Instead, the objective is to maximize the taxpayer's after-tax return or benefits, which may even take noneconomic forms, such as the preference of some clients for either certainty of tax results or to minimize potential disputes with the IRS. This difference in viewpoint—maximizing after-tax benefits as opposed to minimizing tax—is especially important when one realizes that many tax-saving strategies involve some tradeoff with pretax income, either in the form of incurring additional expense, receiving less revenue, or both.

Tax researchers must understand the difference between tax evasion, tax avoidance, and abusive tax avoidance. Tax evasion consists of illegal acts, such as making false statements of fact, to lower one's taxes. Tax advisors must not condone any tax evasion by a client. Tax avoidance seeks to minimize taxes legally, such as avoiding the creation of facts that would result in higher taxes. Tax avoidance is often the objective of tax research. However, in 2003, the IRS began to target "abusive tax avoidance" by promoters of tax shelters and taxpayers investing in transactions which the IRS believes are intentionally misapplying the tax laws.[1]

Tax researchers should also understand how the term "tax research" is used in different contexts. Applied tax research addresses existing tax law, with the objective of

> **QUICK FACTS**
> Tax avoidance seeks to minimize taxes legally.

---

[1] IR–2003-11, Sept. 16, 2003.

determining its impact on a given situation. In this book, the term **tax research** is used solely in the application sense to relate to the tax problems of specific taxpayers, rather than to the problems of society at large. However, theoretical tax research is often policy-oriented research having the objective of providing new information that will help policy makers decide what the tax law ought to be.

TAX RESEARCH CHALLENGES

RESEARCH TIPS

Identifying the relevant facts is critical for an accurate research result.

Tax research is best defined as an examination of all relevant tax laws given the facts of a client's situation, in order to determine the appropriate tax consequences.

Identifying the relevant facts is the first essential part of tax research. Many tax disputes involve questions of fact, rather than questions of law. The term **fact** as used in the definition of tax research includes conclusions, as well as individual events from which those conclusions are drawn.

EXAMPLE: Under the law gifts received are not includable in taxable income (sec. 102), whereas compensation for services is taxable (sec. 61). Does receipt of a diamond necklace constitute an excludable gift or taxable compensation?

Discussion: The result depends upon all events and circumstances relevant to the case. True love suggests the necklace is a gift, whereas a one-evening relationship might suggest the payment of the diamonds is in return for companionship services. Any dispute with the Internal Revenue Service in such a situation is a question of fact since the law is clear that compensation is taxable (Sec. 61), while gifts are not taxable (Sec. 102).

Two other common factual disputes include determining fair market value of property and the amount of deductible business expenses (especially while traveling away from home on business).

Second, the tax researcher must identify the precise legal issues for the given set of facts. Too often there is a tendency among beginning tax researchers to rush into the search for authority without an adequate understanding of the problem and the real issues requiring research. Perhaps the following example can help illustrate the benefit of spending time in the initial steps to determine the relevant facts and legal issues in the tax problem.

EXAMPLE: In *John J. Sexton,*[2] the taxpayer operated refuse dumps and acquired land containing large excavations for use in his dumping business. Land is not depreciable. What should the taxpayer argue to obtain a depreciation deduction?

Discussion: The taxpayer successfully argued before the Tax Court that the major portion of his purchase price was not paid for the acquisition of the land, but rather for the large holes in the land. As the holes were filled in, the taxpayer depreciated the assigned cost of the holes and claimed such depreciation as a current deduction. By characterizing his purchase as a purchase of holes, as opposed to a purchase of land, the taxpayer was able to acquire a valuable tax deduction. Less imaginative taxpayers and tax advisors have easily overlooked this idea.

Third, since tax research is a process by which relevant tax law is applied to a given set of facts, there is a challenge in searching for relevant legal authorities from among the massive quantity of tax materials. To find the authority it helps to have knowledge of how the tax law is organized and skills in careful reading and analysis of the law. The law always controls, even if it contradicts some accounting, economic, social, or moral theory.

---

[2] John J. Sexton, 42 TC 1094 (1964); Acq. 1970-1 C.B.16

Fourth, probably the most difficult challenge in tax research is selecting the correct legal authorities. In some situations, more than one answer may have a reasonable basis in law. The tax researcher may then inform the taxpayer on the relative merits and tax benefits of each defensibly correct option. Usually, however, only one tax result has an appropriate weight of legal authority. Determining the cutoff between a defensible tax treatment and one that is not defensible depends on whether the legal authorities backing the position provide a "realistic possibility of success." Although applying this standard is learned more through experience and professional judgment, some estimate that the evidence should persuasively support winning at least one out of every three times.

Three types of activities involve tax research: tax compliance, tax planning, and tax litigation. In tax compliance engagements tax returns are typically prepared. Sometimes tax compliance is referred to as closed-fact engagements because all the facts have already occurred. In such instances the tax researcher's job is limited to discovery and documentation, since the factual burden of proof generally rests with the taxpayer in the event of audit and litigation. In tax planning engagements (sometimes referred to as open-fact engagements), not all of the relevant facts have yet transpired.

The most common type of tax planning is carefully executed tax avoidance; that is, controlling the facts that actually occur in order to produce an optimal after-tax result for the taxpayer. The rendering of well-researched tax planning advice is generally regarded as the hallmark of a true professional.

Tax accountants generally perform both tax compliance and tax planning work. Lawyers generally handle tax litigation for taking a case to court. Preparation for tax litigation often involves double-checking the prior tax research and digging into more rarely used tax documents that are beyond the practical scope of this text for accountants. If significant litigation potential becomes apparent, the tax accountant or client should consult with an experienced tax attorney.

TAX RESEARCH DATABASES

Tax research databases usually include both primary and secondary authorities. Hard bound paper copy is generally used only for the Code and Regulations and favorite secondary sources, such as a *Masters of Tax Guide*, which summarizes the law. Today's tax professionals generally use tax research databases on either CD-ROM systems, the Internet, or a combination. For example, subscribers to CD-ROM systems receive periodic updates to their CDs from the publisher, and go online to the Internet to check for more current tax changes.

Several publishers produce tax databases. Online legal databases, such as Westlaw and LexisNexis, first developed in the 1970s. These databases generally have the most extensive amount of legal information and are available for subscription on the Web.

Some publishers that were leaders in producing tax services now offer an electronic product with a more advantageous organization for easily finding tax materials and/or more user-friendly search engine results. One example is the Commerce Clearing House (CCH) online system, which contains various tax authorities and government documents such as IRS publications. Another major publisher of an online system is the Research Institute of America's (RIA) Checkpoint service. Since the CPA exam uses a version of the RIA tax service, it is discussed more later in this chapter.

Some popular Internet sites for the tax researcher are presented in Figure 7-1. The Web has enabled Congress, government agencies such as the Internal Revenue Service, and the courts to make their materials more available. Thus, most agencies and courts have their own web sites. On the Web one can obtain primary tax research authorities

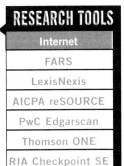

FIGURE 7-1 | INTERNET TAX SITES

Internal Revenue Service	*http://www.irs.gov*
Commerce Clearing House	*http://www.cch.com*
Research Institute of American	*http://www.riahome.com*
Tax and Accounting Sites Directory	*http://www.taxsites.com*
Tax Library	*http://www.taxlibrary.com*
Tax Court Opinions	*http://www.ustaxcourt.gov*
Tax Planning	*http://www.smartmoney.com*
Tax Software	*http://www.intuit.com*
Tax Expert Online	*http://www.kleinrock.com*
American Taxation Association	*http://www.atasection.org*

and IRS publications, as well as federal and state tax forms. In addition, one can access different tax preparation software packages and stay current in new tax law developments by reading recent tax developments or participating in tax discussion newsgroups. One popular site is the IRS's Digital Daily as shown in Figure 7-2. The IRS site provides one with downloadable tax forms and instructions, as well as "plain English" unofficial versions of the Treasury Regulations and daily news updates. A leading index to various tax and accounting sites on the Web is at *http://www.taxsites.com*.

FIGURE 7-2 | IRS HOME PAGE AT *HTTP://WWW.IRS.GOV*

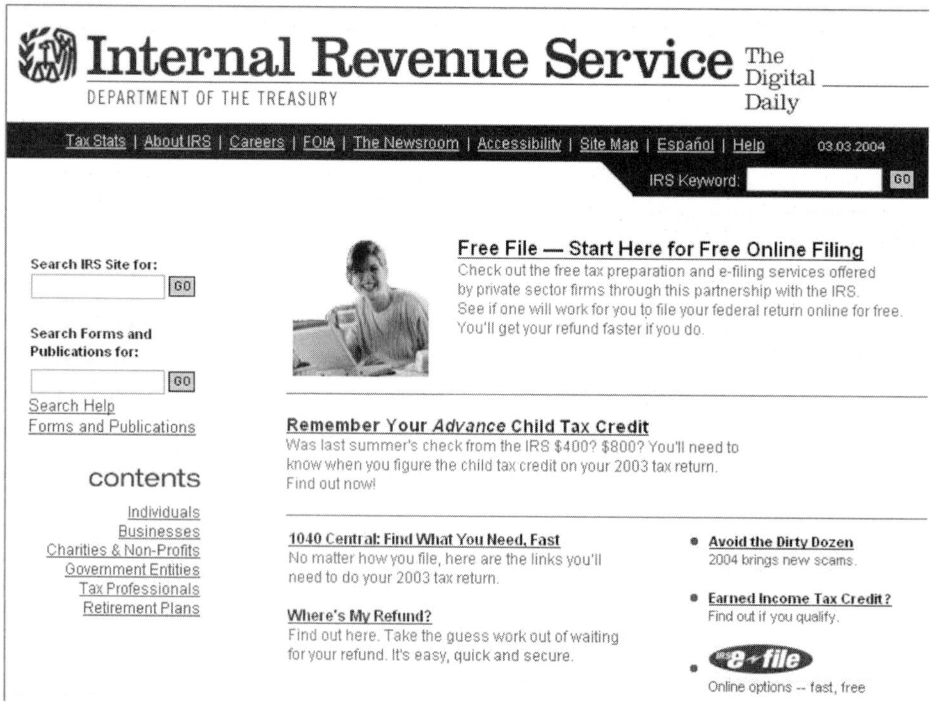

RIA CHECKPOINT

RIA Checkpoint is a total tax database that contains research libraries for federal, state and local, and international, estate planning, pensions, payroll, and Financial Reporting and Management Service by WG&L (Warren Gorman & Lamont). Since we will utilize this database for the tax research process described in this chapter, it is recommended that you access and review RIA Checkpoint's "Demo" and "Getting Started" training tools before proceeding.

The researcher can access RIA Checkpoint through the text's web site located at *http://weirich.swlearning.com*. The opening screen should appear as in Figure 7-3. Once the researcher is at the opening screen, he or she should click on **Training and Tips** at the top to review "Getting Started" and the "Demo," which appear on the left of the screen. The various choices for these practice areas are provided in the drop-down box in the upper-left part of the RIA Checkpoint screen. Usually the researcher wants to limit the search to the federal practice area.

Before the tax research process is explained, the researcher needs to understand the sources of tax authority as well as how to use RIA Checkpoint and other tax services to locate the tax authorities as discussed in the following section.

QUICK FACTS

RIA Checkpoint is a very useful tax research database.

FIGURE 7-3 | RIA CHECKPOINT'S HOME PAGE

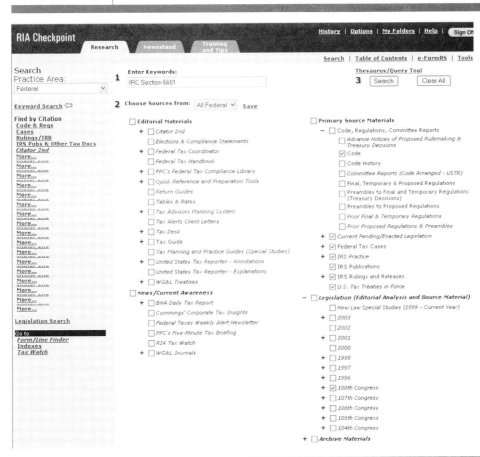

PRIMARY TAX AUTHORITIES

Classifications of tax authorities resemble the classifications of accounting authoritative pronouncements, with primary and secondary authorities. Primary authorities are the statutory law, administrative regulations, and judicial cases. They are created by Congress, the executive branch, and the courts. Thus, primary authority generally comes from the following sources:

- Statutory sources—U.S. Constitution, tax treaties, and statutory tax laws

- Administrative sources—Treasury Regulations and the IRS' revenue rulings and revenue procedures

- Judicial sources—Case decisions from the various courts

The following section provides an overview of the primary sources of tax law. Included are some Practice Exercises for practice locating and finding relevant tax sources. The reader is encouraged to take advantage of RIA's Checkpoint to locate these tax sources. Other services are also presented in order for the future tax researcher to become familiar with all major popular tax research databases.

U.S. Constitution and Tax Treaties

The source of all U.S. federal legal authorities, including tax authorities, is the U.S. Constitution (Art. I, Sec. 8, Cl. 1) and the 16th Amendment to the Constitution. Constitutional research is almost never needed for either compliance or tax planning purposes. However, litigation of selected state taxes sometimes raises Constitutional questions.

If the tax transaction at issue involves a foreign national or arose in a foreign country, tax researchers should begin their research determining if there is any applicable tax treaty The United States has tax treaties with many countries. Although the IRS provides information on its web site indicating which countries have tax treaties with the United States, often tax research databases and secondary sources such as *http://www.taxsites.com* (international page) are valuable in locating the relevant information.

Since relatively few situations require researching tax treaties, this chapter focuses on commonly researched tax authorities for compliance and tax planning: the Code, regulations, and court cases.

The Code

Today the primary statutory law cited on federal taxation is the Internal Revenue Code of 1986 as Amended. It is found in Title 26 of the United States Code. This Internal Revenue Code is more commonly referred to as the Code or IRC. The Code is the statutory foundation of all federal tax authority, except sometimes tax treaties govern certain international issues. When new tax legislation is passed, such as the "Jobs and Growth Tax Relief Reconciliation Act of 2003," the provisions in the law are codified or rearranged logically in the Code.

To locate a given Code provision, researchers are directed to the primary units of the Code, called sections. Code **sections** are uniquely numbered in a consecutive manner throughout the entire Code. Each section number is used only once. Thus, one can use the citation "IRC Sec. 11" instead of the more cumbersome "Subtitle A, Chapter 1, Subchapter A, Part II, Section 11 of the *Internal Revenue Code of 1986 as Amended.*" Notice also that since not all section numbers are used, Congress can add additional sections in the future without the need for renumbering the entire Code. If a Code section refers to one of the organizational divisions of the Code, such as a "part,"the researcher should use the Table of Contents to clarify what Code sections apply.

Finding a specific Code section on a tax research database such as RIA Checkpoint is easiest by using the "Find by Citation" approach, located on the left side of the RIA

Checkpoint screen. After selecting the citation for Code and Regs, the researcher must enter the Code section number in the box requesting the current Code citation.

The tax researcher must always cite to a provision within a Code section with as much precision as possible. Thus, it is essential to know that each section is divided into subsections, paragraphs, subparagraphs, and clauses. Within parentheses following the code section number, subsections generally use lowercase letters, paragraphs use numbers, subparagraphs use capital letters, and clauses use lowercase roman numerals. Only if a Code section existed back under the 1939 codification does the Code not include a small letter before a paragraph number, such as Sec. 212(1) for the deduction of expenses for the production of income.

In tax literature it is generally understood that, unless otherwise stated, references to section numbers concern the *Internal Revenue Code of 1986 as Amended*. Hence, often the prefix IRC is omitted in the citations. See Figure 7-4 for a breakdown of Section 217.

The general rule of a section is usually placed in subsection (a). The tax researcher should read subsection (a) carefully and scan the remaining information to search for the relevant legal information. The Code is typically read by having to jump around within the section and even into other sections, in order to understand the meaning. Sometimes a Code section will explicitly reference another Code provision. More often, however, the researcher must make the effort to connect different sections impacting on the meaning within a Code section. The Code requires careful reading skills. Little words can create big differences in meaning. Thus, sometimes the reader may highlight significant words, so as to place the subsequent lines for reading into proper perspective.

> **EXAMPLE:** How does one read the example provided in Figure 7-4 which reprints part of Section 217 on moving expenses?

> **Discussion:** First read subsection (a) carefully to understand there is a deduction for moving expenses. Then consider how the Code section is organized by scanning the subsections. Subsection (b) defines moving expenses. Subsection (c) provides additional requirements to take the deduction. Note that the paragraphs are further indented. While paragraphs (1) and (2) in subsection (b) stand separately, paragraphs (1) and (2) in subsection (c) are connected with the word "and." The subparagraphs (A) and (B) within both paragraphs of Subsection "c" are connected by the word "or," so that meeting either subparagraph (A) or (B) is sufficient. The language near the end of Sec. 217(c), which returns to a farther left margin, is referred to as Sec. 217(c) "flush language." It is not part of the subparagraph (c)(2)(B) which precedes it.

The Code sometimes defines concepts differently for different parts of the Code.

> **EXAMPLE:** Do related parties for tax purposes include brothers and sisters?

> **Discussion:** Related parties are defined differently in different parts of the Code. Section 267 disallowance of losses between related parties defines related parties in subsection (b) to include brothers and sisters as part of the family relationship for purposes of constructive ownership of stock. Whereas, Sec. 318 on the constructive ownership of stock for purposes of defining related parties for subchapter C does not consider brothers and sisters.

Ready access to the Code is required for the practicing tax researcher. Historically, a tax researcher acquires a new paper-bound edition of the Code after each major change in the law. Commerce Clearing House, Inc. (CCH) and Research Institute of America (RIA) publish a two-volume Code set of books. Today, some tax researchers have paperless offices in which they rely extensively on pulling up the information on computer screens from a tax research database. The Code is reprinted in each of the major tax services, and the individual sections are interspersed within the compilation volumes of a tax service.

RESEARCH TIPS

Always cite as precisely as possible within a Code section.

RESEARCH TIPS

Read relevant provisions of the Code very carefully.

FIGURE 7-4 | ANALYSIS OF A CODE OF A SECTION—SPECIFIC CITATION: SEC. 217

Sec. 217. MOVING EXPENSES.

[Sec. 217(a)]

(a) Deduction allowed.—There shall be allowed as a deduction moving expenses paid or incurred during the taxable year in connection with the commencement of work by the taxpayer as an employee or as a self-employed individual at a new principal place of work.

[Sec. 217(b)]

(b) Definition of moving expenses.—

(1) In general.—For purposes of this section, the term "moving expenses" means only the reasonable expenses-

(A) of moving household goods and personal effects from the former residence to the new residence, and

(B) of traveling (including lodging) from the former residence to the new place of residence.

Such term shall not include any expenses for meals.

(2) Individuals other than taxpayer.—In the case of any individual other than the taxpayer, expenses referred to in paragraph (1) shall be taken into account only if such individual has both the former residence and the new residence as his principal place of abode and is a member of the taxpayer's household.

[Sec. 217(c)]

(c) Conditions for allowance.—No deduction shall be allowed under this section unless—

(1) the taxpayer's new principal place of work—

(A) is at least 50 miles farther from his former residence than was his former principal place of work, or

(B) if he had no former principal place of work, is at least 50 miles from his former residence, and

(2) either—

(A) during the 12-month period immediately following his arrival in the general location of his new principal place of work, the taxpayer is a full-time employee, in such general location, during at least 39 weeks, or

(B) during the 24-month period immediately following his arrival in the general location of his new principal place of work, the taxpayer is a full-time employee or performs services as a self-employed individual on a full-time basis, in such general location, during at least 78 weeks, of which not less than 39 weeks are during the 12-month period referred to in subparagraph (A).

For purposes of paragraph (1), the distance between two points shall be the shortest of the more commonly traveled routes between such two points.

[Sec. 217(d)]

(d) Rules for application of subsection (c) (2).—

(1) The condition of subsection (c)(2) shall not apply if the taxpayer is unable to satisfy the condition by reason of—

———— SECTION 217

———— SUBSECTION (c)

———— PARAGRAPH (2)

———— SUBPARAGRAPH (B)

Practice Exercises | *The Code*

To become more proficient at locating and reading the Code, complete the following exercises.

1. Given a specific citation to the Code, find that authority and related provisions. It helps to use a tax research database, such as the RIA Checkpoint electronic tax infobase, to find reliable information with ease.

   a. What deductions does Sec. 162(a)(2) specifically authorize? What Code provision in another section disallows some of those deductions? Explain.

   _____

   _____

   b. What is the penalty provided under Code Sec. 6662(b)(2)? Where in that Code section is that penalty defined? Explain the definition.

   _____

   _____

2. Find the precise authority to determine whether employer contributions to employees' health and accident plans create gross income for the employee. (*Hint:* Use a tax research database, such as LexisNexis, and use "health plan" as your keyword and the IRS Code as your source.)

   _____

   _____

In order to better understand any new statutory tax law, a tax researcher may need to read Congressional sources. When recently enacted tax legislation is too new for the government to have produced treasury regulations, researchers make more effort to examine Congressional sources to interpret the Code. In Congress, the three major committees considering possible changes in the tax law are the House Ways and Means Committee, the Senate Finance Committee, and a Joint Committee on Taxation. This Joint Committee consists of selected members from both houses of Congress; its role is to produce compromises to reconcile differences in proposed legislation passed by both the House of Representatives and the Senate. Although Congressional hearings address problems, speeches are inserted into the Congressional Record, and Committee Reports may provide some insight into the intent of the law, these sources are rarely used by accountants.

Instead, the best and most convenient source accountants use to understand the law is prepared by the staff of the Joint Committee on Taxation. It focuses on only the parts of the legislation that are actually enacted. Their publication is often referred to as "the Blue-Book." Excerpts of the Blue-Book are provided in the tax services, which are included in the major tax research databases. Tax services are a large multi-volume, comprehensive sets of books, which are organized either topically or annotated by Code section number. For example, both Commerce Clearing House, Inc. (CCH) and Research Institute of America (RIA) have annotated tax services that not only reprint the code, but provide other authorities that interpret the code, such as treasury regulations or sometimes excerpts from the Blue-Book.

RESEARCH TIPS

When researching new Code pronouncements, use congressional sources to acquire more information.

Administrative Authorities, Particularly Treasury Regulations

Once Congress has enacted a tax law, the executive branch of government implements it by interpreting and enforcing the law. Thus, the Treasury Department (of which the Internal Revenue Service is a subdivision) creates tax authority of interest to tax researchers.

Treasury Regulations. Treasury Regulations interpret and clarify the statutory law. Three major types of Treasury Regulations are Proposed, Temporary, and Final Regulations. Proposed regulations often represent trial balloons. After major changes in the Code, the Treasury Department often issues Temporary Regulations without holding public hearings. These Temporary Regulations are legally binding, but expire after three years. Final regulations are issued only after going through the public process for notice and comment.

Two types of Final Regulations are Legislative and Interpretive. Legislative Regulations arise when Congress has delegated specific law-making authority to the Secretary of the Treasury Department within a Code section to create regulations. Legislative Regulations are often described as having nearly the force of statutory law. For example, Section 1445 entitled "withholding of tax on dispositions of United States property interests" has subsection (e) explaining special rules relating to distributions. Paragraph (6) states in relevant part "The Secretary shall prescribe such regulations as may be necessary to carry out the purposes of this subsection… " Interpretive regulations arise under the authority of Section 7805(a), which expressly provides that the Treasury Department Secretary "shall prescribe all needful rules and regulations for the enforcement of this title." The reality is that both types of Treasury Regulations are important sources of administrative law to follow. For example, Sec. 6662(a) provides that intentional disregard of either type of Treasury Regulation will invoke a 20 percent penalty to any tax underpayment, even when no intent to defraud exists.

While some Code sections have many Treasury Regulations, other have no regulations. Treasury Regulations sometimes directly address topics that the relevant Code section did not mention.

> **EXAMPLE:** What type of entertainment expenses are deductible?
>
> **Discussion:** Section 162(a) allows a deduction for ordinary and necessary business expenses. Sec. 274(a)(1)(A) disallows entertainment expenses unless the taxpayer shows the entertainment was directly related to and immediately preceding or following a substantial bona fide business discussion in the active conduct of taxpayer's business. Regulation Sec. 1.274-1 disallows an expenditure for entertainment to the extent that it is lavish or extravagant.

The tax researcher will typically scan the title of the Regulations that interpret a Code section at issue. While most tax research databases attempt to link the Regulations to the related Code section, other services make an effort to link each Regulation to a particular Code subsection. If the title of the Regulation appears to have possible application, the researcher should scan that regulation. Some Treasury Regulations provide clarifying examples.

> **EXAMPLE:** A corporation measures "earnings and profits" under Sec. 312 in order to determine how much of a dividend distribution is taxable. Where in the Regulations is the illustration for adjustment required under subsection (c) for liabilities?
>
> **Discussion:** Reg. Sec. 1.312-4 is entitled "examples of adjustments provided in section 312(c)." However, the name of the Regulation more often does not always indicate whether it has examples as part of the Regulation.

Treasury Regulations are usually first issued in proposed form by publication in the *Federal Register*. Interested parties then have 30 days in which to comment. On occasion, comments received have resulted in modification or withdrawal of the Proposed Regulations. More commonly, the Regulation is then published as a Treasury Decision in the *Federal Register*. This is more commonly known as a Final Regulation, which is later codified into Title 26 of the *Code of Federal Regulations*.

It is important to understand the citation for a Treasury Regulation. Sometimes the beginning of the citation abbreviates reference to *Title 26 of the Code of Federal*

Regulations (CFR). More commonly, abbreviated reference is made to its status as a Treasury Regulation section. Thus, two forms of a citation of the same Regulation are as follows:

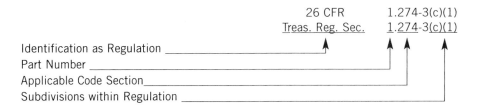

In a Treasury Regulation citation, the corresponding Code section that the Regulation interprets is placed after the decimal point and before the hyphen. Thus, one can tell at a glance that the Regulation just cited applies to Code Sec. 274. However, the subdivisions of the Regulation have no relationship with the subdivisions within the Code section. The "3" after 274 in the Regulation citation means this is the third Regulation issued interpreting Sec. 274.

The initial number for a Regulation before the decimal is called a part number. The **part number** of a Treasury Regulation citation identifies the general area of taxation to which the regulation is related:

Part 1	Income Taxes
Part 20	Estate Taxes
Part 25	Gift Taxes
Part 31	Employment Taxes
Parts 48, 49	Excise Taxes
Parts 301, 601	Administrative and Procedural Rules

Thus, any citation of an income tax Regulation begins with the part number "1" and is followed by a decimal and then the number of the Code section to which it pertains.

Often there is a considerable time lag after enactment of a new tax law and before the Treasury Department's issuance of related Regulations. In such instances, tax researchers are often forced to rely solely on Congressional committee reports for guidance on the statutory provisions. Tax researchers must carefully check that any Treasury Regulations relied upon are up to date, i.e., remain applicable to the current Code section of interest and are not obsolete because of some recent change in the Code language. The Treasury Department is frequently slow to remove or amend Regulations. Commercial tax services are often helpful in pointing out such concerns.

The CPA Exam simulations require the candidate to use a version of the RIA database with the Code and the regulations. Figure 7-5 provides an example simulation similar to the CPA exam.

Revenue Rulings and Revenue Procedures. Revenue Rulings are issued by the Internal Revenue Service (IRS), a division of the Department of the Treasury. Revenue Rulings apply the law to a specific set of facts, unlike the general guidance provided in Treasury Regulations. Revenue Rulings do not carry the same force of authority as do Treasury Regulations. Revenue Rulings often are based on further review of previous Private Letter Rulings from the IRS to taxpayers' requests concerning the tax outcomes of specific proposed transactions.

Revenue Rulings are usually a few pages with subheadings for issues, facts, and law and analysis. For the discussion of the law, the Revenue Ruling will refer to the Code, Regulations, cases, and related Revenue Rulings. When the RIA Checkpoint database reprints a Revenue Ruling, it adds an unofficial headnote summary.

QUICK FACTS
A Treasury Regulation citation identifies the Code section interpreted.

FIGURE 7-5 | AN EXAMPLE OF A CPA EXAM TAX SIMULATION

DIRECTIONS	SITUATION	RESOURCES	ANALYSIS	COMMUNICATION	RESEARCH

Directions

The **Directions** tab informs the candidate as to the instructions or question requirements for this particular case simulation.

Situation

Jim Hawkins is an employee of Protect Security Services, Inc. located in Chicago, Illinois. During the current year, Jim's work assignment was the third shift (12 AM–8 AM) in which he would drive around to various businesses (Protect Security clients) and check for possible property damage and burglars. In addition to Jim's normal pay, Protect Security provides him with $75 in cash each week to cover the cost of food when Jim would stop and eat at restaurants between stops on his shift. Jim believes that his meal allowance is not taxable and requests your assistance with this issue.

Resources

The **Resources** tab provides various resources (tools) that the candidate will utilize in completing the simulation. Here the candidate might find the on-screen calculator, or RIA Checkpoint tax services.

Analysis

Clicking on the **Analysis** tab provides the candidate with detailed information for analysis or completion. This could include the completion of a tax return. Here is where the candidate will input data into drop-down boxes or into Excel spreadsheets.

Written Communication

Written communication is still an integral part of the CPA exam. Under the **Written Communication** tab, the candidate will be required to prepare (type) some form of written communication (i.e., to the client or audit partner) to discuss various tax issues related to the facts presented under the Situation tab.

Research

The **Research** tab is where the candidate will be required to research relevant databases. Candidates will then perform keyword searches utilizing RIA's Checkpoint tax database. Required: For the above given situation (1) list at least three keywords that one would utilize to research the issue; (2) utilize RIA's Checkpoint and perform a keyword search, listing the paragraph numbers of the tax services that seem appropriate for the issue; and (3) identify the primary IRS Code section for this issue.

Since Revenue Rulings are first published in the *Internal Revenue Bulletin* (IRB) and later in the *Cumulative Bulletin* (CB), one might encounter either of the following citations for the same Ruling:

TEMPORARY CITATION: Rev. Rul. <u>2001</u>-<u>34</u>, <u>IRB</u> No. <u>28</u>, <u>31</u>

Year of Issue _____
34th Ruling of Year _____
Internal Revenue Bulletin _____
Number of Weekly Issue _____
Page Number _____

Practice Exercises   *Using Treasury Regulations*

1. Look at Reg. Sec. 1.183-2.

   a. What Code section and language within that Code section does the Regulation interpret?

   _____

   _____

   b. What does the Regulation state are the nine relevant factors?

   _____

   _____

2. Find the Regulation that determines whether educational expenses can qualify as deductible business expenses.

   a. Give the citation for the general rule within that Regulation.

   _____

   _____

   b. Assume Sally is a professor who has a Ph.D. in accounting and teaches tax courses. She decides that it would help her teaching to earn a law degree with a heavy emphasis on tax classes. Can she deduct the cost of the tax courses within the law degree? Explain and cite to specific provisions within the Code and Regulations.

   _____

   _____

3. Find and cite two Proposed Regulations.

   _____

   _____

PERMANENT CITATION: Rev. Rul. <u>2001-34</u>, <u>2001-2</u> <u>C.B.</u> <u>31</u>

Same as Previous Page, 34th Ruling Issued during 2001 _____
Volume Number 2 of 2001 _____
Cumulative Bulletin _____
Page Number _____

The citation to a Revenue Ruling does not reference the Code section that it addresses. However, for the researcher's convenience, sometimes a tax service, such as RIA Checkpoint, will follow the Revenue Ruling citation with the relevant Code section.

Before relying on a Revenue Ruling, always check to make sure that it was neither revoked nor modified subsequent to its initial publication. For convenience, several of the major tax services provide tables that enable the reader to look up the number of any Revenue Ruling to determine its current status.

Revenue Procedures are created by the IRS to announce administrative procedures that taxpayers must follow. Revenue Procedures are similar in weight of authority to Revenue Rulings; they are both issued by the IRS, found in the same sources, and are cited in the same manner except that the prefix "Rev. Proc." is used instead of "Rev. Rul."

The IRS issues many other administrative pronouncements that are sometimes classified as primary authority and published in tax research databases, such as the RIA Checkpoint service. However, often these other administrative pronouncements are

QUICK FACTS
Revenue Rulings and Revenue Procedures represent the IRS's position.

considered nonprimary authority because taxpayers cannot rely upon them, as they lack precedential value. For example, Private Letter Rulings are binding on the IRS only with respect to the particular taxpayer requesting the ruling if all material facts were disclosed. Sec. 6110 expressly prohibits their use as legal precedents by either the IRS or other taxpayers. Another major example is IRS publications, such as Publication 901 on U.S. tax treaties. While one court has stated that taxpayers cannot rely on IRS publications because they do not represent the law, IRS publications are widely used by taxpayers and some tax accountants in small firms. When using a tax research database, one will also find reference to other IRS sources, such as General Counsel Memorandum and Technical Advice Memorandums. However, the accounting researcher should generally focus on the basic primary tax authorities: the Code, Regulations, Revenue Rulings, Revenue Procedures, and cases.

Judicial Sources of Tax Authority. Judicial decisions in common law countries, such as the United States, are part of the law. While Congress sets forth the words of law, and the administrative branch of government is charged with the clarifying interpretation and enforcement of those words, it is the judiciary that has the final say with respect to what the words really mean, as applied in a particular case. Thus, one researches case law to investigate what courts have held the relevant words of law to mean under similar factual circumstances.

Thus, the tax researcher must look to prior judicial decisions in determining the tax consequences of the words of a given Code provision when applied to a particular contemplated or completed transaction.

By consistently treating similar cases in a similar way, the courts establish their interpretations of the statutes as judicial law. The principle that governs the use of prior decisions as law is called *precedent*. The courts use precedents to build stability and order into the judicial system. Decisions concerning similar prior cases are used as guides when deciding current cases. The process of finding analogous cases from the past and convincing the tax authorities of the precedential value of those cases is what judicial tax research is all about.

To appraise the relative authoritative weights of decisions rendered by the various federal courts that hear tax cases, a basic knowledge of the judicial system is necessary. An

RESEARCH TIPS

Research judicial cases to find essential interpretations of the Code and the Treasury Regulations.

Practice Exercises — *Using Revenue Rulings*

Locate the following administrative sources to briefly answer the following questions. Use a tax research database such as RIA Checkpoint to help.

1. Locate Revenue Ruling 2003-25, identify the topic, and find the date of the Revenue Ruling. What Code section is applicable to this topic?

   Topic and date _____

   Code section applicable _____

2. Locate Revenue Procedure 2003-75, identify the topic, and find the date of the Revenue Procedure. What Code section is applicable to this topic?

   Topic and date _____

   Code section applicable _____

3. Find two Revenue Rulings on medical expenses. (If you are using LexisNexis, click on **legal research** and then **Tax law**; use **medical deduction** as your keyword and Revenue Rulings as your source.) Give the full citation within the CB or IRB.

   Most recent Revenue Ruling # _____

   Another Revenue Ruling # _____

outline is presented in Figure 7-6. Each of the courts identified in Figure 7-6 is subsequently discussed along with the information on their citations.

U.S. Tax Court. The United States Tax Court consists of 19 judges, each appointed by the U.S. President for a 15-year term. The Tax Court's web site provides information about each of the judges, as well as recent decisions and rules before the court, and other documents. Judicial hearings are held in several cities throughout the nation, usually with only a single judge present who submits an opinion to the chief judge. These locations are listed on the Tax Court's web site as part of its frequently asked questions. Thus, the client's tax advisor does not necessarily have to travel to the Tax Court's location in Washington D.C.

The Tax Court's chief judge decides whether a case is announcing a new principle in the law so as to classify the case as a "regular decision." Alternatively, if the court is just applying already announced principles to a different set of facts, the case is classified as a "memorandum decision." Sometimes the court decides a case warrants discussion and review by the entire Tax Court. These cases are referred to as "En banc" decisions.

Not having to prepay the amount in dispute with the IRS is a major reason why many taxpayers use the Tax Court to litigate the IRS's audit adjustment. The Tax Court considers only tax deficiencies, not claims for refunds. If a taxpayer prepays the amount in dispute and files a Claim for refund, the taxpayer must use either a U.S. District Court or the U.S. Court of Federal Claims. Unlike all other federal courts, the Tax Court hears only tax cases; consequently, Tax Court judges are usually well acquainted with the tax issues.

QUICK FACTS
Taxpayers in Tax Court do not prepay the taxes in dispute.

FIGURE 7-6 JUDICIAL SYSTEM FOR FEDERAL TAX LITIGATION

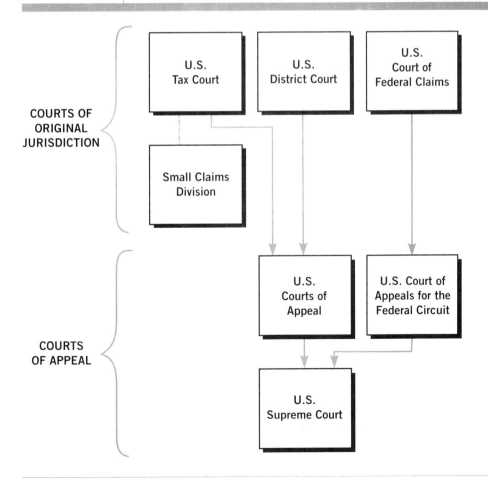

Note that the Tax Court may rule differently on identical fact patterns for two taxpayers residing in different circuit court of appeals jurisdictions, in the event of inconsistent holdings. This is because within each circuit the Tax Court will follow precedents of that Court of Appeals (referred to as the *Golsen* rule).[3]

For most, but not all, regular Tax Court cases that the IRS has lost, the Commissioner will announce either **acquiescence** or **nonacquiescence**. Acquiescence means that the IRS will accept and follow the decision of the court when dealing with cases of similar facts and circumstances. Likewise, nonacquiescence means that the IRS will not follow the court's decision when handling similar cases. This policy of expressing the current position of the IRS applies neither to Tax Court memorandum decisions nor any decisions of any other courts. An acquiescence is not legally binding on the IRS.

> **EXAMPLE:** In *Dixon*,[4] the Supreme Court upheld the IRS's right to retroactively withdraw its announced acquiescence even after it had been relied on by a taxpayer. Therefore, what is the significance of an acquiescence?

> **Discussion:** Announcements of either acquiescence (A or Acq.) or nonacquiescence (NA or Nonacq.), as published in the *Internal Revenue Bulletin* and *Cumulative Bulletin*, are indicative of the current thinking of the IRS and are subject to change at any time.

It is important to note that citations containing the letters USTC do *not* refer to Tax Court cases. Instead, USTC refers to *United States Tax Cases*, which is a special reporter service published by CCH containing all of the tax cases decided by all federal courts other than the Tax Court. Similarly, the comparable RIA series called *American Federal Tax Reports* (AFTR, AFTR2d, AFTR3d) publishes all tax cases, except for those by the Tax Court. Thus, these reporters contain all other federal court decisions concerning taxation: U.S. district courts, court of federal claims, court of appeals, and the Supreme Court.

Second, Tax Court regular and memorandum decisions are reported separately. Regular Tax Court decisions are published by the government under the title *United States Tax Court Reports*, cited T.C. Memorandum decisions by the Tax Court are published by both CCH and RIA in reporters separate from those in which they report other tax cases. Tax Court memorandum decisions published by CCH are in *Tax Court Memorandum Decisions* (TCM), while the RIA series is called *RIA, TC Memorandum Decisions* (RIA T.C. Mem. Dec.). Also, several other major tax services provide loose-leaf copies of both regular and memorandum Tax Court decisions when issued. These memorandum decisions are also included in tax research databases, such as RIA Checkpoint.

Third, prior to 1943, the Tax Court was known as the Board of Tax Appeals. Thus, both regular and memorandum decisions for years prior to 1943 were published by the government under the title *United States Board of Tax Appeals* (BTA).

The citations for court cases generally use the following format: *case name*,—volume number—reporter—initial page number where the case begins—(year of the court's decision). Thus, the year of the court's decision is placed inside the parentheses. If the name of the court is not obvious from the name of the *reporter*, then inside the parentheses is a reference to the court making the decision, then the year of the decision. Also note that the name of a case is capitalized and usually italicized when provided within the discussion of a memo.

The following citations indicate three major reporters where different Tax Court decisions are located in a professional library. Whether one uses electronic tax databases or hardbound books to find the case is irrelevant; the citation is the same.

---

[3] *Jack E. Golsen*, 54 T.C. 742 (1970).
[4] *W. Palmer Dixon*, 381 U.S. 68,85 S.Ct. 1301, 65–1 USTC 9386, 15 AFTR2d 842 (USSC, 1965).

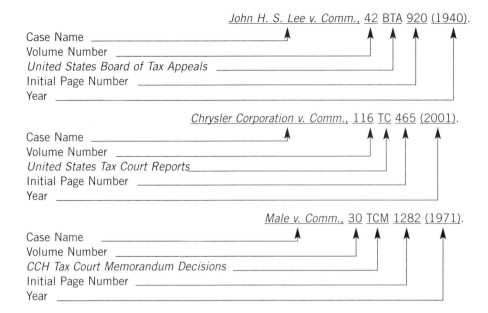

John H. S. Lee v. Comm., 42 BTA 920 (1940).

Case Name
Volume Number
United States Board of Tax Appeals
Initial Page Number
Year

Chrysler Corporation v. Comm., 116 TC 465 (2001).

Case Name
Volume Number
United States Tax Court Reports
Initial Page Number
Year

Male v. Comm., 30 TCM 1282 (1971).

Case Name
Volume Number
CCH Tax Court Memorandum Decisions
Initial Page Number
Year

The Tax Court has a Small Claims Division, which does not publish its decisions because they do not have precedential value. However, sometimes tax research databases such as CCH Tax Research Network will publish such nonprecedential authority. The advantages of a taxpayer electing to have his or her case handled by the Small Claims Division of the Tax Court are the expedited process and less costly procedures. The disadvantage is that no appeal of the decision is permitted. The tax in dispute cannot exceed $50,000 per year for the Small Claims Division of the Tax Court to have jurisdiction.

U.S. District Courts. A taxpayer can sue for a refund of taxes paid in the U.S. District Court. Each state has at least one District Court in which both tax and nontax cases are heard. Only in a District Court can one obtain a jury trial, and even there a jury can decide only questions of fact, not those of law. Appeals of both District Court and Tax Court decisions are made to the U.S. Court of Appeals for the circuit in which the taxpayer lives.

Published decisions of the U.S. District Courts are contained in the _Federal Supplement_ (F. Supp., F. Supp.2d). In addition, the tax decisions of the District Courts are also published in the two special tax reporter series, CCH's _United States Tax Cases_ (USTC) and RIA's _American Federal Tax Reports_ (AFTR, AFTR2d, or AFTR3d). These reporter services are found on their publisher's tax research databases: RIA Checkpoint and CCH Tax Research Network. For purposes of presenting a memo before a court, one refers to the official source in the _Federal Supplement_. In accounting offices, usually it is sufficient to cite to one of the unofficial tax reporters from RIA or CCH.

U.S. Court of Federal Claims. The U.S. Court of Federal Claims is another court hearing tax cases, as well as any other case with claims against the government based on U.S. law. About 25 percent of the U.S. Court of Federal Claims's cases are tax cases. The U.S. Court of Federal Claims's decisions are appealable to the U.S. Court of Appeals for the Federal Circuit. Until 1992 the court was known as the U.S. Claims Court. Until 1982 the predecessor court was called the U.S. Court of Claims and its cases were appealable directly to the U.S. Supreme Court.

Since 1929 decisions of the U.S. Court of Federal Claims and its predecessor courts have been published by West Publishing Company. Decisions rendered between 1929 and 1932 and after 1959 appear in the _Federal Reporter—2d or 3d Series_ (F.2d or F.3d), while those issued between 1932 and 1960 are in the _Federal Supplement_ (F. Supp.) In

Practice Exercises | *Tax Court Cases*

1. Find and read *Erickson Post Acquisition, Inc.*, TC Memo. 2003-218, 86 TCM 111 (2003).

   a. When did the Tax Court issue this memorandum decision?

   _____

   b. What were the issues in this case?

   _____

   c. What did the Tax Court hold?

   _____

2. Find and read a Tax Court regular decision that discusses whether hair transplants are deductible medical expenses.

   a. Give the official citation to the case:

   _____

   b. What did the Tax Court hold?

   _____

   c. If a case presenting similar facts were decided today, would the Tax Court reach a similar conclusion? Explain:

   _____

   _____

addition, the tax decisions of the U.S. Court of Federal Claims and its predecessor court are published in special tax reporters for CCH (USTC) and RIA (AFTR)

When feasible, tax researchers provide information on more than one location for a case. This is known as a parallel citation. The different sources are separated by commas, as shown in the following citation to a tax decision by the U.S. Court of Federal Claims:

> *Okerlund v. U.S.*, 53 Fed. Cl. 341, 90 AFTR 2d 2002-6124, 2002-2 USTC ¶60,447 (Fed. Cls., 2002).

U.S. Courts of Appeals. Both taxpayers and the IRS may appeal decisions of the Tax Court and the District Courts to the U.S. Court of Appeals. These appellate court decisions are officially published in the *Federal Reporter* (F., F.2d, F.3d). Since there are 13 courts of appeals, 11 regional ones plus the D.C. Circuit, plus the Court of Appeals for the Federal Circuit, the citation for the court must identify the specific court of appeals. (Notice that when the name of a specific court is used, the court's name is capitalized.)

Normally, each review by a court of appeals consists of a panel of three judges and is limited to the application of law, not the redetermination of facts. Courts are obligated to follow the decisions of the Supreme Court but not those of the other courts of appeals for the other circuits. However, the Court of Appeals for the 11th Circuit has ruled that it will follow case precedent of the Court of Appeals for the 5th Circuit for those cases decided prior to the creation of the 11th Circuit on October 1, 1981.

District Courts within each individual circuit must follow precedents set by the Court of Appeals for their own circuit. The decisions of other circuit courts of appeals are merely influential, not precedent for district courts outside the jurisdiction of the particular appellate court. Also, as noted earlier, the Tax Court follows the policy of observing precedent set by the appellate court of the circuit in which the taxpayer resides. In this way, consistency in the application of law is maintained between the Tax Court and the District Court of jurisdiction even though an inconsistency may exist in the law's application to taxpayers residing in other circuits. The effect of this system is clear when examining two cases concerning the same issue and facts as to whether the same corporation qualified for Subchapter S status. The Tax Court effectively said "yes" to

QUICK FACTS

Court of appeals decisions provide precedent within each circuit court.

one 50 percent shareholder[5] and "no" to the other 50 percent shareholder,[6] solely because of the difference in where the taxpayers resided.

All decisions, both tax and nontax, of the various courts of appeals are published by West Publishing Company in the *Federal Reporter—2nd series* (F.2d or F.3d). In addition, tax decisions of the courts of appeals are also contained in CCH's *United States Tax Cases* (USTC) and RIA's *American Federal Tax Reports* (AFTR, AFTR2d, or AFTR3d). The following citation refers to a 2001 decision of the U.S. Court of Appeals of the 4th Circuit.

> *United Dominion Industries, Inc. v. U.S.*, 259 F3d 193, 88 AFTR 2d 2001-5323, 2001-2 USTC ¶50,571 (CA-4, 2001).

U.S. Court of Appeals for the Federal Circuit. Although the U.S. Court of Appeals for the Federal Circuit functions at the same level as the regional courts of appeal, its jurisdiction is defined by the trial court chosen by the taxpayer, rather than by geography. It will hear appeals on tax issues only if they arise from decisions of the U.S. Court of Federal Claims. Still, its decisions have nationwide precedential value.

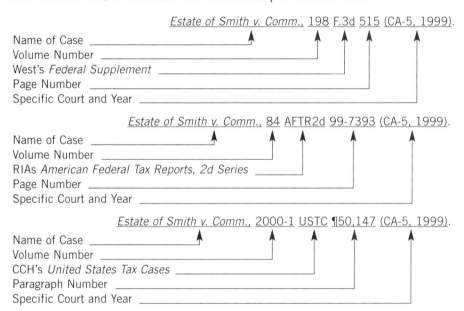

U.S. Supreme Court. The U.S. Supreme Court considers only a handful of tax cases each year. These are generally cases in which courts of appeal have reached different conclusions on the same issue. Either the taxpayer or the IRS can request the Supreme Court to review decisions of any of the courts of appeal. Appeal is by "Writ of Certiorari." If the Court agrees to hear the case, it will grant the Writ (reported as "Cert. Granted"). If the Court refuses, certiorari is denied (reported as "Cert. Den."). Denial of a Writ of Certiorari means the Supreme Court simply does not wish to review the case. The decision of the court of appeals will stand.

After the Supreme Court rules on an issue, all courts are required to follow this precedent as long as the statute remains unchanged. A taxpayer sometimes tries to argue a narrow application of the court's holding or interpretation of the law.

All Supreme Court decisions are published by the U.S. Government Printing Office in *U.S. Supreme Court Reports* (U.S.) and by West Publishing Company in its *Supreme Court Reporter* (S.Ct.). In addition, the tax-related decisions of the Supreme Court are contained in CCH's *United States Tax Cases* (USTC) and RIA's *American Federal Tax Reports* (AFTR, AFTR2d, or AFTR3d). A citation to a case need not include any nonofficial

---

[5] *K. W. Doehring v. Comm.*, 33 TCM 1035, TC Memo. D 74,234.

[6] *P. E. Puckett v. Comm.*, 33 TCM 1038, RIA TC Memo. Dex. 74,2350.

sources for accessing the case; however, it's often helpful to include unofficial sources, as shown in the following example citation to a tax decision of the Supreme Court:

> *United Dominion Industries, Inc. v. U.S.*, 532 US 822, 121 SCt 1934, 87 AFTR 2d 2001, *2001-1 USTC ¶50,430*; (USSC, 2001).

Figure 7-7 provides a summary of tax authorities.

While not every Code section and Regulation has cases interpreting the language in that Code section, most have cases that apply the statutory and administrative law to a particular set of facts. When trying to find these cases the researcher must use a tax research database, such as RIA Checkpoint. One can search directly in RIA's tax service called the *Federal Tax Coordinator* (FTC). Alternatively, when one finds the relevant Code section and provision within it, then one should enter the FTC by selecting the button next to that specific provision. The FTC can provide a drill-down approach to finding relevant annotations of cases that interpret that Code section provision. These annotations provide a one-or two-sentence explanation of the case. Most electronic tax services provide hyperlinks to the authorities discussed. If the case appears potentially relevant, the researcher should then read the entire case to assure its relevance and extract sufficient information to understand the case and generally write a paragraph on that case.

RESEARCH TIPS

Use a tax service to locate relevant cases for an issue.

Another common search method often used to find relevant cases interpreting the Code or regulations is a keyword search. However, this approach may not yield as effective a result. The search engine for different databases does not always search the entire data. Also, a keyword search is more likely to overwhelm the researcher with many documents that are not on point.

Evaluating Different Sources of Tax Authority

Once tax researchers have located authority relevant to a given tax question, they then face what is often the most difficult portion of the task: its assessment. "Authority" is a relative concept. General guidelines are listed below.

1. The Code is the strongest primary authority. However, many questions arise in attempting to apply the words of a Code provision to a given factual situation.

2. Treasury Regulations are the next strongest authority. Although some consider Legislative Regulations of greater weight than Interpretive Regulations, most weigh these types of Regulations similarly.

3. Court decisions interpret Code and Regulations. The court can overturn a Code section only if it is unconstitutional. The court will overturn a Treasury Regulation only if the Regulation is totally unreasonable. Generally, the higher the court, the greater the weight of the precedent.

FIGURE 7-7 | SOURCES OF TAX AUTHORITY

Legislative:	**Internal Revenue Code**
	Congressional Committee reports
Administrative:	Treasury Regulations—Proposed Regs
	Temporary Regs
	Final Regs
	Revenue Rulings
	Revenue Procedures
Judicial:	Tax Court—Regular Decisions
	Memorandum Decisions
	U.S. Court of Federal Claims
	Courts of Appeal
	U.S. Supreme Court

Practice Exercises   *Locating Tax Cases*

1. Locate the following judicial tax cases. Use a tax research database, such as RIA Checkpoint, to access the database.

   a. *United Dominion Industries, Inc. v. U.S.,* 532 US 822, 121 SCt 1934, 87 AFTR 2d 2001, 2001-1 USTC ¶50,430; (2001).

   What was the main issue of the case before the Supreme Court?

   _____

   What did the Supreme Court do with the appellate court's decision?

   _____

   _____

2. Find two state tax cases discussing illegal bribes. Use a tax research database. If you use LexisNexis, click on **legal research** and then **tax law** before using the keywords "illegal bribes" and State Tax Cases as your source.

   Name and citation of case #1 _____

   Name and citation of case #2 _____

4. Published IRS Revenue Rulings and Revenue Procedures are binding on IRS revenue agents, but not on the courts. These sources represent the current official policy of the IRS. Therefore, they carry considerable weight when dealing with IRS employees. Thus, the perception of the weight of authority for Revenue Rulings varies depending on whether the taxpayer is arguing before the IRS or the courts.

RESEARCH TIPS

Use the strongest primary authorities possible to support a position.

The researcher must read the authorities carefully and often distinguish what happened in different courts.

EXAMPLE: How may higher level courts handle the prior court's decision?

Discussion: They may affirm or reverse the prior court's decision, or affirm only part of the case. Sometimes the court may issue the appropriate legal standard and then remand the case back to the prior court for a decision which applies that law.

The researcher must check whether cases continue to have validity. Most often, a citator in a tax research database is used for this purpose. A citator presents the judicial history of a case and traces subsequent judicial references to the case.

EXAMPLE: How does the researcher use the citator in RIA Checkpoint?

Discussion: On the left side of the search screen is a link to the Citator 2nd, where the researcher enters the citation for the case.

While the IRS issues various other administrative pronouncements on tax topics, these are less commonly researched by the professional tax accountant and sometimes classified as secondary authority. Secondary authority on taxation is often helpful in locating and assessing relevant primary tax authority, as well as gaining some insights on the tax issues.

Secondary authority does not carry precedential weight. Secondary authority generally comes from the following sources:

- Other IRS administrative pronouncements, such as Private Letter Rulings

- Tax services, such as Federal Tax Coordinator (FTC) included in RIA's Checkpoint

- Treatises and textbooks

- Tax journals and law reviews

- Tax newsletters and web sites

Secondary authority on tax is often helpful in reporting the opinions, analysis, and research already performed by tax professionals and scholars on a wide variety of tax issues. See Figure 7-8 for a brief listing of some of the more commonly used unofficial secondary tax sources. The ability to use both primary and secondary tax authorities effectively is a necessary skill for the tax researcher.

STEPS IN CONDUCTING TAX RESEARCH

Tax research consists of five basic steps, as explained in Chapter 1. Those steps, as stated in the tax context are:

1. Investigate the facts and analyze the issues.

2. Use a scientific approach to collect the appropriate authorities.

3. Gather and document adequate and representative evidence.

4. Employ logical reasoning in drawing conclusions.

5. Support the validity or reasonableness of the conclusions.

Step 1—Investigate the Facts and Analyze the Issues

Often, tax problems have a way of appearing deceptively simple to taxpayers. Although the taxpayer is usually interested only in the final outcome of a possibly complex chain

FIGURE 7-8 | SELECTED EXAMPLES OF UNOFFICIAL TAX LITERATURE

TAX TREATISES

Bittker & Eustice: *Federal Income Taxation of Corporations and Shareholders*	Warren Gorham & Lamont
McKee, Nelson, and Whitmire: *Federal Taxation of Partnerships and Partners*	Warren Gorham & Lamont
Lerner et al.: *Federal Income Taxation of Corporations Filing Consolidated Returns*	Matthew Bender & Co.

SINGLE-VOLUME TAX REFERENCE BOOKS

Master Federal Tax Manual	Research Institute of America
Master Tax Guide	Commerce Clearing House

COMPREHENSIVE TAX SERVICES

United States Tax Reporter	Research Institute of America
Federal Tax Coordinator 2d	Research Institute of America
Tax Management Portfolios	Bureau of National Affairs, Inc.
Standard Federal Tax Reporter	Commerce Clearing House
Mertens' Law of Federal Income Taxation	Callaghan & Company

PROFESSIONAL TAX JOURNALS

Journal of Taxation	Warren Gorham & Lamont
TAXES—The Tax Magazine	Commerce Clearing House
The Tax Adviser	American Institute of CPAs

TAX NEWSLETTERS

Daily Tax Report	Bureau of National Affairs, Inc.
U.S. Tax Week	Matthew Bender & Co.
Tax Notes	Tax Analysts

Practice Exercises *Evaluating Different Sources*

1. Assume that the taxpayer has a tax issue in which the only authority on point is the following: (1) an unfavorable Circuit Court of Appeals case from the same circuit as the taxpayer's residence and (2) a favorable decision from a district court in another part of the country. What does the researcher advise the taxpayer?

    _____

    _____

2. Assume that the taxpayer has a tax issue in which the only authority on point is the following: (1) an article written by a famous tax lawyer that supports the taxpayer's position and (2) a Revenue Ruling that does not the support taxpayer's position. What does the researcher advise the client?

    _____

    _____

3. Assume that the taxpayer has a tax issue in which the only authority on point is as follows: (1) a Private Letter Ruling that favors the taxpayer's position and (2) a Tax Court regular decision that opposes the taxpayer's position. What does the researcher advise the client?

    _____

    _____

of applicable legal authorities, the tax researcher must always exercise due professional care in acquiring the facts, researching relevant legal issues, documenting the research, and communicating to the client.

> **EXAMPLE:** Taxpayer wants to know how much he can deduct for making a charitable contribution of land costing $100,000, when it has a current fair market value of $250,000.
>
> **Discussion:** The deduction lies somewhere in the range from zero to $250,000, depending upon what additional facts exist. Even the most superficial review of Code Sec. 170 (concerning charitable contributions) reveals that the researcher needs to determine many additional facts just to identify the potential tax issues upon which the amount of any deduction depends. A partial list of such considerations would include whether prior charitable contributions were made during the tax year—and, if so, the amount, nature, and circumstances of each gift; the amount of the individual's adjusted gross income; whether the receiving charitable organization is a public charity as opposed to a private foundation—and, if a public charity, the intended use for the contributed land; and whether or not the contributed land, while in the hands of the taxpayer, would have generated ordinary income or capital gain if the taxpayer had sold the land instead of donating it.

Often preliminary research causes the tax researcher to realize additional facts are needed from the client, which in turn might trigger new issues for research.

> **EXAMPLE:** In attempting to ascertain whether the land contributed was ordinary income or capital gain property, assume the tax researcher discovers that the taxpayer deemed all real estate holdings as investments, despite an extensive history of prior real estate transactions. What is the professional responsibility of the tax professional?
>
> **Discussion:** The central issue is whether the taxpayer's real estate activities constitute a trade or business under Sec. 162(a), and if so, whether the donated land was held for sale in the normal course of the business. Given that the taxpayer is probably deemed under the law to be in the business of selling real estate, the tax professional should conclude that the land in question was held for sale in the

QUICK FACTS
The answer to many tax issues depends on the taxpayer's facts.

normal course of that business. This would result in ordinary income property, thus limiting any possible deduction to the taxpayer's basis in the property— $100,000 in this instance. If the taxpayer's real estate activities constitute only an investment activity and not a trade or business, the taxpayer might be entitled to a deduction for the $250,000 current fair market value of the land, assuming all other necessary conditions were met.

Note that the purpose of these examples was not to discuss the tax law concerning charitable contributions, trade or business, or how property is held, but rather to illustrate the continually unfolding interrelationships between primary tax authorities and relevant facts when identifying and refining the key legal issue to research.

Step 2—Use a Scientific Approach to Collect the Appropriate Authorities

Since taxation is a matter of law, all answers to tax questions must stem from legal authority, either directly or through reasoned implication. However, not all legal authorities are of equal weight. The strength of authorities vary, especially cases and Revenue Rulings that when applied to a set of facts may have significant distinctions compared to the colorable authority.

Step 3—Gather and Document Adequate and Representative Evidence

Because of the enormous volume and the many sources of tax authorities, it is imperative that tax researchers possess a working knowledge of the authoritative tax literature. Such knowledge should include both the source and the location of the authorities. By understanding the hierarchy of tax authorities within the legal system, the researcher can better assess their relative weights. By knowing the manner in which the various authorities are classified and referenced, a researcher can use a more scientific approach to efficiently locate the authorities on specific topics. For these reasons, both the sources and classifications used for the major tax authorities are described in more detail later.

In reaching a solution to a tax issue, the tax researcher will gather relevant tax authorities related to the issue under investigation. In certain cases, no clear solution is apparent due to unresolved issues of law, or perhaps incomplete facts from the client. As in accounting and auditing research, professional judgment in tax also plays an important role in resolving the issue.

Step 4—Employ Logical Reasoning in Drawing Conclusions

In unresolved cases, the tax professional will provide possible legal alternatives to the client with the justification and likely consequences for each alternative. The client, in discussion with the tax professional, will then select the best alternative for the situation.

Step 5—Support the Validity or Reasonableness of the Conclusions

No matter how competently researched, there is little practical impact if the tax research is not effectively communicated to clients. The professional should follow up oral communications with a letter. The goal is to make sure that clients completely understand both the potential benefits and risks of any recommended actions.

Effective communication often requires that the tax researcher tailor the presentation to the intended audience. Judgment is required in determining how much detail to express when preparing any given client letter or document. Whatever the level of technical sophistication of the person for whom the research is performed, generally the communication should set forth at least:

1. A statement of the relevant facts.

2. An identification of the tax issues involved.

3. The researcher's conclusions.

4. The legal authorities and reasoning upon which the conclusions are based.

Guidelines for preparing each section of the research report include the following:

Statement of the Relevant Facts.

1. Include all the facts necessary for answering the tax question(s) at issue.

2. Usually state events in chronological order and give dates for each event.

3. Indicate sources for the facts and give references for any available documentation.

4. Have the client review the written description of the facts for accuracy and completeness.

Identification of the Tax Issues.

1. State each issue as precisely as possible to the most relevant law, referencing the location of particular Code provisions within a section.

2. Tailor the tax issue to the client's specific facts and circumstances that are relevant in the law.

3. Write each issue separately.

4. Arrange the tax issues in a logical order, particularly when the answer to one question raises another question.

Conclusions.

1. State a separate conclusion for each tax issue listed.

2. In addition to the most likely result, indicate any other possible alternatives having a realistic possibility of success and include an assessment of the authoritative legal support underlying each alternative.

3. Sign and date the letter or document.

Authorities and Reasoning.

1. Separately present the authorities and the reasoning underlying each conclusion listed.

2. Concisely summarize the facts and findings, plus a complete citation, for each authority mentioned. Also, note the relative strength of each authority. For court decisions, clarify factors indicating the weight of authority, such as the specific court, the support for the decision (such as the size of the majority opinion or whether the judge's remark was the holding of the court or merely influential passing remarks [dicta]), whether the cited case was upheld on appeal to a higher level court, and how the holding is interpreted in subsequent decisions.

3. Provide a detailed, logical analysis to support each of the research conclusions, using the precise findings of the legal authorities cited. Often the process of expressing one's thoughts in writing aids the identification and elimination of possible gaps in the logic.

> **QUICK FACTS**
> A tax memo states relevant facts, identifies issues, provides conclusions, and supports the researcher's conclusion with authorities and logical reasoning.

DOCUMENTING TAX RESEARCH

Documentation of the relevant law and reasoning to reach a conclusion is an important part of tax research. The reasoning includes writing a discussion of how each potentially relevant legal authority is applied to the set of facts or is distinguishable from them. The reasoning is placed after the conclusion.

Practice Exercises | *Conducting Tax Research and Documenting the Authorities*

If you are able to access a Tax Service, such as FTC on RIA Checkpoint, complete the following activities.

1. Assume that your best friend has a full scholarship offer for playing football at the University of Colorado at Boulder. The scholarship covers tuition, dorm room, and meal costs at the university. Write a brief memo explaining the tax consequences of the scholarship, documenting the relevant authorities.

   _____

   _____

   _____

2. Assume that your older sister agrees to tutor you for a month in math. She normally charges clients $500 for similar services. You would normally charge $100 for your services. Write a brief memo explaining the tax consequences for you and your sister documenting the relevant authorities.

   _____

   _____

   _____

RESEARCH TIPS

Document your tax research in a structured memo for the client.

Written documentation is also important because often the researcher must communicate the research findings to another person in the firm who in turn communicates it to a client. The documentation of the research process is especially important if the client is audited on this issue. If high turnover in the professional staff exists, the person preparing this year's tax return may not be the person who did the return two years ago that is now under audit. Finally, carefully documenting the research also makes pragmatic sense in today's highly litigious environment.

A structured memo format for the completed tax research facilitates a logical approach and helps to ensure that all relevant sources of authority were considered. Figure 7-9 illustrates such a structured format for researching tax questions.

FIGURE 7-9 | BRIEF RESEARCH MEMO ILLUSTRATED

FACTS:

Tim gave Mary a diamond engagement ring worth $2,000 when Mary was a travel companion for Tim's month-long business trip to Europe.

ISSUE:

Can a taxpayer who receives an engagement ring while serving as a travel companion exclude the value of the ring as a gift under Sec. 102(a)?

CONCLUSION:

A taxpayer can exclude the fair market value of an engagement ring as a gift.

REASONING:

Gross income under Sec. 61(a) includes all income, including compensation for services, unless otherwise excluded. The value of a gift is excluded under Sec. 102(a). The U.S. Supreme Court defined a gift as coming from real love and affection, and not from a business relationship in *Comm'r v. Duberstein,* 363 U.S. 278 (1960).

Tim's engagement to Mary suggests true love for transferring the ring, so as to qualify as gift under the analysis of *Comm'r v. Duberstein,* 363 U.S. 278 (1960). The value of the engagement ring is excludable under Sec. 102(a) and not part of Mary's gross income under Sec. 61(a) because it is not compensation for services.

AICPA STATEMENTS ON STANDARDS FOR TAX SERVICES

The AICPA, in order to assist the tax professional, has issued a series of statements on ethical standards in the area of tax services and two interpretations on these standards. These practice standards, called *Statements on Standards for Tax Services* (SSTSs) supplement the *AICPA Code of Professional Conduct* and helps the CPA fulfill his or her professional responsibilities.

> **EXAMPLE:** When preparing or signing a tax return, when must a CPA in good faith not rely, without verification, on information that the taxpayer or third party prepares?

> **Discussion:** If the information appears incorrect, incomplete or inconsistent on its face or on the basis of other facts, the CPA has a duty to make further inquiry (SSTS no. 3).

Other SSTSs address such topics as the use of estimates on the taxpayer's returns, making a departure from a position previously decided by the court or IRS administrative proceedings, and responsibilities after learning about an error on the taxpayer's previously filed tax return. The interpretations discuss the "Realistic Possibility Standard" and "Tax Planning." SSTSs and their interpretations are freely downloadable from the AICPA's web site at *http://www.aicpa.org*, under its materials on taxation. Future tax professionals are encouraged to read these professional authorities and review them in practice when needed.

The enforcement of these SSTSs is recognized as part of the AICPA's Code of Professional Conduct Rule 201, General Standards and Rule 202, Compliance with Standards.

SUMMARY

Tax research is needed for compliance and tax planning. The process of conducting tax research, including its goals and challenges was first discussed in this chapter. Explanations were provided about the significance, citation, and structure of primary tax research authorities, such as the Code, regulations, and cases. Tax research databases, such as RIA Checkpoint, were examined and illustrated. Insights were provided on professionally evaluating different tax authorities so as to comply with legal requirements and avoid penalties, as well as meet professional expectations, as explained in the AICPA Statements on Standards for Tax Services. In the process of understanding tax research, one develops an appreciation for the complexity, excitement, and skills required to become a tax professional.

DISCUSSION QUESTIONS

1. Explain the difference between tax evasion, tax avoidance, and abusive tax avoidance.
2. Identify tax research goals.
3. Identify and explain the basic steps of the tax research process.
4. Which of the following tax sources are primary authorities?
   a. Tax services
   b. Tax Court decisions
   c. Tax newsletters
   d. Internal Revenue Code
   e. Treasury Regulations

5. What are the three major groups of primary tax authority? Describe what is in each group.

6. Differentiate between policy-oriented versus application-oriented tax research.

7. What are the challenges in tax research?

8. Distinguish between tax compliance and tax planning.

9. Identify the differences between a Treasury Regulation and a Revenue Ruling.

10. Explain the meaning of the term "precedent" for tax research.

11. What does it mean when the IRS issues an announcement of nonacquiescence?

12. Identify the three tools that utilize the computer in conducting tax research.

13. What is the source of all primary authorities in tax?

14. Distinguish between two citations when one has "IRB" in it, and the other has a "CB" in it.

15. Where within a tax research database does one find copies of Revenue Procedures?

EXERCISES

1. Access the Internet and complete the following (you may want to use *http://www.taxsites.com* to help you find the materials):
   a. Obtain a copy of your state's 1040 tax form.
   b. Obtain a copy of Publication 597—"Information on the United States–Canada Income Tax Treaty" on the IRS's web site, or locate it by using "International tax sites."
   c. Under "Tax legislation" locate two proposed taxation bills and briefly summarize each.
   d. Under "Tax help, tips and articles," locate two tax articles and briefly summarize.

2. Access the U.S. Code and answer the following (use either a tax research database or a web site, such as *http://uscode.house.gov/usc.htm*):
   a. What is the general content of IRS Code Sec. 61?
   b. What is the general content of IRS Code Sec. 166(d)?
   c. Find the precise authority within the Code that defines "net long-term capital gains."
   d. Find the precise authority within the Code that determines if the gain on the sale of a home is taxable.

3. Access a tax research database and answer the following questions. Then repeat the problem on a different tax research database and compare the ease of use.
   a. Conduct a search of the U.S. Treasury Regulations using the keyword "moving expenses." List three documents from your search and their dates.
   b. Conduct a search of the Internal Revenue Bulletin/Cumulative Bulletin using the keyword "qualified scholarships." List the most recent IRS pronouncement published and its date.
   c. Conduct a search of the Internal Revenue Bulletin/Cumulative Bulletin using the keyword "tuition credit." List the three most recent documents produced from your search.

4. After getting selected in Disney's training program, Minsu became a rock star. His family paid $22,000 to get Minsu trained. How much of these expenses paid by his family are deductible? Reference the specific authority in the Code and regulations.

5. Access the Code of Federal Regulations (CFR) and answer the following (use either on a tax research database or web sites, such as *http://www.gpoaccess.gov/cfr/index.html*):

    a. How may titles are there in the CFR?

    b. Scroll down and search the CFR for IRC Section 217. What did you find?

6. Access the Internet and locate the IRS forms page. Download and print IRS form number 2106 entitled "Employee Business Expenses."

7. Central Michigan Medical Association (CMMA) is planning on hiring a new cardiologist who currently lives in Dallas, Texas. The cardiologist owns a home in Dallas and due to the depressed housing market it would incur a loss of $80,000 if sold. In order for the new doctor to relocate to Michigan, he requests that CMMA reimburse him for the loss to be incurred on the sale of his Dallas home. In conducting tax research, what are some tax issues to consider in regard to the tax treatment for the loss reimbursement? Identify the key issues as precisely as possible.

8. Utilize RIA's Checkpoint or an alternative tax research database and identify the general contents of each of the following Internal Revenue Code sections.

    a. IRC § 62(a)(2)

    b. IRC § 162(e)(4)

    c. IRC § 262(b)

    d. IRC § 6702(a)

9. Utilize RIA's Checkpoint or an alternative tax research database and list the Code sections that highlight the main tax law provisions for the following topics.

    a. Gift tax

    b. Capital gains

    c. Stock dividends

    d. Business energy credits

10. Utilize LexisNexis or an alternative tax research database and identify the general contents of each of the following subchapters of the Internal Revenue Code.

    a. Subchapter A

    b. Subchapter D

    c. Subchapter H

    d. Subchapter O

11. Utilize any tax source to answer the following question. You loaned your roommate $4,500 for next semester's tuition. Your roommate promised to pay you back next summer from his summer employment. However, next summer you realized that your roommate never found a job, but vacationed all summer in Europe. He e-mails you and informs you of his inability to pay off his debt. Can you claim any tax deduction? Focus primarily on the Internal Revenue Code for your research.

12. This exercise requires you to locate the hardbound copies of certain publications and court reporters that are frequently used in tax research. Use your university's library and provide the call number and location in your library (i.e., floor or stack number) for each. If the publication or reporter is not available, so indicate.

    a. RIA United States Tax Reporter

    b. CCH Tax Court Memorandum Decisions

    c. BNA Tax Management Portfolios

    d. Federal Reporter, 3d Series

    e. RIA Tax Coordinator

    f. United States Tax Cases

13. Using your university's library or its web site, list five tax journals in your library and identify the publisher of each journal.

14. Besides Revenue Rulings and Revenue Procedures, identify three other types of documents that the IRS generates.

15. Utilize RIA's Checkpoint or an alternative tax research database and determine for each of the following Code sections how many Treasury Regulations have been issued. Give the total number of such Regulations and also the specific number of the last Regulation.

    a. Sec. 101
    b. Sec. 143
    c. Sec. 183
    d. Sec. 385

16. Utilize RIA's Checkpoint and locate the following court decision: 67 AFTR 2d 91-718. What court heard the case and what was the issue(s) involved?

17. Utilize RIA's Checkpoint U.S. Tax Reporter to determine:

    a. If your school's new basketball player receives an athletic scholarship, is it considered gross income when received by the athlete?
    b. Can the athlete deduct her expenses for such items as clothing, meals, or conditioning camp?

18. Utilize RIA's Checkpoint U.S. Tax Reporter. Locate each of the following topics and provide the first paragraph number listed for each.

    a. Expenses for education
    b. Contributions
    c. Medical deduction
    d. Illegal bribes

19. Isabella Bank loaned Jim Alwood $150,000 for his gardening supplies company. As a result of a drought, the year was a disaster for Alwood. Since he was unable to repay the loan, Isabella Bank accepts the following plan to extinguish the debt: Jim Alwood is to pay cash of $3,000, transfer ownership of the gardening property with a value of $80,000 and a basis of $60,000, and also to transfer to the bank stock with a value of $30,000 and a basis of $45,000. Locate and read the following partial listing of tax authorities to determine how much gross income Alwood should report from the extinguishment of his bank debt:

    Reg. Sec. 1.61-12.;
    Sec. 108;
    James J. Gehl, 102 T.C. 74 (1994);
    Find other relevant sources.

20. Locate three different tax web sites listed in Figure 7-1, and identify three different items available on each web site.

21. The appendix to this chapter provides two additional research cases as practice for the CPA exam. Complete them.

APPENDIX

Tax Research on the CPA Exam

The following two tax simulations, modeled after the CPA exam, will test your understanding of conducting tax research utilizing RIA's Checkpoint database. Figure A7-1 presents the opening screen for a tax simulation. Figures A7-2A and B present the first two opening screens when you click on the "Code" icon in Figure A7-1.

Required: Access RIA Checkpoint and complete the research requested under the Research tab for each simulation in Figures A7-3 and A7-4.

FIGURE A7-1 | OPENING SCREEN FOR TAX SIMULATION

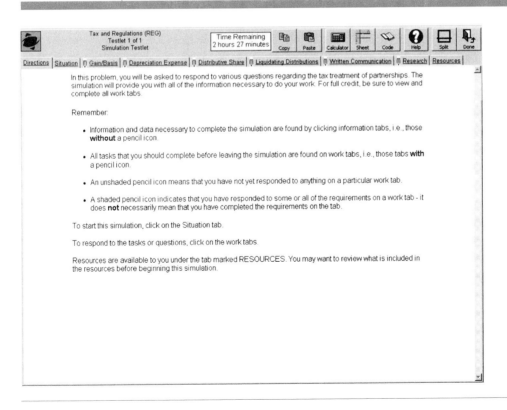

FIGURE A7-2A OPENING SCREENS IN THE "CODE" DATABASE ON THE CPA EXAM

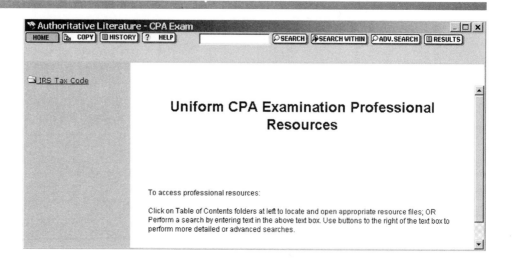

FIGURE A7-2B OPENING SCREENS IN THE "CODE" DATABASE ON THE CPA EXAM

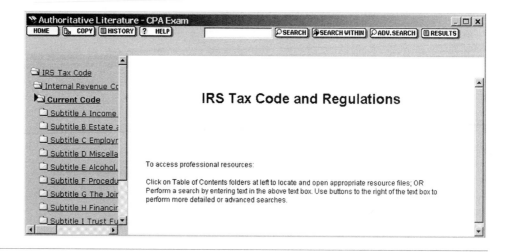

FIGURE A7-3 | TAX SIMULATION 1

DIRECTIONS	The **Directions** tab informs the candidate as to the instructions or question requirements for this particular case simulation.

SITUATION	Jim Hawkins is an employee of Protect Securities Services, Inc. located in Chicago, Illinois. During the current year, Jim's work assignment was the third shift (12 AM–8 AM) in which he would drive around to various businesses (Protect Security clients) and check for possible property damage and burglars. In addition to Jim's normal pay, Protect Security provides him with $75 in cash each week to cover the cost of food when Jim would stop and eat at restaurants between stops on his shift. Jim believes that his meal allowance is not taxable and requests your assistance with this issue.

RESOURCES	The **Resources** tab provides various resources (tools) that the candidate will utilize in completing the simulation. Here the candidate might find the on-screen calculator, or RIA Checkpoint tax services.

ANALYSIS	Clicking on the **Analysis** tab provides the candidate with detailed information for analysis or completion. This could include the completion of a tax return. Here is where the candidate will input data into drop-down boxes or into Excel spreadsheets.

COMMUNICATION	Written communication is still an integral part of the CPA exam. Under the **Communication** tab, the candidate will be required to prepare (type) some form of written communication (i.e., to the client or audit partner) to discuss various issues related to the facts presented under the Situation tab.

RESEARCH	The **Research** tab is where the candidate will be required to research relevant databases. Candidates will then perform keyword searches utilizing RIA's Checkpoint tax database. Required: For the above given situation (1) list at least three keywords that one would utilize to research the issue; (2) utilize RIA's Checkpoint and perform a keyword search, listing the paragraph numbers of the tax services that seem appropriate for the issue, and (3) identify the primary IRS Code section for this issue.

FIGURE A7-4 | TAX SIMULATION 2

DIRECTIONS	The **Directions** tab informs the candidate as to the instructions or question requirements for this particular case simulation.
SITUATION	During the current year, Art Sampson received an award from his employer, the U.S. Navy. The award consisted of $25,000 and a plaque for "Combined Scientific and Technical Contributions of Significant Value to the Navy." Art has been the premier scientist with the Navy for more than 30 years and has received numerous national awards over the years. Since the award was honorary rather than compensatory, Art is of the opinion that the award is tax-free income. This is particularly important to Art, for his regular salary alone places him in the highest tax bracket.
RESOURCES	The **Resources** tab provides various resources (tools) that the candidate will utilize in completing the simulation. Here the candidate might find the on-screen calculator, or RIA Checkpoint tax services.
ANALYSIS	Clicking on the **Analysis** tab provides the candidate with detailed information for analysis or completion. This could include the completion of a tax return. Here is where the candidate will input data into drop-down boxes or into Excel spreadsheets.
COMMUNICATION	Written communication is still an integral part of the CPA exam. Under the **Communication** tab, the candidate will be required to prepare (type) some form of written communication (i.e., to the client or audit partner) to discuss various issues related to the facts presented under the Situation tab.
RESEARCH	The **Research** tab is where the candidate will be required to research relevant databases. Candidates will then perform keyword searches utilizing RIA's Checkpoint tax database. Required: For the above given situation (1) list at least three keywords that one would utilize to research the issue; (2) utilize RIA's Checkpoint and perform a keyword search, listing the paragraph numbers of the tax services that seem appropriate for the issue, and (3) identify the primary IRS Code section for this issue.

Assurance Services and Auditing Research

LEARNING OBJECTIVES

After completing this chapter, you should understand:

- The types of assurance and consulting services, and the applicable standards.

- The environment for the assurance services standard-setting process.

- Authoritative auditing support.

- The Public Company Accounting Oversight Board.

- How to utilize the AICPA's Professional Standards in research.

- The role of auditing in the public sector.

- The hierarchy of the AICPA's Code of Professional Conduct.

- The role of professional judgment in the research process.

- International dimensions of auditing.

Since information technology has had a significant impact on the accounting profession and society in general, the public accounting profession has focused on its willingness and ability to design and offer additional "value-added" services, in addition to such traditional services as tax preparation and auditing. Technological changes have encouraged accounting professionals to transform from "number crunchers and certifiers of information," to "decision support specialists and enhancers of information." Many professionals who keep abreast of the major changes in the profession and technology have adapted their practices and market orientation to these new "value-added" assurance services. Some practitioners are also expanding the area of consulting services offered to clients. As a result, the practitioner/researcher must become aware of these new assurance services and the related authoritative standards and restrictions that apply in offering these services.

ASSURANCE SERVICES

In order to focus on the needs of users of decision-making information and improve the related services that accountants provide, an AICPA Committee conducted research that consisted of assessing customer needs, external factors, information technology, and needed competencies to offer these new "value-added services." These services are referred to as "assurance services," defined as follows:

> Assurance Services are independent professional services that improve the quality of information, or its context, for decision makers.

Notice that this definition of assurance services implies that the service itself will add value to the user, not necessarily just the report. Additionally, an independent professional must offer the assurance services in order to improve the quality of the information or its context. Current examples of such assurance services proposed by the AICPA include CPA WebTrust, CPA ElderCare/Prime Plus, and CPA Performance View services.

Therefore, assurance services are considered three-party contracts—the client, assurer (i.e., accountant), and the third party to whom the accountant is providing assurance. An example of an assurance service engagement is where Consumers Union tests a product and reports the results or ratings in its publication *Consumer Reports*.

Figure 8-1 presents an overview of assurance services versus consulting services. Specific details are provided in the following sections of this chapter. As depicted, the traditional audit service is an attestation function that falls under the broader term of assurance services. As a professional conducting research, one must recognize the professional standards for attestation and consulting engagements.

Consulting Services and Standards

Attestation and audit services are considered special types of assurance services. Consulting services do not fall under the umbrella of assurance services. Historically, consulting services offered to clients (two-party contracts) by CPAs were referred to as management consulting services or management advisory services. These services have

FIGURE 8-1 | ASSURANCE AND CONSULTING SERVICES UMBRELLAS

ASSURANCE SERVICES
(EXAMPLES)

Electronic Commerce

Risk Assessment

Health Care Performance

Information Systems Reliability

Business Procedure

Attestation Services

i.e.,

Audits

Review of Interim Financial Statements

Agreed-upon Procedures Engagement

Reporting on an Entity's Internal Controls

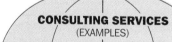

CONSULTING SERVICES
(EXAMPLES)

Litigation Support

Computer Instructions

Market Studies

Logistic Services

Business Validation

Bankruptcy Services

generally evolved from accounting-related matters in connection with audits or tax engagements. In a consulting engagement, the CPA develops findings and conclusions, which are followed with recommendations for the benefit of the client. This is in contrast to an attest engagement (a three-party contract) whereby the CPA reports on the reliability of a written assertion that is the responsibility of a third party. Examples of consulting engagements include litigation support services, computer installation engagements, and various market studies for clients.

The typical consulting engagement is quite similar to the research process presented in this text. The consulting engagement would normally include:

- Determination of the client's objectives.

- Fact-finding.

- Definition of the problem.

- Evaluation of the alternatives.

- Formulation of a proposed action.

- Communication of the results.

- Implementation and follow-up.[1]

Professional standards for consulting services include general standards and specific consulting standards. In rendering professional services (including consulting), general standards of the profession are located in Rule 201 of the AICPA's Code of Professional Conduct as discussed later in this chapter. Additionally, the AICPA has issued Statements on Standards for Consulting Services (SSCS), which provide standards for the practitioner rendering consulting services.

AUDITING STANDARD-SETTING ENVIRONMENT

Auditing is indispensable in a society where credit is extended widely and business failures regularly occur, and where investors wish to study the financial statements of many enterprises. The purpose of the audit report is to add credibility to the financial information. The general environment for auditing is a very dynamic one and is constantly evolving as various factors impact the audit process.

The independent auditor's role serves as a secondary communication function; the audit opinion is expressed on the financial information reported by management. The auditor's primary concern is whether the client's financial statements are presented in accordance with Generally Accepted Accounting Principles (GAAP). The auditor must conduct the audits in a manner that conforms to auditing standards and take actions that are guided by professional ethical standards. Additionally, in nonaudit engagements the accountant must use relevant attestation standards and statements for compilation and review services, as well as standards for accountants' services on prospective financial information (i.e., forecasts and projections).

Attestation Services and Standards

Society increasingly seeks attestation services (a subset of assurance services) from the accounting profession. In the past, attestation services were normally limited to audit opinions on historical financial statements based upon audits that followed Generally Accepted Auditing Standards (GAAS). More recently, professional accountants render

---

[1] AICPA *Professional Standards*, Vol.2, Section CS-100.05.

opinions on other representations, such as reporting on management's report as to the effectiveness of the entity's internal controls, as now required by the Sarbanes-Oxley Act of 2002. Accountants were concerned that existing standards or guidelines did not meet the demands of society. As a result, the AICPA developed attestation standards and related interpretations to provide a general framework for attest engagements.[2]

The term *attest* means to provide assurance as to the reliability of information. The AICPA has defined an attest engagement as follows:

> An attest engagement is one in which a practitioner is engaged to issue or does issue a written communication that expresses a conclusion about the reliability of a written assertion that is the responsibility of another party.[3]

Whether the attestation service is for the traditional audit of financial statements or reporting on an entity's internal control or prospective financial information, the professional accountant must follow certain guidelines and standards in rendering these attestation services. In conducting an attest engagement, the professional accountant reviews and conducts tests of the accounting records deemed necessary to obtain sufficient evidence to render an opinion. Choosing the accounting records and other information to review and deciding the extent to examine them are strictly matters of professional judgment, as many authoritative pronouncements emphasize.

Figure 8-2 presents the major elements of the attestation environment that face accountants in conducting the research for an attest engagement. Figure 8-3 presents an overview of attest engagements and relevant guidelines. The following sections of this chapter provide an overview of the standard-setting environment for attestation services, the auditing standard-setting process, authoritative auditing pronouncements, and the role of professional judgment in the research process. The chapter also includes

FIGURE 8-2 | ATTEST RESEARCH ENVIRONMENT

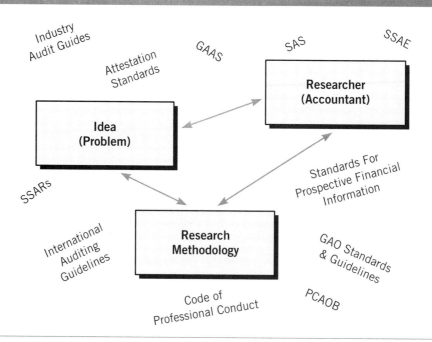

[2] AICPA *Professional Standards*, Vol. 1, Section AT-Introduction.
[3] AICPA *Professional Standards*, Vol. 1, Section AT 100.01.

FIGURE 8-3 | ATTEST ENGAGEMENTS AND GUIDELINES

Attest Engagement	Guidelines	Issued by
Audit and attest services for nonpublic companies	Generally Accepted Audit Standards (GAAS) Statements on Auditing Standards (SASs)	Auditing Standards Board (ASB)
Accounting and Review Review Services	Statements on Standards for Accounting and Review (SSARs)	Accounting and Review Services Committee (ARSC)
Accountant's Services on Prospective Financial Information	Statements on Standards for Accountant's Services on Prospective Financial Information	Auditing Standards Board
Other Attest Services	Statements on Standards for Attestation Engagement	ASB, ARSC, and the Management Consulting Services Executive Committee
Audit and attest services for public companies	Auditing and Related Professional Practice Standards	Public Company Accounting Oversight Board (PCAOB)

a discussion of how the researcher utilizes the AICPA's reSOURCE database in research, a summary of the attestation standards and compilation and review standards, as well as an overview of auditing in the public sector and the international dimensions of auditing. The appendix to this chapter presents examples of simulations similar to the CPA exam that requires one to conduct auditing/attestation research utilizing the AICPA reSOURCE database.

Recently, as the range of attestation services has expanded, many CPAs have found it difficult to apply the basic concepts underlying Generally Accepted Auditing Standards (GAAS) or the Standards of the Public Company Accounting Oversight Board (PCAOB) to various attestation services. Attestation services have included the following examples: reporting on descriptions of the client's system of internal controls, reporting to the client on which computer system is the cheapest or has the most capabilities, reporting on insurance claims data, reporting on compliance with regulatory requirements, or reporting on prospective financial statements. (In one instance, Wilson Sporting Goods requested an accounting firm to attest to the statement that Wilson's Ultra golf ball outdistanced its competitors!)

Consequently, the AICPA has issued *Statements on Standards for Attestation Engagements*, *Statements on Standards for Accounting and Review Services*, and *Statements on Standards for Accountants' Services on Prospective Financial Information* to provide a general framework and set reasonable guidelines for an attest function. The desire is to respond to the changing environment and demands of society.

The broad guidelines for an attest engagement were issued by the AICPA's Auditing Standards Board (ASB) in conjunction with the Accounting and Review Services Committee and the Management Consulting Services Executive Committee. As listed in Figure 8-4, these attestation standards do not supersede any existing standards but are considered a natural extension of the ten generally accepted auditing standards. The design of these attestation standards provides guidance to the professional to enhance both consistency and quality in the performance of attest services.

> **QUICK FACTS**
> AICPA has issued various authorities for different services.

FIGURE 8-4 | ATTESTATION STANDARDS

General Standards

1. The engagement shall be performed by a practitioner or practitioners having adequate technical training and proficiency in the attest function.
2. The engagement shall be performed by a practitioner or practitioners having adequate knowledge in the subject matter.
3. The practitioner shall perform an engagement only if he or she has reason to believe that the subject matter is capable of evaluation against criteria that are suitable and available to users.
4. In all matters relating to the engagement, an independence in mental attitude shall be maintained by the practitioner.
5. Due professional care shall be exercised in the planning and performance of the engagement.

Standards of Field Work

1. The work shall be adequately planned, and assistants, if any, shall be properly supervised.
2. Sufficient evidence shall be obtained to provide a reasonable basis for the conclusion that is expressed in the report.

Standards of Reporting

1. The report shall identify the subject matter or the assertion being reported on and state the character of the engagement
2. The report shall state the practitioner's conclusion about the subject matter or the assertion in relation to the criteria against which the subject matter was evaluated.
3. The report shall state all of the practitioner's significant reservations about the engagement, the subject matter, and, if applicable, the assertion related thereto.
4. The report shall state that the use of the report is restricted to specified parties under the following circumstances:
   - When the criteria used to evaluate the subject matter are determined by the practitioner to be appropriate only for a limited number of parties who either participated in their establishment or can be presumed to have an adequate understanding of the criteria.
   - When the criteria used to evaluate the subject matter are available only to specified parties.
   - When reporting on subject matter and a written assertion have not been provided by the responsible party.
   - When the report is on an attest engagement to apply as-agreed-upon procedures to the subject matter.

Source: AICPA Professional Standards, Vol. 1, AT Section 101.

Auditing Standards

Auditing standards differ from audit procedures in that auditing standards provide measures of the quality of performance, whereas audit procedures refer to the specific acts or steps to perform in an audit engagement. Auditing standards do not vary; they remain identical for all audits. Audit procedures often change, depending on the nature and type of entity under audit and the complexity of the audit.

In contrast to generally accepted accounting principles (GAAP), which is not identified with exactness, the AICPA has formally adopted ten broad requirements for auditors to follow in examining financial statements. These ten requirements, referred to as the *Generally Accepted Auditing Standards* (GAAS), are listed in Figure 8-5. In addition to the issuance of GAAS, the AICPA published a series of *Statements on Auditing Standards* (SASs). These SASs supplement and interpret the ten generally accepted auditing standards by clarifying

FIGURE 8-5 | GENERALLY ACCEPTED AUDITING STANDARDS

General Standards

1. The examination is to be performed by a person or persons having adequate technical training and proficiency as an auditor.
2. In all matters relating to the assignment, an independence in mental attitude is to be maintained by the auditor or auditors.
3. Due professional care shall be exercised in the performance of the audit and the preparation of the report.

Standards of Field Work

1. The work is to be adequately planned, and assistants, if any, are to be adequately supervised.
2. A sufficient understanding of the internal control structure is to be obtained to plan the audit and to determine the nature, timing, and extent of the tests to be performed.
3. Sufficient competent evident matter is to be obtained through inspection, observation, inquiries, and confirmation to afford a reasonable basis for an opinion regarding the financial statements under audit.

Standards of Reporting

1. The report shall state whether the financial statements are presented in accordance with generally accepted accounting principles.
2. The report shall identify those circumstances in which such principles have not been consistently observed in the current period in relation to the preceding period.
3. Informative disclosure in the financial statements are to be regarded as reasonably adequate unless otherwise stated in the report.
4. The report shall contain either an expression of opinion regarding the financial statements, taken as a whole, or an assertion to the effect that an opinion cannot be expressed. When an overall opinion cannot be expressed, the reasons therefore should be stated. In all cases where an auditor's name is associated with financial statements, the report should contain a clear-cut indication of the character of the auditor's work and the degree of responsibility the auditor is taking.

Source: AICPA Professional Standards, Vol. 1, AU Section 150.

the audit procedures or prescribing the auditor's report in both form and content. SASs serve as the primary authoritative support in conducting an audit and are a major source of authoritative information when conducting auditing research. These SASs were incorporated into the AICPA's loose-leaf service, *Professional Standards*, which provided a continuous codification of SASs. However, the PCAOB is currently reviewing and updating these standards, as discussed later in this chapter.

Various forms of GAAS are also recognized by governmental and internal auditors. The General Accounting Office (GAO), through the Comptroller General of the United States, has issued *Governmental Auditing Standards*, often referred to as the Yellow Book. The Institute of Internal Auditors has also issued auditing standards, called the *Standards for the Professional Practice of Internal Auditing*, under which internal auditors operate.

AUDITING STANDARD-SETTING PROCESS

Concern has always existed as to who should set auditing standards for the independent auditor. Prior to establishment of the SEC, Congress debated having audits conducted by governmental auditors. However, the auditing standard-setting process remained in the private sector. Until recently, SASs were created by the Auditing Standards Board (ASB) as the AICPA's senior technical committee on auditing standards. However, in addition, the staff of the Auditing Standards Division of the AICPA issued auditing interpretations on the application of SASs. The interpretations are not considered as authoritative as a SAS. However, auditors must justify any departure from an auditing interpretation issued by the Auditing Standards Division of the AICPA. Other publications of the Auditing Standards Division include a number of Industry Audit Guides and Statements of Position.

The Sarbanes-Oxley Act of 2002 transferred the responsibility for auditing and attestation standard setting for public companies to the Public Company Accounting Oversight Board (PCAOB), as explained in the next section. An overview of the current hierarchy of authoritative auditing support is presented in Figure 8-6. The auditor needs to understand each of the sources listed, particularly the PCAOB's auditing standards and the predecessor SASs by the AICPA.

Unlike an audit that expresses whether the financial statements are in conformity with GAAP, the accountant's examination of prospective financial statements provides assurance only as to whether (1) the prospective financial statements conform to the AICPA's guidelines, and (2) the assumptions used in the projections provide a reasonable basis for a forecast or projection. The accountant must provide a report on any attestation service provided, as described in the various attestation and auditing standards. (See Figure 8-7)

Public Company Accounting Oversight Board

RESEARCH TIPS

Use the Public Company Accounting Oversight Board (PCAOB) authorities for auditing public companies.

The Public Company Accounting Oversight Board (PCAOB or Board) has the legal responsibility under the Sarbanes-Oxley Act to establish GAAS, attestation, ethics, and quality control standards for those accounting firms auditing public companies. This Board has adopted a rule that requires all registered public accounting firms to adhere to the Board's auditing and related practice standards in connection with the preparation or issuance of any audit report for an issuer and in their auditing and related attestation practices. Going forward, the Board's new standards are called *Auditing and Related Professional Practice Standards*.

Standards for auditors of nonpublic companies are currently within the domain of the AICPA. The reconstituted mission of the AICPA's Auditing Standards Board (ASB) includes the following three main issues:

FIGURE 8-6 | AUDITING AUTHORITATIVE SUPPORT

Primary Authoritative Support
A. General Application
    1. Generally Accepted Auditing Standards (ASB)
    2. Statements on Auditing Standards (ASB)
    3. Auditing and Related Professional Practice Standards (PCAOB)
    4. Auditing Interpretations
    5. AICPA Code of Conduct
    6. Internal Auditing Guidelines

B. Special Application to Certain Entities
    1. Industry Audit Guides
    2. Statements of Position of the Auditing Standards Division
    3. GAO-Government Auditing Standards

Secondary Authoritative Support
A. Audit Research Monographs
B. AICPA Audit and Accounting Manual
C. Journal articles and textbooks

FIGURE 8-7 | AICPA AUDIT AND ACCOUNTING GUIDES

Agriculture Producers and Agriculture Cooperatives
Airlines
Audit Sampling
Banks and Savings Institutions
Brokers and Dealers in Securities
Casinos
Common Interest Realty Associations
Consideration of Internal Control Structures in a Financial Audit
Construction Contractors
Credit Unions
Employee Benefit Plans
Entities with Oil and Gas Producing Activities
Federal Government Contractors
Finance Companies
Health Care Organizations
Investment Companies
Not-for-Profit Organizations
Personal Financial Statements
Property and Liability Insurance Companies
Prospective Financial Statements
State and Local Governmental Units
Use of Real Estate Appraisal Information

---

1. To develop auditing, attestation, and quality control standards for nonissuer engagements such as privately held commercial entities, not-for-profit organizations, and governmental entities.

2. To contribute to the development and issuance of high-quality national and international auditing and assurance standards.

3. To respond to the needs for practical guidance in implementing professional standards.

The PCAOB's interim standards adopted the AICPA's auditing, attestation, and quality control standards, as well as the AICPA's ethics and independence standards. Thus,

Practice Exercises   *Auditing Standards*

1. Access the AICPA's web site (*http://www.aicpa.org*) and locate the ASB under auditing and attestation standards. Examine the approved highlights of the ASB. What were the last three auditing standards issued by the ASB?

    _____

    _____

    _____

2. Access the PCAOB's web site (*http://www.pcaobus.org*) and list two new or proposed auditing standards issued by the PCAOB.

    _____

    _____

the PCAOB uses the AICPA standards, as of April 2003, as the authoritative standards for public company audits until superseded or amended by the PCAOB.

Benchmarking (Performance Measurement)

A typical extension of the audit is providing the assurance service of "benchmarking," whereby the practitioner provides quality information as to management's strategies and performance in relation to other similar companies. Benchmarking is a performance measurement tool used in conjunction with improvement initiatives to measure comparative operating performance and to identify best practices. Benchmarking issues have studied such areas as accounting and financial systems, acquisitions, business facilities management, corporate downsizing, and foreign currency, as well as a host of other topics. Various Internet sites currently provide benchmarking surveys (i.e., *http://www.Benchnet.com*).

Benchmarking has benefited clients for many years, and for many accounting firms this assurance service has also improved the audit function. As corporations have reengineered their processes, accounting firms are involved in a continuous process of reengineering their audit methodologies in order to become more efficient. This reengineered audit methodology includes more emphasis on the following three basic components: strategies and business process analysis, risk assessment, and business measurement.

The first component, strategies and business process analysis, includes a thorough understanding of the client—the client's strategies, objectives, and management processes to maintain its competitive advantage; the client's business risks associated with these elements; and how the client is responding to these risks. The output from this first component of the audit methodology is to compare the client's elements to industry standards or best practices in order to assess the client's effectiveness in these areas. Such an in-depth analysis has a significant impact on the scope of the audit. PricewaterhouseCoopers' Internet applet called Edgarscan is an excellent tool for performance measurement or benchmarking activities. If you have not done so yet, please view the demo of Edgarscan that is available at the web site for this text: *http://weirich.swlearning.com*.

The second component of the reengineered audit methodology is risk assessment. Based on the auditor's understanding of the client's strategies, objectives, processes, and related business risks, the auditor must determine whether the client has appropriate controls to mitigate the risks. This detailed assessment of the client's risk profile has a major impact on the audit plan for the client. Risk assessment consists of the process of identifying and analyzing both internal and external risks and threats to achieving an entity's goals and objectives. The auditor can perform risk assessment either on the level of the whole enterprise or on just a specific application or transaction. Processes for both enterprise-level and application-level risk assessment form the basis for determining how to manage risk. The auditor will then assign more audit effort to the high risk areas within the client's operations.

The third major component of the reengineered audit methodology is business measurement. Here the auditor not only focuses on the financial statement numbers, but also the client's accounting recognition practices, the quality of earnings, and financial and nonfinancial performance measures. Benchmarking also aids in business measurement. The result of this audit methodology is not only a report on the fairness of the entity's financial statements, but also constructive advice for improvement in the client's operations and performance. This assurance service of benchmarking along with related tools, such as Edgarscan, is having a significant impact on improving client operations and the business audit methodology of accounting firms.

Another excellent tool for benchmarking activities is Thomson ONE (Thomson Analytic). Access to the Business School Edition is at this text's web site, *http://weirich. swlearning.com*. Thomson Analytics provides a professional research tool to access a full range of fundamental information, earnings estimates, various market data, and other source documents on a variety of companies. Figure 8-8 provides the opening screen upon clicking on the Thomson Analytics at the Thomson ONE web site.

RESEARCH TIPS

Use Benchmarking as a performance measurement tool to measure comparative operating performance and to identify best practices.

RESEARCH TOOLS

Internet
FARS
LexisNexis
AICPA reSOURCE
PwC Edgarscan
Thomson ONE
RIA Checkpoint SE
ACL
i2

QUICK FACTS

Audits now place more emphasis on strategies and business process analysis, risk assessment, and business measurement.

RESEARCH TOOLS

Internet
FARS
LexisNexis
AICPA reSOURCE
PwC Edgarscan
Thomson ONE
RIA Checkpoint SE
ACL
i2

Practice Exercises *Benchmarking Activities*

1. After reviewing the PwC's Edgarscan tutorial at this text's web site, access the Edgarscan software at *http://www.edgarscan.pwcglobal.com* and answer the following:

   a. On the opening screen enter "Nike" and click on **search**. Locate Nike Inc. and click on the name. How does Nike rank in comparison to other companies in its Standard Industrial Classification with respect to the following items?

Item	Value	Rank
Receivables	_____	_____
Gross Margin	_____	_____
Financing Activities	_____	_____

   b. On the opening screen click on **Benchmarking Assistant.** Enter "Ford Motor Co." into the name field and click on **search**. Proceed to click on the company name, which moves it to the right side of the screen under "selected." Click on **Find Peers** and select General Motors, Spartan Motors, and Chrysler Corp. Now click on **graphs** and for the most recent fiscal year end compare the companies as to the following:

	Total Debt	Inventory	Retained Earnings
Ford Motor	_____	_____	_____
General Motors	_____	_____	_____
Spartan Motors	_____	_____	_____
Chrysler Corp.	_____	_____	_____

2. Access Thomson ONE, open up Thomson Analytics, and conduct the following:

   Enter CAT in the entry lookup (Caterpillar, Inc.). Click **GO**.

   a. Briefly summarize the business description.

   _____

   _____

   _____

   b. What is the industry?

   _____

   c. Click on **Peers**.

   _____

   1. List the peer companies.

      _____ _____ _____

      _____ _____ _____

   2. For Caterpillar and each peer company, list the current sales.

      CAT _____ _____ _____

      _____ _____ _____

   3. For current sales, select the peer mean and median.

      Peer mean _____ Per median _____

   4. Comment as to how dominant Caterpillar is in relation to the peer set.

      _____

      _____

FIGURE 8-8 | OPENING SCREEN FOR THOMSON ONE (THOMSON ANALYTICS)

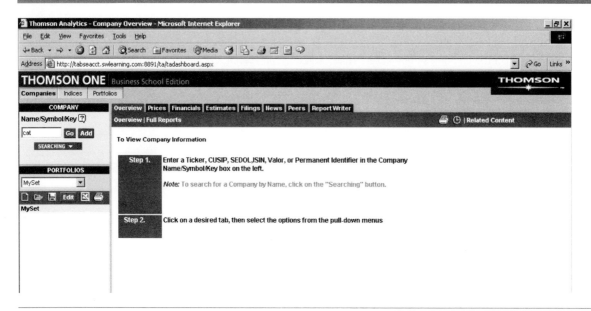

AICPA reSOURCE Database

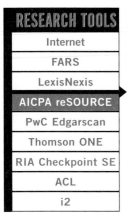

RESEARCH TOOLS

Internet

FARS

LexisNexis

AICPA reSOURCE

PwC Edgarscan

Thomson ONE

RIA Checkpoint SE

ACL

i2

The AICPA reSOURCE database includes a comprehensive compendium of the AICPA literature consisting of *Professional Standards*, *Accounting Trends and Techniques*, *Technical Practice Aids*, *Auditing and Accounting Guides*, and *Audit Alerts*. The Professional Standards segment of this database is also utilized on the CPA exam in conducting auditing research.

To conduct auditing research utilizing either the AICPA's online reSOURCE database or the CD version would consist of the following steps. The opening screen of the online version of the database appears in Figure 8-9. The table of contents (TOC) appears on the left side of the screen. Clicking on the + box next to a phrase will expand the TOC section. Clicking on Professional Standards will result in the screen shown in Figure 8-10.

Note the tabs across the top of the screen. A brief explanation of the main tabs is as follows.

Home Tab. Provides a listing of the AICPA's literature available in this database.

Search Tab. (Figure 8-11) A general search allows you to conduct a single word or phrase search. The researcher simply enters the word(s) she or he wants to search for and clicks the Search button. A list of the results will be displayed.

An advanced search allows the researcher to focus a search on a list of options. From the drop-down list he or she can select from the following options: "All words"—each word must be present in the document; "Any words"—at least one of the words must be present; "Exact phrase"—each word must be present in the exact order typed; "Boolean search"—allows one to search utilizing Boolean operators.

Results Tab. After one conducts a keyword(s) search, this tab provides a list of hits that match the search. To view a hit, one simply clicks on the link. One should also note in this tab the professional literature location is provided as to where in the database the hit comes: *Professional Standards*, *Accounting Trend and Techniques*, *Technical Practice Aids*, *Audit and Accounting Guides*, or *Audit Alerts*.

Documents Tab. This tab provides a list of the documents that contain one's search word(s).

FIGURE 8-9 AICPA PROFESSIONAL STANDARDS OPENING SCREEN

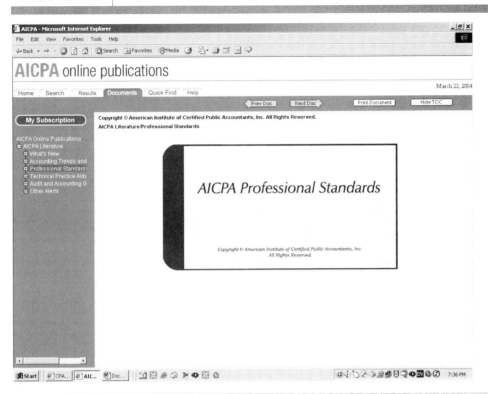

FIGURE 8-10 DETAILS OF PROFESSIONAL STANDARDS DATABASE

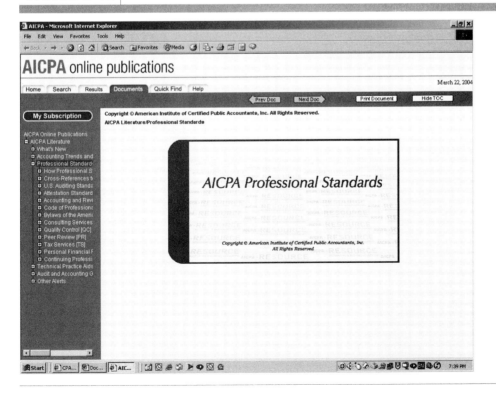

FIGURE 8-11 | SEARCH TAB

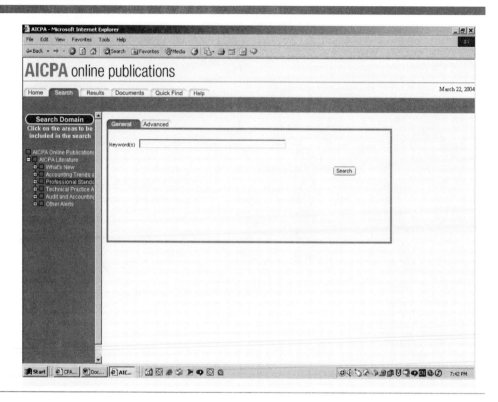

FIGURE 8-12 | AICPA AUDITING STANDARDS SEARCH REQUEST

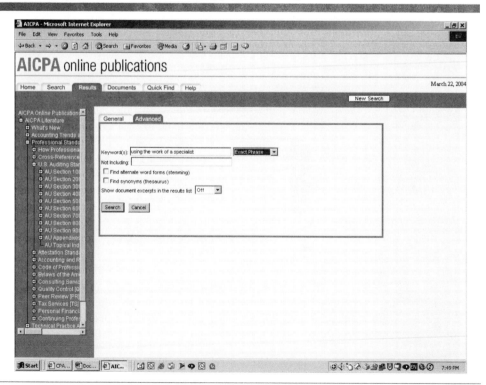

FIGURE 8-13 | AICPA AUDITING STANDARDS SEARCH RESULTS

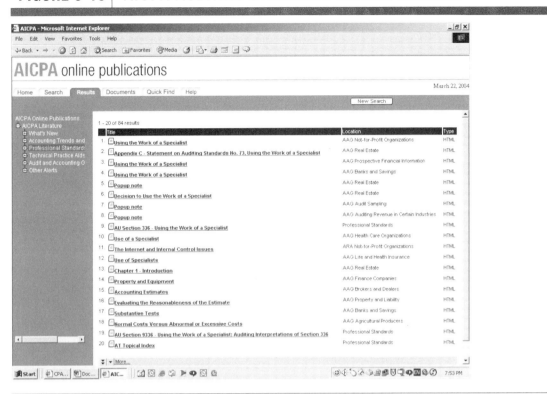

FIGURE 8-14 | AICPA AUDITING STANDARDS EXAMPLE

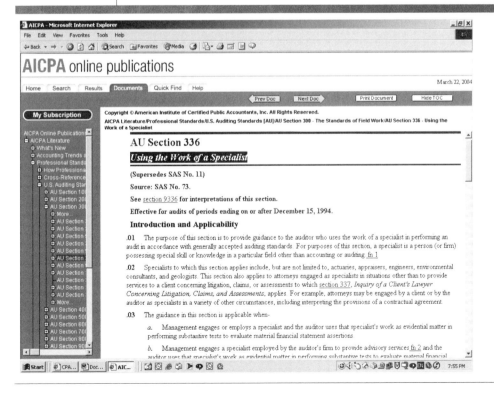

Example: If, as an auditor, I am searching for the appropriate professional literature related to the use of a specialist on the audit engagement, I would enter the phrase "using the work of a specialist" in the advanced search screen (see Figure 8-12). Figure 8-13 provides me with a listing of my hits and where the hits are located. Scrolling down to item 9 indicates that this hit is from the Professional Standards; clicking on the hit opens that particular standard (Figure 8-14).

Practice Exercises   *AICPA reSOURCE Database*

If you have access to the AICPA reSOURCE database, attempt to complete the following practice exercises. (*Note:* You can also complete these exercises with a hard copy of the AICPA Professional Standards.)

1. You have been requested by a potential client to conduct an "agreed upon procedures engagement" related to the client's pension plan. Access the AICPA's database and determine what type of service this is—audit, attestation, or a consulting engagement. Also identify the specific standard governing this type of service.

   Type of engagement: _____

   Related standard(s): _____

2. When is it appropriate to issue an adverse audit opinion? Cite the specific Professional Standard section used for your answer.

   An adverse opinion is appropriate when: _____

   _____

   Specify the Professional Standard section: _____

3. Utilize the AICPA database to answer the following issue brought to you by a co-worker. The co-worker believes that only the general standards of the AICPA Code of Professional Conduct apply to consulting engagements. Are there any other general standards that apply to a consulting engagement in addition to the general standards of the Code?

   Are additional general standards applicable? _____

   If additional standards apply, list the appropriate standard(s) titles: _____

   _____

CODE OF PROFESSIONAL CONDUCT

A distinguishing mark of any profession is the establishment and acceptance of a code of professional conduct. Such a code outlines a minimum level of conduct that is mandatory and enforceable upon its membership. A code of ethics emphasizes both the profession's responsibility to the public as well as to colleagues. Every CPA in the practice of public accounting must become familiar with the AICPA Code of Professional Conduct and its applicability to audit, tax, and consulting services.

The AICPA Code of Professional Conduct consists of Principles, Rules, Interpretations, and Ethics Rulings. The Principles serve as the basic framework for the Rules. The Rules are mandatory and enforceable. Periodically, the Professional Ethics Division of the AICPA issues Ethics Rulings and Interpretations for the purpose of clarifying the Code. The Interpretations render guidance to the accountant as to the scope and applicability of the Rules. Ethics Rulings help to clarify specific situations confronted by the accountant. Figure 8-15 depicts the hierarchy of these components.

Departure from the Rules may result in disciplinary action unless the accountant can justify the departure under the circumstances. Disciplinary action may lead to suspension

QUICK FACTS
The AICPA Code of Professional Conduct includes enforceable Rules.

| **FIGURE 8-15** | HIERARCHY OF THE AICPA'S CODE OF PROFESSIONAL CONDUCT |

Level 1   **Principles**—The Principles provide the framework for the development of the Rules.

Level 2   **Rules**—The Rules serve as the enforceable part of the Code that governs the professional services of the AICPA members.

> Official Section of the Code

Level 3   **Interpretations of the Rules of Conduct**—Interpretations are those that have been adopted by the professional ethics division's executive committee to provide guidelines as to the scope and application of the Rules.

Level 4   **Ethics Rulings**—The Ethics Rulings consist of formal rulings made by the professional ethics division's executive committee. Their Rulings summarize the application of the Rules and Interpretations to particular factual circumstances.

> Members who depart from interpretation of rulings must justify such departures.

or termination of AICPA membership. Furthermore, a violation of professional conduct may result in revocation of a CPA certificate or license to practice by a state board of accountancy. In many cases, the revocation is also sanctioned by the Securities and Exchange Commission.

Although the AICPA's Code of Professional Conduct applies to all members, certain rules are specifically applicable to the independent auditor. Rule 202 requires compliance with the standards and is stated as follows:

> **Rule 202—Compliance with standards.** A member who performs auditing, review, compilation, management consulting, tax, or other professional services shall comply with standards promulgated by bodies designated by Council.[4]

Rule 203 generally prohibits the auditor from expressing an opinion that financial statements are in conformity with generally accepted accounting principles (GAAP) if the statements contain any departure from the official pronouncements of the Financial Accounting Standards Board, its predecessors, or the Governmental Accounting Standards Board. Rule 203 is stated as follows:

> **Rule 203—Accounting principles.** A member shall not (1) express an opinion or state affirmatively that the financial statements or other financial data of any entity are presented in conformity with generally accepted accounting principles or (2) state that he or she is not aware of any material modifications that should be made to such statements or data in order for them to be in conformity with generally accepted accounting principles, if such statements contain any departure from an accounting principle promulgated by bodies designated by Council to establish such principles that has a material effect on the statements taken as a whole. If, however, the statements or data contain such a departure and the member can demonstrate that due to unusual circumstances the financial statements would otherwise have been misleading, the member can comply with the rule by describing the departure, its approximate effects, if practicable, and the reasons why compliance with the principle would result in a misleading statement.[5]

As noted in the above two rules, it is important to emphasize that the CPA must comply with generally accepted auditing standards (GAAS) or PCAOB standards and also have familiarity with generally accepted accounting principles (GAAP) when expressing an audit opinion. Therefore, the practitioner should master the research methodology in order to determine if the audit is in compliance with GAAS and the entity is following GAAP.

> **QUICK FACTS**
>
> An audit opinion requires the CPA to comply with GAAS or PCAOB standards, and review GAAP.

---

[4] AICPA *Professional Standards,* Vol. 2, Section ET-202.

[5] AICPA *Professional Standards,* Vol. 2, Section ET-203.

Rule 203 was clarified with the issuance of the following two Interpretations:

Interpretations under Rule 203—Accounting principles:

203-1—Departures from established accounting principles. Rule 203 was adopted to require compliance with accounting principles promulgated by the body designated by Council to establish such principles. There is a strong presumption that adherence to officially established accounting principles would in nearly all instances result in financial statements that are not misleading.

However, in the establishment of accounting principles it is difficult to anticipate all of the circumstances to which such principles might be applied. This rule therefore recognizes that upon occasion there may be unusual circumstances where the literal application of pronouncements on accounting principles would have the effect of rendering financial statements misleading. In such cases, the proper accounting treatment is that which will render the financial statements not misleading.

The question of what constitutes unusual circumstances as referred to in Rule 203 is a matter of professional judgment involving the ability to support the position that adherence to a promulgated principle would be regarded generally by reasonable men as producing a misleading result.

Examples of events which may justify departures from a principle are new legislation or the evolution of a new form of business transaction. An unusual degree of materiality or the existence of conflicting industry practices are examples of circumstances which would not ordinarily be regarded as unusual in the context of Rule 203.

203-2—Status of FASB and GASB interpretations. Council is authorized under Rule 203 to designate bodies to establish accounting principles. Council has designated the Financial Accounting Standards Board (FASB) as such a body and has resolved that FASB Statements of Financial Accounting Standards, together with those Accounting Research Bulletins and APB Opinions which are not superseded by action of the FASB, constitute accounting principles as contemplated in Rule 203. Council has also designated the Governmental Accounting Standards Board (GASB), with respect to Statements of Governmental Accounting Standards issued in July 1984 and thereafter, as the body to establish financial accounting principles for state and local governmental entities pursuant to rule 203.

In determining the existence of a departure from an accounting principle established by a Statement of Financial Accounting Standards, Accounting Research Bulletin or APB Opinion encompassed by Rule 203, or the existence of a departure from an accounting principle established by a Statement of Governmental Accounting Standards encompassed by Rule 203, the division of professional ethics will construe such Statements, Bulletin or Opinion in the light of any interpretations thereof issued by the FASB or the GASB.[6]

As a result, the recognition of the FASB, its predecessors, and the GASB as the designated bodies in setting GAAP, and the due process that these organizations conduct, their pronouncements are placed in Level One in the Hierarchy of GAAP as identified in Chapter 4.

> **QUICK FACTS**
>
> Interpretation of the AICPA's Rules of Conduct provide guidelines as to the scope and application of the Rules.

AUDITING IN THE PUBLIC SECTOR

Government officials and the general public are concerned about how the public's money was spent and whether government is achieving its goals funded by taxpayer dollars. Thus, to a large degree, the standards and guidelines used in a governmental audit are similar

---

[6] AICPA *Professional Standards*, Vol. 2, Section ET 203.

to auditing requirements in the corporate sector. Federal, state, and local governments have historically placed substantial reliance on the auditing requirements of the AICPA's Auditing Standards Division. However, various governmental regulatory bodies have addressed specific governmental audit concerns.

The GAO's *Government Auditing Standards* (fourth revision in 2003), commonly referred to as the "Yellow Book," are applicable to all governmental organizations, programs, activities, and functions. They have the objective of improving the quality of governmental audits at the federal, state, and local levels. These governmental standards were founded on the premise that governmental accountability should go beyond identifying the amount of funds spent, to measure the manner and effectiveness of the expenditures. Therefore, these standards provide for an audit scope to include financial and compliance auditing as well as auditing for economy, efficiency, and effectiveness of program results. Under federal legislation, federal inspector generals must follow these GAO auditing standards. Also, these standards are audit criteria for federal executive departments and agencies.

Currently, three audit levels affect governments. The first level consists of the generally accepted auditing standards (GAAS) issued by the AICPA. Building upon the AICPA standards are the *Government Auditing Standards* and federal audit requirements. The *Government Auditing Standards*, considered add-ons to GAAS, are also known as "Generally Accepted Government Auditing Standards" (GAGAS) promulgated under the auspices of the U.S. General Accounting Office by the Government Auditing Standards Advisory Board. The federal requirements are found in the OMB Circular A-133, *Audits of States, Local Governments, and Non-Profit Organizations*.

Other major audit guidelines for nonprofit organizations are listed in Figure 8-16. The issuance of the Single Audit Act of 1984 (Public Law 98–502), was particularly important because it incorporated the concept of an entity-wide financial and compliance "single audit." This Act requires an annual audit of any state or local government unit that receives federal financial assistance. The single audit concept thus eliminates the need for separate financial and compliance audits conducted by the various federal agencies from whom the entity has received funding. By Congressional directive, the Director of the Office of Management and Budget (OMB) has the authority to establish policy and guidelines and the mechanisms to implement single, coordinated financial and compliance audits of grant recipients on a government-wide basis.

| FIGURE 8-16 | MAJOR GUIDELINES FOR PUBLIC SECTOR AUDITING |

GAO   (General Auditing Office)
             Government Auditing Standards ("The Yellow Book")

OMB   (Office of Management and Budget)
             "Single Audit Act"

AICPA   (American Institute of CPAs)
             Attestation Standards
             Generally Accepted Auditing Standards (GAAS)
             Audit Guides: Audits of Not-for-Profit Organizations
                             Audits of Federal Government Contractors
                             Audits of State and Local Governmental Units
                             Audits of Health Care Organizations
             Statements of Position

ACCOUNTING SERVICES

In response to the needs of nonpublic clients,[7] regulatory agencies, and the investing public, the public accounting profession offers compilation or review services to clients, rather than conducting a more expensive audit examination in accordance with GAAS. Compilation and review of financial statements are defined as follows:

> **Compilation**—a service presenting, in the form of financial statements, information that is the representation of management without undertaking to express any assurance on the statements.

> **Review**—a service performing inquiry and analytical procedures that provide the accountant with a reasonable basis for expressing limited assurance that there are no material modifications that should be made to the statements in order for them to be in conformity with generally accepted accounting principles or, if applicable, with another comprehensive basis of accounting.[8]

QUICK FACTS

For reviews, use AICPA Statements on Standards for Accounting and Review Services.

Therefore, the basic distinction between these two services is that a review service provides limited assurance about the reliability of unaudited financial data presented by management, whereas a compilation engagement provides no assurance as to the reliability of the data. In a compilation the CPA prepares financial statements only from information supplied by management. The CPA in a compilation need not verify this information furnished by the client and therefore provides no assurance regarding the validity of this information.

The AICPA established guidance for the public accountant for compilation and review services with the issuance of Statements on Standards for Accounting and Review Services (SSARS). To date, the committee has issued ten statements:

1. "Compilation and Review of Financial Statements," Dec. 1978.

2. "Reporting on Comparative Financial Statements," Oct. 1979.

3. "Compilation Reports on Financial Statements Included in Certain Prescribed Forms," Dec. 1981.

4. "Communication Between Predecessor and Successor Accountants," Dec. 1981.

5. "Reporting on Compiled Financial Statements," July 1982.

6. "Reporting on Personal Financial Statements Included in Written Financial Plans," Sept. 1986.

7. "Omnibus Statement on Standards for Accounting and Review Services," Nov. 1992.

8. "Amendment to Statement on Standards for Accounting and Review Services No. 1, Compilation and Review of Financial Statements," Oct. 2000.

9. "Omnibus Statement on Standards for Accounting and Review Services—2002," Nov. 2002.

10. "Attestation Standards: Revision and Recodification," Jan. 2003.

---

[7] The distinction between a public versus nonpublic client is based on whether the entity's securities are traded publicly on a stock exchange or in the over-the-counter market.

[8] Accounting and Review Services Committee, *Statement on Standards for accounting and review services, No. 1,* "Compilation and Review of Financial Statements," AICPA, 1978.

INTERNATIONAL AUDITING

The International Federation of Accountants (IFAC) has had a broad objective to develop a worldwide accounting profession with harmonized standards. To meet the objective relating to auditing standards, the IFAC established the International Auditing Practices Committee (IAPC) to develop and issue International Standards on Auditing (ISAs) on the form and content of audit reports.

The purpose of the International Standards is to improve the uniformity of auditing practices throughout the world. Additionally, the IAPC issues International Auditing Practice Statements (IAPSs) that provide practical assistance in implementing the International Standards, but do not have the authority of the International Standards. Currently, the IFAC has established the International Auditing and Assurance Standards Board (IAASB) that has the responsibility of developing international auditing standards.

The International Standards on Auditing apply to every independent audit of financial information regardless of the type or size of the entity under audit. However, within each country, local regulations govern. To the extent that the ISAs conform to the specific country's regulations, the audit will be considered in accordance with the Standards. In the event that the regulations differ, the members of the IAASB will work towards the implementation of the Standard, if practicable, within the specific country.

ROLE OF JUDGMENT IN ACCOUNTING AND AUDITING RESEARCH

Accountants and auditors exercise professional judgment in considering whether the substance of business transactions differs from the form, in evaluating the adequacy of disclosure, in assessing the probable impact of future events, and in determining materiality limits. This informed judgment on the part of the practitioner is the foundation of the accounting profession. In providing an attest engagement, the result is often the rendering of a considered opinion or principled judgment. In effect, the auditor gathers relevant and reliable information, evaluates and judges its contents, and then formalizes an opinion on the financial information or statements.

A review of current authoritative literature reveals that certain pronouncements on generally accepted accounting principles (GAAP) require disclosure on the applicable accounting principle for a given business transaction. Other pronouncements provide only general guidelines and in some cases suggest acceptable alternative principles. The process of applying professional judgment in choosing among alternatives is not carried out in isolation, but through consultation with other professionals knowledgeable in the area. In rendering his or her professional judgment, the accountant/auditor must exercise critical-thinking skills in the development of a solution or opinion.

QUICK FACTS
Disclosure of accountancy principles varies depending on the authority and accounting judgment.

Statement on Auditing Standards No. 5 makes the following point on the use of professional judgment in determining conformity with GAAP:

.04 The auditor's opinion that financial statements present fairly an entity's financial position, results of operations, and changes in financial position in conformity with generally accepted accounting principles should be based on his judgment as to whether

(a) the accounting principles selected and applied have general acceptance;

(b) the accounting principles are appropriate in the circumstances;

(c) the financial statements, including the related notes, are informative of matters that may affect their use, understanding, and interpretation;

(d) the information presented in the financial statements is classified and summarized in a reasonable manner; that is, neither too detailed nor too condensed; and

(e) the financial statements reflect the underlying events and transactions in a manner that presents the financial position, results of operations, and changes in financial position stated within a range of acceptable limits; that is, limits that are reasonable and practicable to attain in financial statements. [Emphasis added][9]

In order to render an opinion based upon professional judgment, the auditor often considers the opinions of other professionals. In such cases, the practitioner can use several published sources to determine how others have dealt with specific accounting and reporting applications of GAAP. The AICPA publishes *Technical Practice Aids*, which contains the "Technical Information Service." This service consists of inquiries and replies that describe an actual problem that was encountered in practice and the interpretation and recommendations that were provided along with relevant standards and other authoritative sources.

ECONOMIC CONSEQUENCES

Since time is a scarce commodity, the auditor should weigh the cost/benefit tradeoffs in extending the audit research process. The researcher should address the problem until eliminating all reasonable doubt relating to the issue, recognizing the hidden costs of making an improper audit decision. Besides the legal damages from an association with a negligent audit, the auditor can face criminal penalties; SEC, FTC, and other government sanctions; loss of reputation among the auditor's peers; and a significant loss of existing clients in a competitive environment.

SUMMARY

This chapter has presented an overview of assurance services, the attestation standard-setting environment, accounting services, and professional ethics. Familiarity with this information, in particular the authoritative pronouncements that exist, will aid the practitioner in the research process.

In researching an accounting or assurance services issue, the practitioner will be called upon to use professional judgment in the decision-making process. Experience is undoubtedly the primary factor in developing good professional judgment. However, this text presents a research methodology that should aid in the application of professional judgment.

DISCUSSION QUESTIONS

1. What is an assurance service engagement?
2. Define an attest engagement. Is an audit engagement an attest service?
3. Identify three other attest services in addition to the normal financial statement audit.
4. Differentiate between auditing standards and attestation standards.
5. What guidelines exist for the performance of accounting and review services?
6. Differentiate between auditing standards and auditing procedures.

---

[9] AICPA *Professional Standards*, Vol. 1, Section AU-411-04.

7. Discuss the relationship between generally accepted auditing standards (GAAS) and Statements on Auditing Standards (SAS).

8. Discuss the applicability of the first and third general standards of GAAS to accounting and auditing research.

9. Discuss the historical relationship of the Auditing Standards Board, Auditing Standards Executive Committee, and Committee on Auditing Procedure. Also, list the authoritative pronouncements issued by each body.

10. What is the PCAOB? What standards does it issue?

11. State the objective of the Single Audit Act. When is this act applicable?

12. List the primary auditing guidelines for public sector auditing.

13. Explain the importance of the Code of Professional Conduct in the performance of an audit.

14. Explain the significance of Rules 202 and 203 of the AICPA's Code of Professional Conduct.

15. How may accounting or auditing research aid the practitioner in complying with Rules 202 and 203 of the Code of Professional Conduct?

16. What role does professional judgment play in the daily activities of the accountant or auditor?

17. What authoritative auditing literature that has general applicability in practice is considered primary authoritative support?

18. What guidelines are available for the accountant in serving the needs of the non-public client?

19. What authoritative body exists as to the development of international auditing standards?

EXERCISES

1. a. Utilizing PricewaterhouseCoopers' Edgarscan, locate the most recent 10-K filing for a public company and summarize its Management's Discussion and Analysis Section (MD&A).

   b. For the company selected in (a), utilize the benchmarking tool of Edgarscan and report the results of five different ratios for the most current quarter and full year.

2. a. Select a publicly traded company in the airlines industry. Using Price-waterhouseCoopers' Edgarscan and the selected company's home page, prepare a listing of management's mission and business strategies by highlighting the entity's business units, product lines, customers, competition, joint ventures, and any other pertinent information as to business strategies. (*Hint:* Use Edgarscan to find the most recent 10-K filing for the company in addition to the company's home page).

   b. Utilize the benchmarking tool of Edgarscan; select three competitors to the company selected in (a) and prepare a benchmarking report on five attributes comparing the selected company with its competition.

3. Utilizing Figure 2–3 (Universal Elements of Reasoning), identify the eight elements for the following:

   A prospective client has requested a report as to the reliability of its electronic commerce activities on the Internet. You are trying to decide the type of assurance service engagement this would involve.

4. Access the Web site *http://www.Benchnet.com,* and report on three benchmarking and best practices surveys in progress.

5. Access the Web site *http://www.riskmetrics.com*, and report on three different risk-metrics products available.

6. Access Thomson ONE and enter BA in the entry lookup (Boeing Co.).

    a. Click on **News** and summarize the two most recent news headlines about Boeing.

    b. Click on **Related Content** and determine the Return on Assets and Return on Equity ratios for the most current year.

    c. Click on the **Financials** tab and determine the amount of inventory reported for the most current fiscal year.

APPENDIX

CPA Exam Audit Simulation

Following are examples of two simulations similar to those appearing on the CPA exam. Review the opening screens and utilize the AICPA reSOURCE database to answer the questions in the two simulations.

FIGURE A8-1 | SIMULATION SCREEN FOR AUDITING AND ATTESTATION

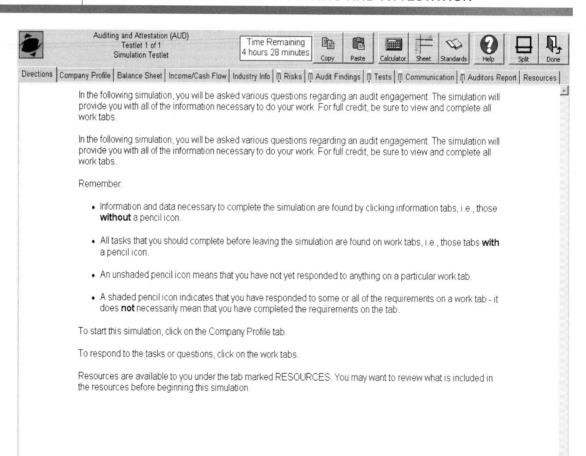

FIGURE A8-2 | OPENING SCREEN AFTER CLICKING ON THE "STANDARDS" ICON

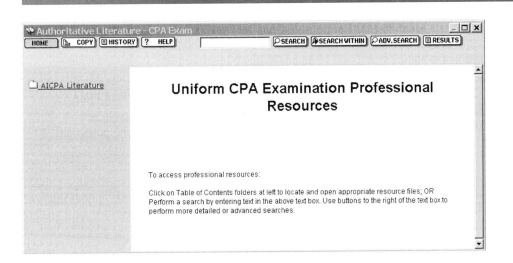

FIGURE A8-3 | OPENING SCREEN AFTER CLICKING ON "AICPA LITERATURE" IN FIGURE A8-2

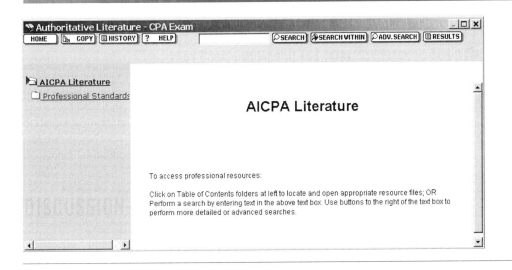

FIGURE A8-4 | SIMULATION 1

DIRECTIONS	The **Directions** tab informs the candidate as to the instructions or question requirements for this particular case simulation.
SITUATION	In addition to completing the audit of Jack's Manufacturing Inc. for the coming year, your firm has also been requested to review the interim financial statements for the first three quarters of the year. The engagement partner has requested your assistance in preparing a draft of the appropriate report for the review.
RESOURCES	(i.e., Financial Statements, Industry Information on Figure A8-1) The **Resources** tab provides various resources (tools) that the candidate will utilize in completing the simulation. Here the candidate might find the financial statements, industry information, or audit workpapers needed to complete various tasks.
ANALYSIS	(i.e., Risks, audit findings, and audit tests on Figure A8-1) Clicking on one of these tabs provides the candidate with detailed information for analysis or completion. Here is where the candidate might input data into drop-down boxes.
COMMUNICATION	Written communication is still an integral part of the CPA exam. Under this tab, the candidate will be required to prepare (type) some form of written communication (i.e., to the client or audit partner) to discuss various accounting, auditing, or tax issues related to the facts presented under the Situation tab.
RESEARCH	Here is where the candidate will be required to research relevant databases. Candidates will then perform keyword searches utilizing AICPA's Checkpoint tax database.

Required: For the above given situation, (1) list at least three keywords that one would utilize to research the issue, (2) utilize the AICPA's database by clicking on the "Standards" icon in Figure A8-1 and perform a keyword search. Cut and paste an example of the report to present to the partner as an example report on interim financial statements.

FIGURE A8-5 | SIMULATION 2

DIRECTIONS	The **Directions** tab informs the candidate as to the instructions or question requirements for this particular case simulation.
SITUATION	You are a new staff auditor for a large-sized client that has two subsidiaries located in foreign countries. Since your firm does not have offices near these subsidiaries, your firm will be using other auditors to aid you in the audit of the parent company. The audit partner on the engagement has requested your assistance as to the type of audit report necessary in order to share responsibility with these other auditors.
RESOURCES	(i.e., Financial Statements, Industry Information in Figure A8-1) The **Resources** tab provides various resources (tools) that the candidate will utilize in completing the simulation. Here the candidate might find the financial statements, industry information, or audit workpapers needed to complete various tasks.
ANALYSIS	(i.e., Risks, audit findings, and audit tests in Figure A8-1) Clicking on one of these tabs provides the candidate with detailed information for analysis or completion. Here is where the candidate might input data into drop-down boxes.
COMMUNICATION	Written communication is still an integral part of the CPA exam. Under the Communication tab, the candidate will be required to prepare (type) some form of written communication (i.e., to the client or audit partner) to discuss various accounting, auditing, or tax issues related to the facts presented under the Situation tab.
RESEARCH	Here is where the candidate will be required to research relevant databases. Candidates will then perform keyword searches utilizing AICPA's Professional Standards database. Required: For the above given situation, (1) utilize the AICPA's database by clicking on the "Standards" icon in Figure A8-1 and perform a keyword search. Identify the authoritative literature citation for your answer as to a shared audit report. (2) Cut and paste an example of the report to present to the partner as an example report on sharing audit responsibility for the consolidated financial statements.

Refining the Research Process

LEARNING OBJECTIVES

After completing this chapter, you should understand:

- How to execute the five basic steps in the research process introduced in Chapter 1.
- The process of identifying the issues or problems to research.
- How to review related accounting, tax, or auditing literature and then collect the evidence.
- Using keyword searches and a reference matrix of authorities.
- The importance of using professional judgment in evaluating the results of research.
- How a client letter and research memorandum document the results of research.
- Lessons learned from the example and research on the CPA exam.
- How to "remain current" with the ever-expanding body of authorities.
- International complexities in the global business economy.

Prior chapters have laid the foundation for conducting effective and efficient applied accounting, tax, and auditing research. Recall the basic five-step research process introduced in Chapter 1, as well as various research databases and tools to use.

This chapter expands upon the application of the five research steps by applying them to a comprehensive problem that illustrates the research process in various areas of accounting and tax through an integrated problem. Specific steps and procedures for conducting and documenting the research process are summarized in Figure 9-1, which presents a flow chart providing an overview of the complete research process. Execute each step and document the findings for every research project.

METHOD OF CONDUCTING RESEARCH

Accountants are confronted with problems relating to the proper accounting treatment for given transactions or the proper financial presentation of accounting data and disclosures. The focus of the research will determine what appropriate alternative principles exist and potential authoritative support for those alternatives. Apply professional judgment in selecting one accounting principle from the list of alternatives. Always use a systematic method for conducting research.

The following example problem demonstrates the application of the research methodology depicted in Figure 9-1. Think through each part of the problem and research steps in order to comprehend the complete research process.

> **EXAMPLE:** Sony is a Japanese multinational company that decided to expand its entertainment business in the United States. Therefore, Sony purchased CBS Records and Columbia pictures to form Sony Music and Sony Pictures. Because of these acquisitions, Sony assumed debt of $1.2 billion and allocated $3.8 billion to

RESEARCH TIPS

Summary of Steps in Conducting Research

Step 1. Identify the Issues or Problem

Step 2. Collect the Evidence

Step 3. Analyze the Results and Identify Alternatives

Step 4. Develop the Conclusions

Step 5. Communicate the Results

FIGURE 9-1 | OVERVIEW OF THE RESEARCH PROCESS

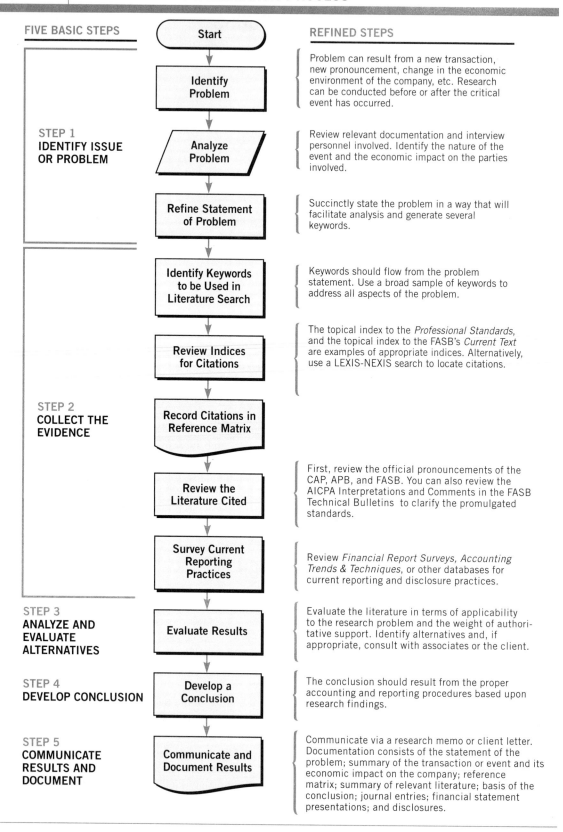

FIVE BASIC STEPS

REFINED STEPS

Start

Identify Problem

Problem can result from a new transaction, new pronouncement, change in the economic environment of the company, etc. Research can be conducted before or after the critical event has occurred.

STEP 1
IDENTIFY ISSUE OR PROBLEM

Analyze Problem

Review relevant documentation and interview personnel involved. Identify the nature of the event and the economic impact on the parties involved.

Refine Statement of Problem

Succinctly state the problem in a way that will facilitate analysis and generate several keywords.

Identify Keywords to be Used in Literature Search

Keywords should flow from the problem statement. Use a broad sample of keywords to address all aspects of the problem.

Review Indices for Citations

The topical index to the *Professional Standards*, and the topical index to the FASB's *Current Text* are examples of appropriate indices. Alternatively, use a LEXIS-NEXIS search to locate citations.

STEP 2
COLLECT THE EVIDENCE

Record Citations in Reference Matrix

Review the Literature Cited

First, review the official pronouncements of the CAP, APB, and FASB. You can also review the AICPA Interpretations and Comments in the FASB Technical Bulletins to clarify the promulgated standards.

Survey Current Reporting Practices

Review *Financial Report Surveys, Accounting Trends & Techniques*, or other databases for current reporting and disclosure practices.

STEP 3
ANALYZE AND EVALUATE ALTERNATIVES

Evaluate Results

Evaluate the literature in terms of applicability to the research problem and the weight of authoritative support. Identify alternatives and, if appropriate, consult with associates or the client.

STEP 4
DEVELOP CONCLUSION

Develop a Conclusion

The conclusion should result from the proper accounting and reporting procedures based upon research findings.

STEP 5
COMMUNICATE RESULTS AND DOCUMENT

Communicate and Document Results

Communicate via a research memo or client letter. Documentation consists of the statement of the problem; summary of the transaction or event and its economic impact on the company; reference matrix; summary of relevant literature; basis of the conclusion; journal entries; financial statement presentations; and disclosures.

goodwill. On Sony's Annual Report filed with the SEC, it reported only two industry segments—electronics and entertainment. While Sony Music was profitable, however, Sony Pictures had produced continued losses of approximately $1 billion.

Sony's founder, Akio Morita, has asked your firm, XYZ, to have its CPAs identify and explain any potential accounting or tax concerns from these facts, but does not want you to worry about consolidations.

Step 1—Identify the Issues or Problems

To start the research, reread the problem provided to establish the facts and identify the issues or problems in clear and concise statements. Approach this task systematically by using the following three-part approach:

1. Make a preliminary identification of the problem.

2. Analyze the problem.

3. Refine the statement of the problem.

Make a Preliminary Identification of the Problem. First, recognize potential problems in accounting, tax, and auditing. Often company management, such as the controller or tax director, initiates this research process.

Because initial statements of potential problems are usually very general and vague, subsequent problem analysis and refining the statement of the problem is crucial.

> **EXAMPLE:** Can Sony write down or amortize the goodwill?
>
> Did Sony's financial statement presentation of two industries comply with relevant authorities?

Analyze the Problem. Analyzing the problem often requires one to go back and acquire more information or facts. Certain types of facts, such as related-party situations and dates, are almost always relevant.

Problem analysis is similar to an auditor conducting the planning for an audit. The auditor will acquire more information about the business. One might look at the relevant corporate web sites to acquire some insights. If one looks closely at the web sites, they usually offer a link to "About" the company, which explains more about the history and current structure of these companies.

> **EXAMPLE:** Corporate web sites are available for Sony, Sony Online Entertainment, Sony Music, and Sony Pictures.

A researcher might also look at the SEC filings, such as Form 20-F, the annual report for a foreign-owned entity. Included in this report is such information as the company's management, the board of directors, key information about the company's financial data, operating and financial revenue prospects, major shareholders and related party transactions, and qualitative and quantitative disclosures about the market risk, and the Code of Ethics for senior financial officers.

> **EXAMPLE:** Sony has filed form 20-F for several years. These are publically available on the Web.

Basic knowledge of the law and professional authorities helps one to determine what additional facts one needs to acquire. Thus, a professional often refines the problem analysis after conducting some research in Step 2 (Collect the Evidence). The professional may also need to ask the client for additional specific information.

> **EXAMPLE 1:** Since the treatment for goodwill changed in 2001 for accounting purposes and 1993 for tax purposes, the year for Sony's acquisitions is critical. Assume the desired analysis is for the current year (although you can actually look up the real year on the Web).

EXAMPLE 2: The XYZ, CPAs, review Sony's Form 20-F and find the following information:

- When Sony purchased the motion pictures operations, it projected a loss for only 5 years, since it assumed that the motion pictures entertainment would become profitable.

- Sony suffered a significant loss after amortization and the costs of financing the acquisition for the past four years. Moreover, in the current year, Sony Pictures sustained a loss of nearly $450 million, double the amount that Sony had planned. To date, Sony Pictures have had total net losses of nearly $ 1 billion.

- Early in the year, Sony declared that it had written down $2.7 billion of goodwill associated with the acquisition of Sony Pictures.

- Sony combined the results of Sony Music and Sony Pictures together and reported them as Sony Entertainment. Sony Entertainment showed little profit; Sony's consolidated financial statements did not disclose the losses from Sony Pictures.

Refine the Statement of the Problem. After the preliminary problem identification and problem analysis using the initial research, restate the research problems with more sophisticated references incorporating the critical facts and the main authorities. Here is where the researcher would also start to list keywords to enter into the various databases or web sites to begin the research process.

EXAMPLE 1: Determine whether an annual write-down of goodwill and its impairment is necessary under FAS 142 for an acquisition of a company with continued losses.

EXAMPLE 2: Determine whether financial statement disclosures of two segments are needed when one industry has two businesses with different financial trends, to avoid misleading financial statement users under Securities Exchange Act section 13(a).

Step 2—Collect the Evidence

The collection of evidence generally involves (1) a review of related accounting, tax, or auditing authorities and (2) sometimes a survey of present practice.

Review the Authorities. Remember that the accounting and auditing pronouncements have a hierarchical structure of authority and are classified into primary or secondary sources. Begin the review of authorities with the highest level authorities, statutory law for tax, and official standard-setting bodies for accounting—generally the FASB or, in certain cases, the SEC, GASB, or others. Note the scope of any authorities or pronouncements reviewed. Save time by first scanning potential authorities for their relevance. Avoid making detailed reviews of authorities and pronouncements that are not applicable to the specific issues and facts, for the transaction under investigation.

Do not completely ignore pronouncements that may not specifically address the research problem, but are "colorable authorities" (those having potential application) or are related to it. Review them for possible references to other appropriate sources; discussions within these authorities or pronouncements may add insights into the problem at hand. These sources may aid the development of a solution by analogy. If the primary sources are not on point, extend the search to secondary authorities such as industrial practices, published research studies, and other respected sources. Begin the review of primary sources with those that have the highest level of authority, as indicated by the law or the hierarchy of GAAP. After exhausting the primary sources, proceed to secondary sources.

Developing keywords from the issues is essential to locating relevant authoritative literature. A statement of the problem generates the initial keywords necessary to access the appropriate sections of the authorities and professional literature. Sometimes one

QUICK FACTS

Summary of Step 1: Identify the Issues or Problems

1. Make a preliminary identification of the problem
2. Analyze the problem
3. Refine the statement of the problem

FIGURE 9-2 | BRAINSTORMING POTENTIAL KEYWORDS FOR THE EXAMPLE

Accounting Authorities Search:

Goodwill

Impairment

Segment Disclosure

Write down

Financial statements disclosure

Business combination

Tax Authorities Search:

Amortization

Goodwill

Business Knowledge Search:

Sony

Sony Music

Sony Entertainment

Sony Pictures

identifies additional keywords after the search has begun, as one acquires more knowledge about various "terms of art."

From the analysis and statement of the problem stated previously, the researcher can identify the keywords in Figure 9-2 for a literature and web site search.

Use Keywords to Locate Relevant Authorities. Finding relevant legal and professional authorities is akin to traveling through a maze. The researcher may encounter cross-references that circle back to original starting points or keywords that prove useless in the search. Conduct the search for authorities and literature carefully and systematically to avoid making the process frustrating and inefficient. For accounting research, use the FASB's Current Text in the FARS database to systematically conduct the literature search.

One potential path through the Current Text for accounting authorities is shown in the diagram in Figure 9-3. Sometimes a diagram aids the researcher in conducting and documenting an efficient literature search. The starting point for the search is the list of keywords identified from the statement of the problem. Review these terms for relevant citations, cross-references to other terms in the Current Text, whether broader, narrower, or related terms. Examine these additional terms for potential citations. List the Current Text citations in logical order, using the hierarchy of relevant authorities, such as for GAAP or legal authorities. Always start with the highest level of primary authority. Use lesser authorities to explain or further interpret part of the stronger authority.

FIGURE 9-3 | ACCOUNTING KEYWORD/CITATION DIAGRAM FOR THE EXAMPLE

Keyword	Reference Descriptions	Citation
Goodwill	Goodwill and Other Intangible Assets	FAS 109, par 263, FAS 142, par B220
Write Down		No relevant citation
Impairment	Goodwill and relevant impairment test Recognition and measurement of an impairment loss	FAS 142, par B159 167, and 205 FAS 142, par 29
Financial Statement disclosures	Recognition and measurement	CON 5, par 7
Segment disclosure	Disclosure of segments	FAS 131, par 90-96, 101 FAS 14, par 22, 27
Business Combination	Business Combination	FAS 141

After identifying all relevant citations, locate and review the authoritative sources and literature. Do not rely on summaries, even if this is the firm's practice. Reference the primary authorities as precisely as possible, such as sections of the *FASB Accounting Standards—Current Text*, paragraphs within an FAS, or subparagraph within a relevant IRC provision for tax.

For accounting research, use the Topical Index of the Current Text to locate specific paragraphs within this section. The paragraph references are located in the Topical Index under the relevant keyword. Construct a reference matrix similar to that shown in Figure 9-4 to facilitate identification of section references and original pronouncements.

EXAMPLE ON GOODWILL: The following is a summary of the relevant portions on goodwill from the accounting literature and tax authorities:

ACCOUNTING FOR GOODWILL: Goodwill is a separate line item in the statement of financial position. (FAS 141, par 43.) Goodwill is NOT amortizable on Business Combinations after June 30, 2001. (FAS 141, par 18.) Not amortizing goodwill represents that goodwill is an intangible asset with an indefinite useful life.(FAS 141, par 16.)

Each reporting unit must annually test goodwill for potential impairment, or more frequently if the events and circumstances change. (FAS-142, par 26 & 28.) A reporting unit is defined in FAS-131, par 16 to include a segment of an operating unit for which disclosure is needed. The notes to the financial statements must disclose each goodwill impairment loss in accordance with FAS 131, par 47, if the loss is probable and can be reasonably estimated. The impairment is measured by comparing the fair value to the reported carrying value of goodwill. (FAS 142, par 19.)

Goodwill recognized prior to the effective date of FAS 142 (Dec. 15, 2001) is accounted for in accordance with APB-17, which presumed that goodwill had a finite life and mandated an arbitrary ceiling of 40 years for amortization.

TAX TREATMENT OF GOODWILL: Goodwill is amortizable under IRC section 197(a), as defined under IRC section 197(d)(1)(A). However, the tax-payer must acquire the goodwill after the enactment of this Code section, IRC sec. 197(c)(1)(A), and the taxpayer must hold the amortizable intangible asset in connection with the conduct of a trade or business. Goodwill is defined as "the value of a trade or business attributable to the expectancy of continued customer patronage" under Reg. sec. 1.197- 2(b)(1).

EXAMPLE ON SEGMENT DISCLOSURE: The following is a summary of the relevant portions of segment disclosure from the accounting and SEC accounting literature:

FIGURE 9-4 | REFERENCE MATRIX FOR THE EXAMPLE

Keyword	Current Text Section	FASB Statement
Goodwill	G40.116	FAS 141, par 43
Business Combination	B51.156	FAS 141, par 43
	B51.160	FAS 141, par F1
Financial Statement	G40.142	FAS 142, par 43
Impairment	G40.116-.137	FAS 142, par 18-38
Segment	S30.113-116	FAS 131, par 14-17

A public business enterprise must report in its annual financial statements information about operating segments. (FAS 131, par 9). The objective of segment disclosure is to provide users of financial statements with information about the business' different types of business activities and different economic environments. Operating segments earn revenues and expenses, have results regularly reviewed by management, and have discrete financial information available. (FAS 131, par 10.) Operating segments should exist if the revenue is 10% or more of the combined revenues, or assets are 10% or more of the combined assets.

The type of segment information to disclose includes general information such as the types of products and services from which each reportable segment derives its revenues; information about the reported segment profit or loss, segment assets, and the basis of measurement; reconciliations of the totals of segment revenues, reported profit or loss, assets, and other significant items to corresponding business enterprise amounts; and interim period information.

The Exchange Act of 1934 (1934 Act), Section 13(a) requires that every issuer of a security must periodically file reports with the SEC, complying with the Section 12 requirements. The periodic reports must include any information to ensure the required financial statements are not misleading in light of the circumstances. (1934 Act Rule 12[b]-20 [17 C.F.R. sec. 40.12b-20].) 1934 Act Rules 13a-1 and 13a-16 require foreign-owned companies with registered securities to file Form 20-F, the annual financial statements. The SEC issued an interpretive release that the disclosure is intended to give the investor an opportunity to see the company through the eyes of management by providing both a short- and long-term analysis of the business . . . (Rel. No. 33-6835, 34-26831 [May 18, 1989].)

RESEARCH TIPS

After reviewing relevant sections in the Current Text, read the Original Pronouncement that is on point.

After reviewing relevant sections in the Current Text on each topic, the researcher should read relevant Original Pronouncements—FASB Statement No. 141 on goodwill and FAS 131 on segment disclosure—to obtain additional insight into the background and rationale underlying these key standards.

Review the Accounting Literature. After the researcher has used the FASB's Financial Accounting Research System (FARS Online) to find relevant, authoritative citations to

FIGURE 9-5 | FARS INITIAL MENU

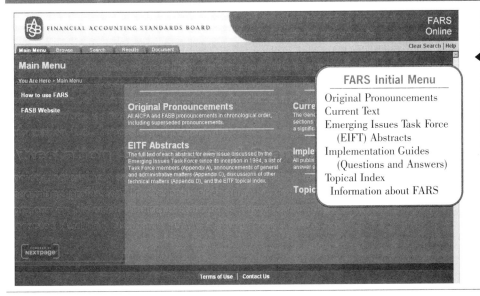

RESEARCH TOOLS

Internet

FARS

LexisNexis

AICPA reSOURCE

PwC Edgarscan

Thomson ONE

RIA Checkpoint SE

ACL

i2

help solve research dilemmas, LexisNexis provides an alternative location where FARS contains very limited information.

Opening FARS Online provides a menu similar to that found in Figure 9-5. The researcher can select Original Pronouncements, Current Text, EITF Abstracts, Implementation Guides (Questions and Answers), Topical Index, and Information about FARS. Researchers unfamiliar with a database may wish to start the process of using FARS by clicking on a tutorial or explanation of the database, such as the "About FARS" icon.

After becoming familiar with the FARS process, the researcher should then click on the Topical Index icon as shown in Figure 9-5, revealing an alphabetical listing of links to relevant topics, as shown in Figure 9-6. The researcher then clicks on the **G** icon to find *Goodwill*, and the FARS program creates a Topical Index (shown in Figure 9-7).

Focus on "Goodwill" by scrolling down in Figure 9-7 and click on **Section G40.116-137** of the Current Text. This process locates the authoritative language found in Figure 9-8.

Alternatively, click directly on the icon under the Current Text Section of FARS "G40 Goodwill and Other Intangible Assets" (Figure 9-9) or under the Original Pronouncements Section of FARS "FAS142" (Figures 9-10 and 9-11). One could click directly on the "General Standards" icon in the Current Text Section and then scroll down to to produce the Original Pronouncements "FAS 142" on Goodwill as shown in Figure 9-11.

Survey Present Practice. In addition to a review of authorities, particularly for accounting and auditing research, Step 2 also includes collecting the evidence to determine how other companies with similar circumstances or transactions have handled the accounting and reporting procedures. This survey could include a review of *Accounting Trends and Techniques* or *Financial Reporting Surveys,* as well as a discussion of the issue with colleagues via the Internet. However, one must exercise care in protecting client confidentiality. Thus, one normally does not discuss any specifics with professionals outside of one's accounting firm.

Sometimes, the researcher will take advantage of the many available relevant web sites and other accounting, tax, and auditing resources available on the Internet. Researchers

FIGURE 9-6   FARS LINKS TO RELEVANT TOPICS

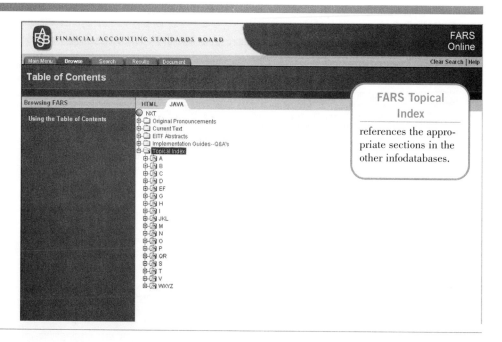

FIGURE 9-7 | FARS TOPICAL INDEX EXAMPLES

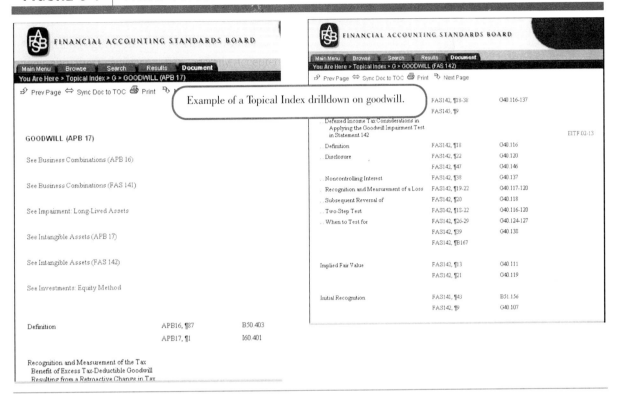

Example of a Topical Index drilldown on goodwill.

FIGURE 9-8 | SECTION G40. 116-137 OF THE *CURRENT TEXT ON GOODWILL*

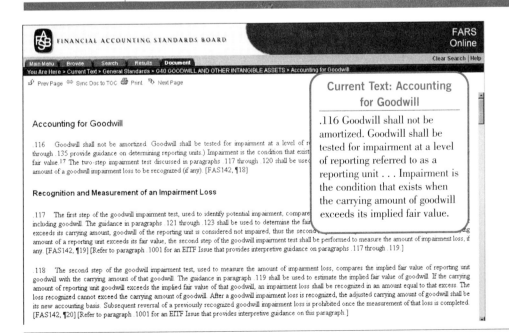

FIGURE 9-9 | FARS "G40 GOODWILL AND OTHER INTANGIBLE ASSETS"

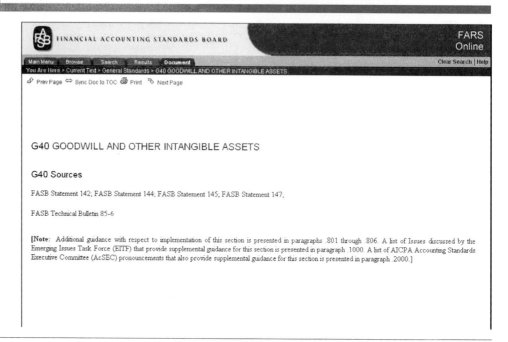

FIGURE 9-10 | FASB ORIGINAL PRONOUNCEMENTS MENU

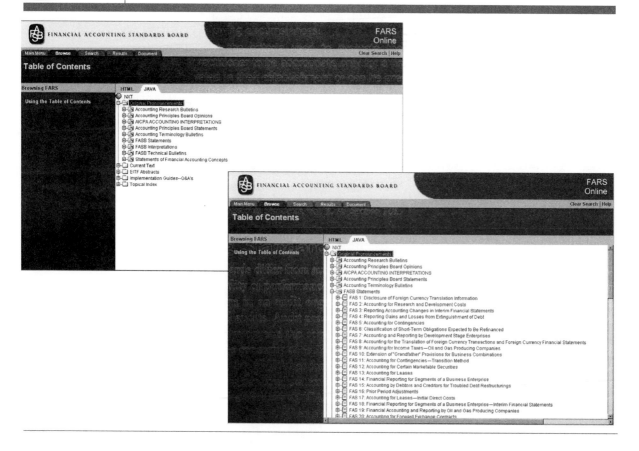

FIGURE 9-11 ORIGINAL PRONOUNCEMENTS "FAS 142" ON GOODWILL

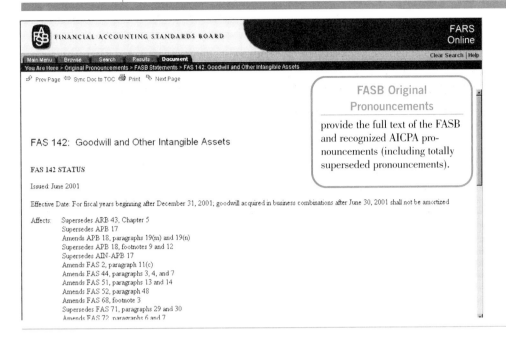

can make "hot links" to valuable web sites, such as the information in government agencies (e.g., the EDGAR database available from the SEC), financial markets and services (e.g., the New York and American Stock Exchanges), professional organizations (e.g., the AICPA and Institute of Management Accountants), and search tools and engines (e.g., Yahoo! and Infoseek). Reviewing these web sites can help the researcher quickly find the latest information on the topic in question.

> **EXAMPLE:** Using the Google search engine to search for the topic "Goodwill and other intangible assets" derives a total of 157,000 hits, as shown in Figure 9-12. One of the earliest links appearing provides a summary of FASB Statement No.142 as shown in Figure 9-13.

A researcher should investigate the significant businesses within the relevant industry. One could also use LexisNexis, clicking Business > Accounting > Industry Comparison to see various articles on a business.

> **EXAMPLE:** An article shows that Sony Music is the second largest music company.

Step 3—Analyze the Results and Identify Alternatives

Exercise professional judgment in evaluating results and identifying alternatives. Review the evidence carefully and identify a tentative conclusion for each issue raised. Furthermore, evaluate the quality and amount of authoritative support for each alternative. Sometimes a researcher reviews the evidence with other accountants knowledgeable in the field.

> **EXAMPLE:** Recall the refined statement of the problem for Sony was whether an annual write-down of goodwill was necessary under FAS 142 for an acquisition of Sony Picture, after continued losses. The second concern was whether financial statement disclosures of Sony and Sony Entertainment were adequate under Securities Exchange Act section 13(a) when Sony Entertainment had two businesses (music and pictures) with different financial trends.

QUICK FACTS

Summary of Step 2: Collect the Evidence

1. Review accounting, tax, or auditing authorities
2. Sometimes survey present practice

FIGURE 9-12 | GOOGLE "GOODWILL" SEARCH

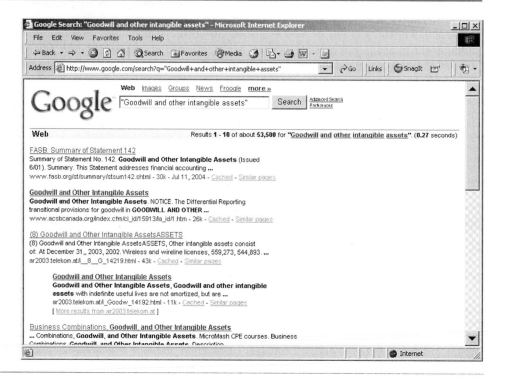

FIGURE 9-13 | SUMMARY OF FASB STATEMENT NO. 142

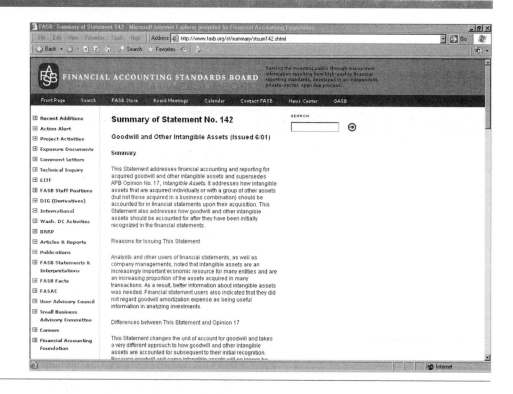

Additional facts were identified through the examination of related documents and discussion with persons involved. The following determinations were made applying the authorities previously discussed to the facts:

1. The carrying value of Sony Pictures exceeded its fair value; the carrying amount of Sony Pictures' goodwill exceeded the implied fair value of Sony Pictures' goodwill. The impairment of goodwill loss was probable and can be reasonably estimated under FAS 142.

2. Sony should report separately information on each operating segment that met any of the 10% quantitative thresholds under FAS 131.

3. Sony may NOT combine Sony Music and Sony Pictures as one reportable segment, for any of the following reasons: They do not have similar economic characteristics, these businesses are not similar in the nature of the products, the nature of the production processes, the type or class of customer for their products and services, and the methods used to distribute their products.

4. Sony should disclose Sony Music and Sony Pictures segmental information, providing the types of products from which each reportable segment derives its revenues; information about their reported segment profit or loss; any reconciliations needed of the total segment revenues; and interim period information.

5. The amount assigned to goodwill acquired was significant in relation to the total cost of acquiring Sony Pictures; therefore, Sony must disclose the following information for goodwill in the notes to Sony Entertainment's financial statements: (1) the total amount of goodwill and the expected amount deductible for tax purposes and (2) the amount of goodwill by reportable segment.

6. The accounting literature search provides authoritative support for recognizing, writing down goodwill of an acquired entity with continuous losses. When a loss is probable and can be reasonably estimated, write down goodwill. FAS 141 and FAS 142 address the impairment of goodwill and its disclosure. On the other hand, FAS 131 and FAS 141 all require that Sony provide separate financial reporting for Sony Pictures because Sony Pictures and Sony Music don't share similar economic characteristics.

Step 4—Develop the Conclusion

Develop a well-reasoned, well-supported conclusion as to the appropriate resolution of each issue. In the illustrative problem, the authoritative literature found through the research process supports the write-down of the goodwill of an acquired entity with continuous loss. The amount is equal to the difference between the carrying value of goodwill and the fair value. The financial statement disclosure of only two industries when one industry has two businesses with different financial trends is misleading under Securities Exchange Act section 13(a).

The conclusion is often placed after the statement of the issue. If there is more than one issue, provide more than one conclusion. Conclusions are generally very short statements.

EXAMPLE

• Issue 1: Whether an annual write-down of goodwill and its impairment is necessary under FAS 142 for an acquisition of a company with continued losses.

CONCLUSION: FAS 142 requires the write-down of goodwill of an acquired entity with continuous losses.

• Issue 2: Whether financial statement disclosures of two segments are needed when one industry has two businesses with different financial trends, to avoid making misleading financial statement to users under Securities Exchange Act section 13(a).

CONCLUSION: The financial statement disclosure of only two industries when one industry has two businesses with different financial trends is misleading under Securities Exchange Act section 13(a) and needs revising under FAS 131.

Step 5—Communicate the Results

Once the researcher has determined a solution to the research problem, he or she should present the conclusion concisely and clearly to the client, often in a short client letter.

Thorough documentation is a crucial part of the entire research process. The following information is included in a longer memo form documentation:

1. A statement of the the relevant facts and the issues or problems.

2. A summary of the conclusions.

3. References to legal and authoritative literature used, along with a brief explanation of the relevant parts of the authority.

4. The application of authorities, including a description of the authoritative support for each alternative, as well as an explanation of why the alternatives were discarded and the recommended principle or procedure was selected.

More detailed documentation exists in a research memorandum, such as shown in Figure 9-14.

Accounting firms have slightly different structures for their memos and documentation approaches. An example of a documentation worksheet that an accounting firm might use to organize the pertinent research information for its records is shown in Figure 9-15. Given the time pressures within the profession, sometimes the relevant portions of the authorities are simply copied and pasted into a document, and then attached to the document worksheet. While the authors advocate as much precision as possible, given current practices in accounting research, the example document worksheet provides the authors' view of the absolute minimum documentation needed for general references to the accounting authorities, rather than references to the precise paragraphs.

Although most accountants do not currently cite precisely where in the accounting authority the support for the statement arises, the authors expect that level of precision will increase in future years. The combination of more documentation requirements and potential penalties for lack of due professional care should motivate an increased level of precision and sophistication in referencing the authorities. The lack of citing within the standard creates the appearance of using a summary of the standard, rather than the primary source document. A more detailed process is more likely to assure the reviewer that the researcher has an understanding of relevant details within the standard.

LESSONS LEARNED AND RESEARCH ON THE CPA EXAM

Make the example in this chapter even more valuable by looking up each authority cited. This process of reading the authorities will give the researcher a better feel for the real research process.

The inspiration for this case example arose from SEC Accounting and Auditing Enforcement Release No. 1061. While the case oversimplifies the facts, it lays a foundation from which the reader is encouraged to tackle the entire case.

Not all accountants will have work involving public companies with complex problems; however, an understanding of sophisticated SEC accounting research is important for comprehending the potential regulatory environment that all accountants could face if additional crises arise in the profession.

FIGURE 9-14 | MEMORANDUM

RE: Sony's Goodwill and Segment Reporting

FACTS:

Sony is a Japanese multinational company that decided to expand its entertainment business in the United States. Therefore, Sony purchased CBS Records and Columbia pictures to form Sony Music and Sony Pictures. Because of these acquisitions, Sony assumed debt of $1.2 billion and allocated $3.8 billion to goodwill. On Sony's Annual Report filed with the SEC, it reported only two industry segments—electronics and entertainment. Sony Music was profitable; however, Sony Pictures had produced continued losses of approximately $1 billion.

When Sony purchased the motion pictures operations, it projected a loss for only five years, since it assumed that the motion pictures entertainment would become profitable. However, Sony suffered a significant loss after amortization and the costs of financing the acquisition for the past four years. Moreover, in the current year, Sony Pictures sustained a loss of nearly $450 million, double the amount that Sony had planned. To date, Sony Pictures has had total net losses of nearly $ 1 billion.

Early in the year, Sony declared that it had written down $2.7 billion goodwill associated with the acquisition of Sony Pictures. Sony combined the results of Sony Music and Sony Pictures together and reported them as Sony Entertainment. Sony Entertainment showed little profit; Sony's consolidated financial statements did not disclose the losses from Sony Pictures.

ISSUES:

1. Whether an annual write-down of goodwill and its impairment is necessary under FAS 142 for an acquisition of a company with continued losses.
2. Whether financial statement disclosures of two segments are needed when one industry has two businesses with different financial trends, to avoid misleading financial statement users under Securities Exchange Act section 13(a).

CONCLUSIONS:

1. FAS 142 requires the write-down of goodwill of an acquired entity with continuous losses.
2. The financial statement disclosure of only two industries when one industry has two businesses with different financial trends is misleading under Securities Exchange Act section 13(a) and needs revising under FAS 131.

AUTHORITIES ON GOODWILL:

ACCOUNTING FOR GOODWILL: Goodwill is a separate line item in the statement of financial position. (FAS 141, par 43.) Goodwill is *not* amortizable on Business Combinations after June 30, 2001. (FAS 141, par 18.) Not amortizing goodwill represents that goodwill is an intangible asset with an indefinite useful life. (FAS 141, par 16.)

Each reporting unit must annually test goodwill for potential impairment, or more frequently if the events and circumstances change. (FAS-142, par 26 & 28.) A reporting unit is defined in FAS-131, par 16 to include segments of an operating unit for which disclosure is needed. The notes to the financial statements must disclose each goodwill impairment loss in accordance with FAS 131, par 47, if the loss is probable and can be reasonably estimated. The impairment is measured by comparing the fair value to the reported carrying value of goodwill. (FAS 142, par 19.)

Goodwill recognized prior to the effective date of FAS 142 (Dec. 15, 2001) is accounted for in accordance with APB-17, which presumed that goodwill had a finite life and mandated an arbitrary ceiling of 40 years for amortization.

TAX TREATMENT OF GOODWILL: Goodwill is amortizable under IRC section 197(a), as defined under IRC section 197(d)(1)(A). However, the taxpayer must acquire the goodwill after the enactment of this Code section, IRC sec. 197(c)(1)(A), and the taxpayer must hold the amortizable intangible asset in connection with the conduct of a trade or business.

FIGURE 9-14 | MEMORANDUM (CONTINUED)

Goodwill is defined as "the value of a trade or business attributable to the expectancy of continued customer patronage" under Reg. sec. 1.197- 2(b)(1).

AUTHORITIES ON SEGMENT DISCLOSURE:

A public business enterprise must report in its annual financial statements information about operating segments. (FAS 131, par 9.) The objective of segment disclosure is to provide users of financial statements with information about the business's different types of business activities and different economic environments. Operating segments earn revenues and expenses, have results regularly reviewed by management, and have discrete financial information available. (FAS 131, par 10.) Operating segments should exist if the revenue is 10% or more of the combined revenues, or assets are 10% or more of the combined assets.

The type of segment information to disclose includes general information such as the types of products and services from which each reportable segment derives its revenues; information about the reported segment profit or loss, segment assets, and the basis of measurement; reconciliations of the totals of segment revenues, reported profit or loss, assets, and other significant items to corresponding business enterprise amounts; and interim period information.

The Exchange Act of 1934 (1934 Act), Section 13(a) requires that every issuer of a security must periodically file reports with the SEC, complying with the Section 12 requirements. The periodic reports must include any information to ensure the required financial statements are not misleading in light of the circumstances. (1934 Act, Rule 12[b]-20 [17 C.F.R. sec. 240.12b-20].) 1934 Act Rules 13a-1 and 13a-16 require foreign-owned companies with registered securities to file Form 20-F, the annual financial statements. The SEC issued an interpretive release that the disclosure is intended to give the investor an opportunity to see the company through the eyes of management by providing both a short and long term analysis of the business. . . (Rel. No. 33-6835, 34-26831 [May 18, 1989].)

APPLICATION OF AUTHORITIES:

1. The carrying value of Sony Pictures exceeded its fair value; the carrying amount of Sony Pictures' goodwill exceeded the implied fair value of Sony Pictures' goodwill. The impairment of goodwill loss was probable and can be reasonably estimated under FAS 142.
2. Sony should report separately information about each operating segment that met any of the 10% quantitative thresholds under FAS 131.
3. Sony may NOT combine Sony Music and Sony Pictures as one reportable segment for any of the following reasons: They do not have similar economic characteristics: these businesses are *not* similar in the nature of the products, the nature of the production processes, the type or class of customer for their products and services, and the methods used to distribute their products.
4. Sony should disclose Sony Music and Sony Pictures segmental information, providing the types of products from which each reportable segment derives its revenues, information about their reported segment profit or loss, any reconciliations needed of the total segment revenues, and interim period information.
5. The amount assigned to goodwill acquired was significant in relation to the total cost of acquiring Sony Pictures, therefore, Sony must disclose the following information for goodwill in the notes to Sony Entertainment's financial statements: (1) the total amount of goodwill and the expected amount deductible for tax purposes and (2) the amount of goodwill by reportable segment.
6. The accounting literature search provides authoritative support for recognizing writing down goodwill of an acquired entity with continuous losses. When a loss is probable and can be reasonably estimated, write down goodwill. FAS 141 and FAS 142 address the impairment of goodwill and its disclosure. On the other hand, FAS 131 and FAS 141 require that Sony provide separate financial reporting for Sony Pictures. Sony Pictures and Sony Music don't share similar economic characteristics.

FIGURE 9-15 | MINIMUM DOCUMENTATION WORKSHEET OF ACCOUNTING/AUDITING RESEARCH

Client information

Name: Sony Corporation of America

Address: 550 Madison Ave, 33rd Floor New York, NY 10022-3211

Client code #118

I. Problem Identification or Statement of the Problems:

Whether an annual write-down of goodwill under FAS 142 was necessary for an acquisition of a company with continued losses.

Whether financial statement disclosures of only two industries when one industry had two businesses with different financial trends violated FAS 131 and was misleading under Securities Exchange Act section 13(a).

Contact Person (Client): Akio Morita—Chairman Kimiko Tanaka— Administrative Assistant

II. Research Evidence (Keywords Utilized):

Disclosure
Goodwill
Impairment
Segment disclosure
Business Combination

References (Citations):

FASB 131, par. 13-31
FASB 141, par. 14-18
    par. 43, 47, 50, F1
FASB 142
APB 16
IRC section 197
1934 Exchange Act Section 13 (a)

Database (library resources) Utilized:

FARS Database
FASB Stds-Current Text
Accounting Trends and Techniques
RIA Checkpoint
Internet sites

III. Alternatives Available:

No other alternatives are permissible.

IV. Conclusions:

FAS 142 requires the write-down of goodwill of an acquired entity with continuous losses.

The financial statement disclosure of only two industries when one industry has two businesses with different financial trends is misleading under Securities Exchange Act section 13(a) and needs revising under FAS 131.

While the CPA Exam research questions will present shorter questions, with more limited authorities than provided in the full databases, the process is similar. However, the AICPA's Test Tips for CPA exam candidates notes the following software limitations: (1) misspelled keywords used in the search engine are not corrected, (2) the search engine results may require scrolling down a window, (3) there is no back button in the authoritative literature, but one can use the history button to list recently visited pages, and (4) one can copy and paste only one paragraph at a time from the authoritative literature.

REMAINING CURRENT

Remaining current with the ever-expanding accounting, tax, and auditing authorities is essential. Adopt some of the following techniques to save valuable professional time.

1. **Use checklists**—Use a checklist for remaining current. Accountants prepare listings of new pronouncements and update them periodically with indications as to which clients a pronouncement may affect. Pronouncements having no direct immediate impact on any client are placed in a "rainy day" reading file.

RESEARCH TIPS

Remaining current
about authorities
will make future
research projects
easier.

2. **Prepare summary of authorities**—Prepare summaries of new authorities at specific intervals and distribute to all staff members. Such memos identify and describe new legal authorities and pronouncements.

3. **Read periodicals**—Successful accountants regularly read many business and accounting periodicals that summarize and explain new authorities. For example, reading *The Wall Street Journal*, the AICPA's *Journal of Accountancy*, and a leading professional publication in one's particular area, such as *Management Accounting* or *Tax Adviser*, helps the professional remain current.

4. **Review accounting newsletters**—Many organizations publish accounting or tax newsletters to update practitioners on current events. Major newsletters by organizations include the following:

   - *FASB Status Report.* This monthly publication, issued by the Financial Accounting Standards Board, covers FASB official actions and releases. It periodically reports the agenda of the FASB in addition to summary comments on recently issued statements, exposure drafts, or technical bulletins.

   - *Action Alert.* The FASB issues a weekly publication on actions and future meetings.

   - *GASB Action Report.* Similar in content to the FASB newsletter, the Governmental Accounting Standards Board issues quarterly reports of the GASB comments on GASB statements, exposure drafts, interpretations, or technical bulletins.

   - *The CPA Letter.* This newsletter, published by the AICPA, contains current information concerning the profession. Such topics include AICPA board business, new pronouncements on accounting and auditing, disciplinary actions against members, upcoming events, and briefs on events in Washington.

5. **Use the Internet**—Use the newsgroups on the Internet to keep abreast of topics of interest to one and one's clients. Some practitioners have developed personal web pages that capture relevant information on a timely basis, which they then review.

Remaining knowledgeable on every detail of all the new authorities is impossible. However, every practitioner must develop and consistently use techniques to keep as current as possible, especially with authorities and pronouncements that directly affect his or her clients. Failure to remain current could violate one's professional responsibilities and lead to penalties, lawsuits, and other potential problems.

INTERNATIONAL COMPLEXITIES

In an increasingly global economy, one may also desire to research the legal and professional authorities in another country, in order to have a more sophisticated discussion with accounting professionals in other countries.

One should not assume that all parts of the world have as much professional commitment and as many potential penalties to ensure due diligence in researching and applying the appropriate authorities. Thus, increasingly, accountants are accessing the authorities in other countries to ask other professionals very sophisticated questions.

LexisNexis has various international legal authorities, useful particularly for tax research in another country. One is increasingly able to acquire a subscription on the Web to foreign tax services, such as CCH Canadian. Access an index to web sites in foreign countries, such as *http://www.taxsites.com*, that may have relevant accounting, tax, and auditing authorities.

QUICK FACTS

International
complexities
usually require
extensive research.

The International Accounting Standards Board has a web site offering summary information and subscription access to its full set of standards.

Various secondary literature is also increasingly available. The World Catalog, accessible through some university libraries, is a window to the world's libraries. It was built by the Online Computer Library Center member libraries.

SUMMARY

The professional accountant who remains current and has developed skills in researching accounting, tax, and auditing issues increases management's confidence and respect in his or her work as an accountant, tax professional, or auditor. One who follows the advice in this text is more easily able to fulfill his or her professional role, which includes that of a competent researcher in accounting, tax, and auditing matters.

Follow the five-step research process to (1) identify the issues or problems, (2) collect the evidence, (3) analyze the results and identify the alternatives, (4) develop the conclusion, and (5) communicate the results.

DISCUSSION QUESTIONS

1. What is the focus of accounting, tax, and auditing research?
2. What three-part approach is used to identify the precise problem or issue?
3. Explain two ways to collect evidence.
4. How are keywords used to evaluate and collect evidence?
5. What is the purpose of a research memorandum?
6. What are two common causes of accounting problems?
7. What should be included in the documentation of the research process?
8. What are some basic ways of keeping current with the authoritative literature?

EXERCISES

1. Look at 17 CFR 229.306 and explain what the audit committee must do. Hint: Use *http://www.taxsites.com > regulations* or search for the Code of Federal Regulations available at the National Archives and Records Administration web site.
2. Look up SEC Accounting and Auditing Enforcement Release No. 1062. What did that SEC release discuss? Hint: While the SEC web site has many releases, it is often more productive to use a subscription service with a stronger index. LexisNexis and CCH Business Research Network are examples of two databases having many SEC releases.
3. Does a tax treaty exist between the United States and Japan? If so, when was it signed?
4. List the competitor companies to Sony Music and how they rank. Identify your sources.
5. **Major Research Problem:** Johnson Realty, Inc., is a regional real estate firm. Andrea Johnson incorporated the firm eleven years ago. She is the founder, president, and

the majority stockholder. Recently, Johnson decided to expand her successful local real estate firm into a regional operation. She established offices in major cities across the Midwest. Johnson Realty, Inc. leased the office space. The standard lease agreement included a ten-year, noncancelable term and a five-year option renewable at the discretion of the tenant.

Two years ago the residential home market was depressed in the Midwest due to movement of factory jobs abroad, a shaky economy, and tight credit policies. Therefore, Johnson decided to eliminate 10 offices located in depressed economic areas that she believed would not recover in the housing market during the next five years. This year, Johnson Realty, Inc. closed the 10 offices. Johnson Realty, Inc., however, was bound by the lease agreements on all these offices. The company subleased four of the 10 offices but continued to make lease payments on the six remaining vacated ones.

Johnson Realty properly classified the lease commitments as operating leases. The controller for the company, Calvin Brain, expressed concern to Johnson about the proper accounting for the lease commitments on the six remaining offices available for subleasing. Brain believes they must recognize that the future lease commitments are a loss for the current period. However, Johnson disagrees and believes that the rental payments are period costs to recognize as an expense in the year paid. Johnson is confident that the company can sublease the vacant offices within the next year, and avoid booking a loss and corresponding liability in this accounting period. She has, however, given Brain the job of researching this problem and making a recommendation supported by current authoritative accounting pronouncements. Brain has asked your firm, XYZ, CPAs, to help in the development of the recommendations.

Complete all steps of this research problem, documenting each step.

APPENDIX

Common Abbreviations Used in Accounting, Tax, and Auditing Citations

Abbreviation	Title of Pronouncement
AAG-NPO	Audit and Accounting Guide: Audits of Certain Not-for-Profit Organizations
AAG-SAM	Audit and Accounting Guide: Audit Sampling
AAG-SLG	Audit and Accounting Guide: Audits of State and Local Governmental Units
ACC-PB	Accounting Standards Division Practice Bulletins
ACC-SOP	Accounting Standards Division Statements of Position
ACIJ	AICPA Accounting Interpretations
APB	Accounting Principles Board Opinions
APBS	Accounting Principles Board Statements
ARB	Accounting Research Bulletins
ATB	Accounting Terminology Bulletins
AUD-SOP	Auditing Standards Division Statements of Position
AUG-AIR	Industry Audit Guide: Audits of Airlines
AUG-COL	Industry Audit Guide: Audits of Colleges and Universities
AUG-VHW	Industry Audit Guide: Audits of Voluntary Health and Welfare Organizations

Common Abbreviations Used in Accounting, Tax, and Auditing Citations (continued)

Abbreviation	Title of Pronouncement
AUIJ	AICPA Auditing Interpretations
CASB	Cost Accounting Standards Board Standards
CASB-I	Cost Accounting Standards Board Interpretations
EPS	Computing Earnings
ET-INT	Ethics Interpretations of Rules of Conduct
ET-RLNG	Ethics Rulings
ET-RULE	Code of Professional Conduct—Rules
FAC	Financial Accounting Standards Board Statements of Financial Accounting Concepts
FAS	Financial Accounting Standards Board Statements of Financial Accounting Standards
FASEITF	Financial Accounting Standards Board Emerging Issues Task Force Consensus
FASI	Financial Accounting Standards Board Interpretations
FAST	Financial Accounting Standards Board Technical Bulletins
GAC	Governmental Accounting Standards Board Statement of Financial Accounting Concepts
GAS	Governmental Accounting Standards Board Statements on Governmental Accounting Standards
GASI	Governmental Accounting Standards Board Interpretations
GAST	Governmental Accounting Standards Board Technical Bulletins
GUD-PFS	Personal Financial Statements Guide
IAS	International Accounting Standards
IAU	International Statements on Auditing
IAU/RS	International Statements on Auditing/Related Services
IRC	Internal Revenue Code
NCGA	National Council on Governmental Accounting Statements
NCGAI	National Council on Governmental Accounting Interpretations
PFP	Statements on Responsibilities in Personal Financial Planning Practice
QC	Statements on Quality Control Standards
QCI	Quality Control Standards Interpretations
QR	Standards for Performing and Reporting on Quality Reviews
QRI	Quality Review Interpretations
REV. PROC.	Revenue Procedures
REV. RUL.	Revenue Ruling (IRS)
SAR	Statements on Standards for Accounting and Review Services
SARI	Accounting and Review Services Interpretations

Common Abbreviations Used in Accounting, Tax, and Auditing Citations (continued)

Abbreviation	Title of Pronouncement
SAS	Statements on Auditing Standards
SEC-AAER	Accounting and Auditing Enforcement Releases
SEC-FRR	Financial Reporting Releases
SEC-SAB	Staff Accounting Bulletins
SECSK	Regulation S-K
SECSX	Regulation S-X
SSAE	Statement on Standards for Attestation Engagements
SSAEI	AICPA Attestation Engagements Interpretations
SSCS	Statements on Standards for Consulting Services

Fraud and Other Investigative Techniques

LEARNING OBJECTIVES

After completing this chapter, you should understand:

- The definition of fraud.

- Different types of fraud.

- The components of the Fraud Triangle.

- The utilization of ACL and i2 Analyst Notebook in fraud investigations.

- An overview of a fraud examination and business investigation.

- The use of computer technology in fraud examinations/investigations.

Picture yourself when a client requests your help to determine if evidence exists of vendor kickbacks to certain employees in the purchasing department. Perhaps a company's legal counsel has hired you to determine whether an officer of the company has any hidden assets as a result of an embezzlement scheme he or she carried out. Maybe you need to conduct background checks (due diligence checks) on potential strategic partners of a proposed joint venture. Sound like interesting assignments? These are just a few examples of engagements of value-added services offered by accounting firms to their clients. Other common engagements of a fraud auditor/examiner in relation to an audit client could include the following:

- Providing assistance to the audit team in assessing the risk of fraud and illegal acts.

- Providing assistance to the audit team in investigating potential fraud or illegal acts.

- Conducting fact-finding forensic accounting studies of alleged fraud that could include bribery, wire fraud, securities fraud, money laundering, retail fraud, theft of intellectual property, and other fraud investigations.

- Conducting due diligence studies that could include public record checks or background checks on individuals in a hiring situation or on entities in a potential acquisition.

- Consulting as to the implementation of fraud prevention, deterrence, and detection programs.

These examples of fraud engagements demand that the investigator possess unique research skills in addition to the traditional skills presented in the previous chapters of this book.

In addition to the typical accounting, auditing, and tax services rendered by accountants, the profession is rapidly moving into additional value-added services known as fraud investigations (or litigation support), or the broader, more comprehensive term of forensic accounting. The terms "forensic accounting" or "litigation support" generally imply the use of accounting in a court of law. Thus, the services of an accountant in a fraud investigation or court case are often referred to as forensic accounting or litigation support services.

Fraud is a major problem for most organizations. Newspapers and business periodicals provide plenty of stories about major frauds. A review of such articles would reveal

> **QUICK FACTS**
>
> Forensic accounting is the use of accounting in a court of law.

that fraud is not perpetrated against only large organizations. One report in a business magazine has estimated that 80 percent of all crimes involving businesses are associated with small businesses. Although the full impact of fraud within organizations is unknown, various national surveys have reported that annual fraud costs to U.S. organizations exceed $600 billion (or six percent of their revenues) and are increasing!

Fraud examinations and background (due diligence) checks are not easy tasks. One must have the proper training, skills, and experience to conduct a successful fraud investigation. Many fraud investigators currently working in CPA firms obtained their experience working with various federal and local agencies, such as the Internal Revenue Service (IRS), the Federal Bureau of Investigation (FBI), or various levels of police work. Others obtained their knowledge of fraud examination skills by attending conferences or seminars conducted by organizations such as the Association of Certified Fraud Examiners.

This chapter presents a basic overview of fraud and common red flags that may indicate its occurrence. Additionally, the chapter explains the basic steps of a financial fraud examination, and the investigative techniques a forensic accountant may use. Since no two fraud investigations are alike, this chapter will provide a heightened awareness of the environment of fraud and present basic techniques for a fraud investigation. Also, with advances in technology, fraud examination is increasingly becoming more high tech. Thus, the chapter will highlight the use of computer software and the Internet as tools in fraud investigations. Discussion will focus on two major software products (ACL and i2's Analyst Notebook) that are utilized in fraud investigations.

DEFINITION OF FRAUD

In simplest terms, fraud is commonly defined as intentional deception, or simply lying, cheating, or stealing. *Black's Law Dictionary* defines fraud as:

> A generic term, embracing all multifarious means which human ingenuity can devise, and which are resorted to by one individual to get advantage over another by false suggestions or by suppression of truth. It includes all surprise, trickery, cunning, dissembling, and any unfair way by which another is cheated.

Concern about fraud exists with investors, creditors, customers, government entities, and others. Major financial statement frauds such as Enron, Sunbeam, WorldCom, and others have raised the importance of fraud prevention and detection.

Various laws that relate to fraud are often complex. The fraud examiner must become aware of the different types of frauds and will often request the legal assistance of an attorney. However, the different fraud-related laws have a common legal definition. As defined by the U.S. Supreme Court, fraud includes the following elements:

- A misrepresentation of a material fact
- Known to be false
- Justifiably relied upon
- Resulting in a loss

Thus, a fraud examination involves various procedures of obtaining evidence relating to the allegations of fraud, conducting interviews of selected witnesses and related parties, writing reports as to the findings of the examination, and, in many cases, testifying in a court of law as to the findings. A sufficient reason or suspicion (predication) is the basis for beginning a fraud examination. Often this predication is based upon circumstantial evidence that a fraud has likely occurred. An employee complaint, or unusual or unexplained trends in financial ratios may raise a suspicion that something is wrong. The fraud examination is conducted to prove or disprove the allegations.

TYPES OF FRAUDS

Statement on Auditing Standards No. 99, *Consideration of Fraud in a Financial Statement Audit*, distinguishes between two categories of financial statement fraud: *fraudulent financial reporting* and *misappropriation of assets*.

The first category of fraud is referred to as *fraudulent financial reporting*, which is usually committed by management in order to deceive financial statement users. Thus, fraudulent financial reporting (management fraud) refers to actions whereby management attempts to inflate reported earnings or other assets in order to deceive outsiders. Examples of management fraud would include overstating assets/revenues, price fixing, contract bidding fraud, or understating expenses/liabilities in order to make the financial statements look better than they really are. Figure 10-1 presents details of two examples of enforcement actions by the SEC relating to management fraud. Fraudulent financial reporting is generally the most costly type of fraud.

The second category of fraud is referred to as *misappropriation of assets*, more commonly known as employee fraud. Misappropriation of assets (employee fraud) refers to actions of individuals whereby they misappropriate (steal) money or other property from their employers. Various employee fraud schemes could include embezzlement, theft of company property, kickbacks, and others as listed in Figure 10-2. Misappropriation of assets is generally the most common type of fraud.

One common categorization of fraud is by industry classification, such as financial institution fraud, health care fraud, or insurance fraud. Another classification of fraud (Albrecht, et al.)[1] uses six types:

- **Employee Embezzlement**—Fraud in which employees steal company assets either directly—stealing cash or inventory—or indirectly—taking bribes or kickbacks.

- **Management Fraud**—Deception by top management of an entity primarily through the manipulation of the financial statements in order to mislead users of those statements.

- **Investment Scams**—The sale of fraudulent and often worthless investments. Such frauds would include telemarketing and Ponzi scheme type frauds.

- **Vendor Fraud**—Fraud resulting from overcharging for goods purchased, shipment of inferior goods, or nonshipment of inventory even when payment has been received.

- **Customer Fraud**—Fraud committed by a customer by not paying for goods received or deceiving the organization in various ways to get something for nothing.

- **Miscellaneous Fraud**—This category is a catch-all category for frauds that do not fit into one of the previous five categories. Examples would include altering birth records or grade reports.

Although there are many different types and categories of fraud, a fraud examiner should approach each engagement in a systematic manner, as explained in this chapter.

THE FRAUD TRIANGLE

Why do individuals commit fraud? Probably the most common reason is that the perpetrators are greedy and believe that they will not get caught. Various researchers, including criminologists, psychologists, sociologists, auditors, police detectives, educators, and others have studied this issue. They have concluded that three basic factors determine whether an individual might commit fraud. These three factors comprising the fraud

---

[1] Albrecht, W. Steve, Gerald W. Wernz, and Timothy L. Williams. *Fraud: Bringing Light to the Dark Side of Business,* (Burr Ridge, Ill.: Richard D. Irwin, Inc., 1995).

FIGURE 10-1 | EXAMPLES OF MANAGEMENT FRAUD

Case 1

The SEC brought an enforcement action that permanently barred senior officers and directors of Solucorp Industries, Ltd. from serving as officers or directors of any publicly traded company as a result of their fraudulent conduct.

The SEC alleged that certain members of Solucorp's senior management and directors claimed in press releases and other publicly disseminated materials to have contracts that either did not exist or were subject to undisclosed material contingencies, or that provided revenues materially below those announced by the company. The Complaint also alleged that senior management falsified Solucorp's financial statements by improperly recognizing as revenue license fees that were subject to material contingencies.

The final judgment against Solucorp and senior management permanently enjoined the company from any further violations of the antifraud provisions of the Exchange Act, and also permanently barred the defendants from ever serving as officers or directors of a publicly traded company.

Source: Accounting and Auditing Enforcement Release No. 1849; August 25, 2003.

Case 2

On April 8, 2004, the SEC filed three accounting fraud actions against Ira Zar, former CFO at Computer Associates International, Inc., David Rivard, and David Kaplan, former vice presidents of finance at Computer Associates. The SEC's Complaint alleged that Zar, Rivard, and Kaplan participated in a widespread practice that resulted in the improper recognition of revenue by Computer Associates.

Specifically, the Commission alleged that Computer Associates engaged in a practice in which the company held its books open after the end of each quarter and improperly recorded, in that elapsed quarter, revenue from contracts that had not been finalized and executed before the expiration of the quarter. As a result of the improper practice, Computer Associates made material misrepresentations and omissions about its revenue and earnings in Commission filings and other public statements. It is also alleged that the defendants each mislead Computer Associates outside auditors regarding the existence of such illegal activities.

Each defendant consented to entry of a permanent injunction prohibiting him from further violations of the securities laws.

Source: Accounting and Auditing Enforcement Release No. 1988, April 8, 2004.

> **QUICK FACTS**
>
> The fraud triangle consists of motivation (pressure or incentive), perceived opportunity, and rationalization.

triangle include (1) motivation (perceived pressure or incentive), (2) perceived opportunity, and (3) rationalization.[2] All three elements generally exist in the typical fraud.

The first element of the fraud triangle is motivation based on perceived pressure or incentive to commit a fraud. An individual's motivation can change due to external forces. An individual who is honest one day might commit fraud the next day due to external pressures. These pressures include financial pressures, vices, and work-related pressures. Typical financial pressures include excessive debt resulting from unexpected high medical bills, uncontrolled spending with credit cards, lifestyles beyond one's means, or outright greed. Vices may include addiction to gambling, drugs, or alcohol. The individual having a vice is sometimes motivated by this pressure to commit a fraudulent act in order to support his or her addiction. Work-related pressures could include not receiving desired job recognition, being overworked and underpaid, or not getting an expected promotion. A formerly honest individual may turn to fraud in order to get even with his or her employer.

The motivation based on perceived pressure or incentive for top management to commit financial statement fraud (management fraud) may include obtaining a bonus or

---

[2] More detailed discussion of the fraud triangle can be found in the following: Bologna, G. Jack, and Robert J. Lindquist, *Fraud Auditing and Forensic Accounting*, 2e, (New York, John Wiley & Sons, Inc., 1995); Albrecht, W. Steve, *Fraud Examination*, (Cincinnati, Thomson South-Western, 2003); and *Fraud Examiners Manual*, 2003 Edition, Association of Certified Fraud Examiners.

FIGURE 10-2   COMMON EXAMPLES OF FRAUD ACTIVITIES

Misappropriation of Assets:

Account	Schemes
Cash	Skimming
	Forgery
	Kiting
	Phony Refunds
	Larceny
	Fraudulent Disbursements
Accounts/Rec.	Lapping
	Fictitious Write-offs
Purchases/Inventory	Duplicate Payments
	Nonexistent Vendor
	Kickbacks
	Misdirected Shipments
	Theft
Fixed Assets	Unauthorized Personal Use of Assets
	Fictitious Burglary
Payroll	Phantom Employees
	Falsified Time Cards

Fraudulent Financial Reporting:

Fictitious Revenues—recording of sales of goods or services that never occurred
      —timing differences, recognizing revenue in improper periods

Asset Overstatement—recording certain assets as market values rather than
      the lower of cost or market

Unrecorded Liabilities and Expenses—not recording an environmental contingency
      that is probable and reasonably estimable

Improper Disclosures—not disclosing related party transactions or other significant events

Corruption:

Conflict of Interest
Bribery
Illegal Gratuities
Economic Extortion

---

stock option based on the company's financial results, the company's stock price, or meeting regulatory requirements. Similarly, when there are dramatic changes in the organization, such as reengineering or a potential merger, such changes can lead to uncertainty as to the future. This may motivate an individual to become dishonest in order to survive within the organization.

    The second element of the fraud triangle is perceived opportunity. All employees have opportunities to commit fraud against their employers, suppliers, or other third parties, such as the government. Perceived opportunity is often driven by the access an individual has to the entity's assets or financial statements, the skill of the individual to exploit the opportunity to commit fraud, and, in certain cases, by the individual's seniority or trust within the organization. Many corporate frauds have occurred due to breaches of trust by employees and management to whom access privileges were granted. If an individual believes that the opportunity exists to commit a fraud, conceal the fraud in some way from others, and avoid detection and punishment, the probability of the individual committing

RESEARCH TIPS

Examine the fraud probability to plan the fraud investigation.

fraud increases. When an individual's professional aspirations are being met, generally the individual is content. However, when the aspirations are not met, unconventional means that may include fraud are sometimes sought.

Conditions (red flags) that may provide the opportunity for fraud include:

- Negligence on the part of top management to enforce ethical standards, or to discipline an individual who commits a fraud.

- Major changes in the entity's operating environment.

- Nonenforcement of mandatory vacations for employees, thereby preventing others from filling in during absences.

- Lack of supporting documentation for transactions.

- Lack of physical safeguards over assets.

Effective internal control is an important factor in limiting fraud. The fraud examiner must pay attention to the entity's internal controls and evaluate the weaknesses or red flags that provide the opportunity for fraud.

The third element of the fraud triangle is an individual's rationalization for the actions taken. If an individual can rationalize that questionable actions taken were not wrong, he or she might justify in his or her mind any improper behavior. Common rationalizations for fraud activity include such statements as: "I work long hours and am treated unfairly by my employer; the company owes me more," "I will use the funds only for my current financial emergency and will pay them back later," or, "The federal government foolishly wastes my money and therefore, I will not report my extra income this year on my tax return—besides, no one gets hurt." What the individual is attempting to do is to rationalize away the dishonesty of any wrongful action.

Individuals use many other rationalizations when committing fraud. However, an important factor, which the fraud examiner will evaluate, in minimizing illicit actions is an individual's personal integrity. An individual's strong personal standards of ethics can offset the desire to rationalize the fraud activity. The tone set by top management as to proper ethical conduct can have a major impact on actions taken by employees.

Most frauds result when the three elements of the fraud triangle combine: motivation (pressure or incentive), opportunity, and rationalization. If an organization is able to control or deny any of the three elements of the fraud triangle, the likelihood for fraud decreases. Knowledge of these three elements provides the fraud examiner with a better understanding of different approaches to take in the investigation.

Fraud comes in many forms and thus the fraud examination must be tailored to the specific circumstances. Following is an overview of a typical financial statement fraud examination.

OVERVIEW OF A FINANCIAL FRAUD EXAMINATION

Over the years, independent auditors often have not met the expectations of third parties in detecting material fraud when conducting audits of financial statements. Fraud auditing encourages the detection and prevention of fraud. In such an environment, the fraud auditor possesses the skills of a well-trained auditor combined with the skills of a criminal investigator.

To further clarify the auditor's responsibility to discover fraud in a financial statement, SAS No. 99 provides guidance. The auditor has a responsibility to plan and perform the audit in order to obtain reasonable assurance that the financial statements are free of material misstatement, whether caused by error or fraud. Therefore, the auditor/fraud examiner must understand the characteristics and types of fraud, be able to assess fraud risks or red flags, design an appropriate audit, and report the findings on possible fraud to management or the appropriate levels of authority. Specifically, the auditor needs to assess the risk of material misstatement of the financial statements due to the possibility of fraud. The assessment would include attempts to answer the following questions: What types of fraud risk exist? What is the actual and potential exposure to the fraud? Who are the perpetrators? How difficult is it to identify and prevent the fraud? What is the company doing to prevent fraud now, and how effective are these measures? This risk assessment then aids the auditor in designing the audit procedures to be performed.

In conducting the risk assessment of material misstatement due to fraud, the auditor would evaluate fraud risk factors (red flags) that relate to the two basic categories of financial statement fraud—fraudulent financial reporting and misappropriation of assets. A fraud risk factor is a characteristic that provides a motivation or opportunity for fraud to occur, or an indication that fraud may have occurred. The risk factors that relate to financial reporting fraud are placed into the following three groups:

1. **Incentives/Pressures.** This group of risk factors relates to the financial stability or profitability of the entity, excessive pressure on management or operating personnel to meet expectations of third parties or financial targets, or when the personal situation of management or the board of directors is threatened by the entity's financial performance. Examples of specific red flags would include the following: a high degree of competition or market saturation along with declining profit margins, perceived or real adverse effects of reporting poor financial results, or personal guarantees by management or board members for debts of the entity.

2. **Opportunities.** These factors relate to the nature of the industry or the entity's operations that provide the opportunity to engage in fraudulent financial reporting. Examples would include significant or highly complex transactions, major operations conducted across international borders, or deficiencies in internal controls.

3. **Attitudes/Rationalization.** This category of risk factors reflects the attitude or rationalization by board members or management to justify or rationalize their motive to commit fraudulent financial reporting. Examples of red flags here would include: ineffective communication or enforcement of ethical standards and excessive interest by management in maintaining or increasing the entity's earnings trend. [3]

Risk factors relating to misstatements arising from the misappropriation of assets are classified into two groups: **susceptibility of assets to misappropriation,** which relates to the nature of the organization's assets and the probability of theft; and **controls,** which relate to the lack of controls for preventing or detecting the misappropriation of assets. Examples of red flags for the susceptibility of assets include large amounts of cash on hand; easily convertible assets, such as bearer bonds or diamonds; or lack of ownership identification of fixed assets that are very marketable.

Although fraud is usually concealed, the presence of risk factors (red flags) may alert the fraud auditor to the possibility that fraud may exist within the company. If such conditions exist, and a risk assessment warrants, the auditor should discuss them with management and/or legal counsel. If the conclusion reached is that fraud is likely, a fraud examination would commence. The basic steps of the fraud examination are as follows:

1. Identify the Issue/Plan the Investigation

2. Gather the Evidence/The Investigation Phase

3. Evaluate the Evidence

4. Report Findings to Management/Legal Counsel

RESEARCH TIPS

Examine one's incentives, pressures, opportunities, and attitudes to identify potential fraud.

QUICK FACTS

Red flags alert the auditor to potential fraud.

---

[3] AICPA, SAS No. 99, *Consideration of Fraud in a Financial Statement Audit,* October, 2002.

Step 1—Identify the Issue/Plan the Investigation

Based upon the circumstances indicating the possibility of fraud, the client and/or the client's legal counsel would usually contact the fraud examiner to conduct a fraud examination. Management's suspicions as to the possibility of fraud could come from a number of sources, such as improprieties noted by fellow employees, observation of an employee's lifestyle that is inconsistent with his or her income, or issues resulting from an internal or external audit that has identified missing documents. Not all suspicions result in a finding of fraud, but by pursuing the evidence and anomalies, the fraud examiner can make a reasoned determination as to its existence. If fraud exists and is not pursued, it will probably continue and more likely increase over time. Based upon the circumstantial evidence, the fraud examiner would create a hypothesis as to when the potential fraud occurred, how it was committed, and by whom.

Step 2—Gather the Evidence/ The Investigation Phase

Although different investigation methods exist, the objective of the investigation phase is to gather appropriate evidence in order to determine whether a fraud has occurred or is occurring. Investigations are often contentious and generate a great deal of uneasiness for all parties involved. Each investigation is different and the suspects and witnesses will often react differently. One mistake in the investigation can jeopardize the entire process.

Also included in the investigation phase is the identification of resources to utilize in the investigation. The fraud examiner would need to know what resources are available—primary, secondary, or third parties. Various types of resources are discussed later in the chapter.

The investigation technique used will often depend on the type of evidence the fraud examiner is attempting to gather. One approach is to classify the evidence into four types with the related investigative techniques to gather the evidence as follows:[4]

Type of Evidence	Investigative Technique
1. Documentary Evidence (hardcopy or electronic)	Examination of documents, Searches of public records, Searches of computer databases, Analysis of net worth, or Analysis of financial statement
2. Testimonial Evidence	Interviewing, Interrogations, or Polygraph tests
3. Observational Evidence (Investigator's personal observation)	Physical examination—counts/inspections, Surveillance (close supervision of suspect during examination period)
4. Physical Evidence (i.e., tire marks or fingerprints)	Use of forensic expertise

Two examples of gathering evidence as to the existence of fraud are presented below.

Case 1. Management has experienced lower profit margins than expected. In this investigation, the fraud examiner might review inventory procedures to determine whether employees are stealing inventory. The investigation might identify shrinkage in the actual counts of high-dollar inventory items, and a review of surveillance records may show whether anyone has removed inventory during off hours.

Case 2. A co-worker has reported that an employee appears to be living well above his known means. In such a case, the fraud investigator might review payment records to determine whether sales proceeds were diverted into an employee's personal

---

[4] Albrecht, et al., op.cit.

account. A net worth analysis can also identify inconsistencies, and a review of the suspect's brokerage statements (with legal permission) may show whether the deposit dates correspond to the dates when questionable business transactions occurred.

The investigation phase of the examination requires strong analytical skills. These skills are important in the analysis of the financial information and other data for any trends or anomalies.

In gathering testimonial evidence, interviewing skills are critical for the fraud examiner. Interviewing skills require an ability to extract testimonial evidence from collaborators, co-workers, or others related to the case, as well as the suspect, in hopes of obtaining a confession. Fraud-related interviews are carefully planned question-and-answer sessions designed to solicit information relevant to the case.

Also, information technology skills are required in order to search public records and other electronic databases in the gathering of evidence for the investigation. The use of computer databases and software in evidence gathering for a fraud investigation is discussed later in this chapter.

Step 3—Evaluate the Evidence

After completing a thorough investigation, the fraud examiner will evaluate the evidence in order to determine whether the fraud has occurred or is still occurring. One can draw sound, documented conclusions only if the information was properly collected, organized, and interpreted. Once fraud is discovered, the fraud examiner attempts to determine the extent of the fraud. Was it an isolated incident? Was there a pattern connecting each incident? When did the fraud begin? By identifying how long and to what extent the fraud occurred, the investigator may be able to provide critical information to help the client recover missing funds from the perpetrator or an insurance company.

Step 4—Report Findings to Management/Legal Counsel

Upon completing the evaluation of the evidence, the fraud examiner needs to document the results of the investigation and prepare a report on the findings. The report should use the writing concepts discussed in Chapter 2. Any report should use coherent organization, conciseness, clarity, standard English, responsiveness, and a style appropriate to the reader.

At times, the client's legal counsel may request the fraud examiner serve as an expert witness in a court case. A fraud examiner might win or lose a court case against a perpetrator depending upon the accuracy and technical rigor of the fraud examiner's investigation and report. However, the fraud examiner's report needs to avoid rendering his or her opinion as to the guilt or innocence of the suspect. The report should state only the facts of the investigation and the findings. The report should present answers as to *when* the fraud occurred, *how* it was committed, and by *whom*.

Since fraud investigations are considered litigation support services, which are considered consulting services, the CPA/fraud investigator needs to adhere to professional standards during the investigation, as well as in developing the report. Relevant standards and guidance issued by the AICPA's Management Consulting Services Committee and related subcommittees include the following:

- Statement on Standards for Consulting Services No. 1, *Consulting Services: Definition and Standards.*

- Consulting Services Special Report 93-1, *Application of AICPA Professional Standards in the Performance of Litigation Services.*

- Consulting Services Special Report 93-2, *Conflicts of Interest in Litigation Services Engagements.*

- Consulting Services Practice Aid (Cons. Serv. Prac. Aid) 96-3, *Communicating in Litigation Services: Reports.*

- Cons. Serv. Prac. Aid 97-1, *Fraud Investigations in Litigation and Dispute Resolution Services.*
- Cons. Serv. Prac. Aid 98-1, *Providing Bankruptcy and Reorganization Services.*
- Cons. Serv. Prac. Aid 98-2, *Calculations of Damages from Personal Injury, Wrongful Death and Employment Discrimination.*
- Cons. Serv. Prac. Aid 99-1, *Alternative Dispute Resolution Services.*
- Cons. Serv. Prac. Aid 99-2, *Valuing Intellectual Property and Calculating Infringement Damages.*
- Cons. Serv. Prac. Aid 02-1, *Business Valuation in Bankruptcy.*

Practice Exercises   *Fraud Investigations*

1. Access a recently issued SEC Accounting and Auditing Enforcement Release related to a fraud action (*http://www.sec.gov/divisions/enforce/friactions.shtml*), and determine the following:

   Incentive(s)/Pressure to commit the fraud: _____

   _____

   Accounting Issue(s): _____
   Motive for the fraud: _____

2. Access the Association of Certified Fraud Examiners' web site (*http://www.cfenet.com*) and complete the following:

   a. List three qualifications for becoming a CFE:

   _____

   _____

   _____

   b. List three items located in the ACFE's resource library:

   _____

   _____

   _____

3. Locate four web sites on fraud and briefly describe the contents of the site.

   Site #1   Web address: _____
             Contents: _____

   Site #2   Web address: _____
             Contents: _____

   Site #3   Web address: _____
             Contents: _____

   Site #4   Web address: _____
             Contents: _____

BUSINESS INVESTIGATIONS

In addition to a fraud examination, professional accountants sometimes provide a related service to help management minimize their business risks. This service is referred to as business or due diligence investigations. At times, a client may need help to verify information about an organization before entering into a joint venture or corporate merger. Or perhaps the client needs a background information check before hiring a new corporate officer or other employee. In other situations, the client may need to know about any related parties associated with the corporation or the reputation of a potential new vendor. In each of these examples, a business or individual background investigation might prove valuable in obtaining desirable information for managing business risks.

In most types of investigative work, one needs to have a "documents state of mind." Many types of documents, or "paper trails," exist that the investigator can use to gather facts about the issue under investigation. Such documents are classified as either primary or secondary sources. A typical secondary source would include a newspaper article about a company acquiring a subsidiary or doing business in a certain country.

Primary documents are readily available in many types of investigations. For example, if one is attempting to gather background information on a new corporate executive, typical primary sources would include voter registrations, tax records for property ownership, civil and criminal lawsuits, and divorce and bankruptcy records. Corporations have similar types of paper trails. For example, an entity's articles of incorporation are roughly equivalent to an individual's birth certificate.

In gathering background information, the investigator typically follows a technique referred to as "working from the outside in." This technique is depicted with concentric circles, with the larger circle representing the secondary sources as illustrated in Figure 10-3. The middle circle contains the primary sources that often substantiate the

RESEARCH TIPS

Develop a "documents state of mind" to show a paper trail.

FIGURE 10-3 INVESTIGATIVE TECHNIQUE—"WORKING FROM THE OUTSIDE IN"

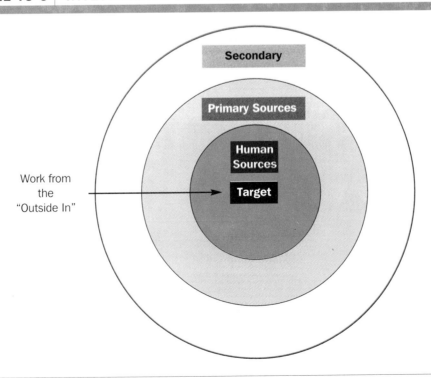

secondary information. The inner circle could include personal interviews for facts concerning the target or the issue under investigation. In many investigations, the investigator needs to use creativity in gathering and analyzing the data.

COMPUTER TECHNOLOGY IN FRAUD INVESTIGATIONS

In the information technology age, fraud potential is wider in scope. However, new tools and techniques exist to detect and combat this expansion of fraud. Uncovering signs of fraud among possibly millions of transactions within an organization requires the fraud examiner to use analytical skills and work experience to construct a profile against which to test the data for the possibility of fraud. Three important tools for the fraud examiner are data mining software, public databases, and the Internet.

Data Mining Software

Data mining software is a tool that models a database for the purpose of determining patterns and relationships among the data. This tool is an outgrowth of the development of "expert systems." Computer-based data analysis tools can prove invaluable when examining for possible fraud. From the analysis of data, the fraud examiner can develop fraud profiles from the patterns existing within the database. Through identifying and understanding these patterns, the examiner may uncover fraudulent activity. The use of data mining software also provides the opportunity to set up automatic red flags that will reveal discrepancies in data that should be uniform. Some of the common features of data mining software include the following:

- **Sorting**—arranging data in a particular order such as alphabetically or numerically.

- **Occurrence selection**—querying the database to select the occurrences of items or records in a field.

- **Joining files**—combining selected files from different data files for analysis purposes.

- **Duplicate searches**—searching files for duplication, such as duplicate payments.

- **Ratio analysis**—performing both vertical and horizontal analyses for anomalies.

Following is a brief description of some of the more common commercial data mining software products used by fraud examiners.

WizRule. This software package is used for many different applications, such as data cleaning (searching for clerical errors) or anomaly detection in a fraud examination. The program is based on the assumption that in many cases, errors are considered as exceptions to the norm. For example, if Mr. Johnston is the only salesperson for all sales transactions to certain customers and a sales transaction to one of the customers is associated with salesperson Mrs. Allen, the software could identify the situation as a "deviation" or a suspected error.

WizRule is based on a mathematical algorithm that is capable of revealing all the rules of a database. The main output of the program analysis is a list of cases found in the data that are unlikely to be true in reference to the discovered rules. Such cases are considered suspected errors.

Financial Crime Investigator. This is a program that is a systematic approach for investigating, detecting, and preventing contract and procurement fraud. The software, using artificial intelligence, provides instructions on how to query databases to find fraud indicators and match them to the appropriate fraud scheme. It provides a detailed work plan to investigate each scheme, converts probable schemes to the related criminal offenses, outlines an investigative plan for each offense based on the elements of proof, and generates interview formats for debriefing anonymous informants for each contract fraud scheme.

IDEA (Audimation Services, Inc.). This product is a powerful generalized audit software package that allows the user to display, analyze, manipulate, sample, or extract data from files generated by a wide variety of computer systems. The software provides the ability to select records that match one's criteria, check file totals and extensions, and look for gaps in numerical sequences or duplicate documents or records. The investigator can conduct fraud investigations; perform computer security reviews by analyzing systems logs, file lists, and access rights; or review telephone logs looking for fraudulent or inappropriate use of client facilities.

Monarch. This software program allows the investigator to convert electronic editions of reports from programs such as Microsoft Access into text files, spreadsheets, or tables. Monarch can then break this information into individual reports for analysis.

ACL for Windows. ACL Services Ltd., the developer and marketer of ACL for Windows, is considered the market leader in data inquiry, analysis, and reporting software for the auditing profession. ACL's clients include many of the Fortune 100 companies, governmental agencies, and many of the largest international accounting firms. In the software category of fraud detection and prevention, ACL for Windows is the most commonly used software package.

This software product allows the fraud examiner to perform various analytical functions without modifying the original data. The software can sort data on multiple levels as well as locate numerical gaps in the sequencing of data. Graphical display options allow the investigator to create graphs from the Histogram, Stratify, Classify, or Age commands. ACL is very beneficial in fraud detection due to its ability to quickly and thoroughly analyze a large quantity of data in order to highlight those transactions often associated with fraudulent activity.

As a world leader in data inquiry, analysis, and reporting software, ACL is very effective in such areas as identifying trends and bringing to the auditor/fraud examiner's attention potential problem areas, highlighting errors, or potential fraud by comparing files with end-user criteria, and identifying control concerns. Specifically in fraud detection, ACL can identify suspect transactions by performing such tests as matching names between employee and paid vendor files, identifying vendor price increases greater than an acceptable percent, identifying invoices without a valid purchase order, or identifying invoices with no related receiving report.

As the forensic accountant attempts to sort through a massive volume of data in order to detect the possibility of fraud, ACL is a major software product available for the fraud examiner. Accompanying this text is ResearchLink, a web site that contains ACL Desktop Edition, Version 8 software. ResearchLink also contains "ACL in Practice," a tutorial that provides real-world data analysis scenarios at a fictional company, Metaphor Corporation. Download ACL onto your computer and begin the tutorial "ACL in Practice" in order to become familiar with ACL's analysis and reporting capabilities using real-word data. It is suggested that you print out this tutorial prior to beginning your review of ACL. To install ACL Desktop Edition Full Educational Version, simply follow the two basic installation instructions:

1. Close all Windows applications.
2. At http://weirich.swlearning.com, click on ResearchLink. Follow the on-screen instructions to download and install ACL. A successful installation will provide an opening screen as illustrated in Figure 10-4.

Please review this demo. Selected end-of-chapter questions will quiz you as to the use of ACL for fraud detection. This tutorial will require a considerable amount of time to complete; therefore, plan accordingly. The comprehensive tutorial will explain how to manage a data analysis project consisting of the following six phases:

RESEARCH TOOLS

Internet

FARS

LexisNexis

AICPA reSOURCE

PwC Edgarscan

Thomson ONE

RIA Checkpoint SE

ACL

i2

QUICK FACTS

Software can often assist in highlighting transactions often associated with fraudulent activities.

FIGURE 10-4 | OPENING SCREEN OF ACL SOFTWARE

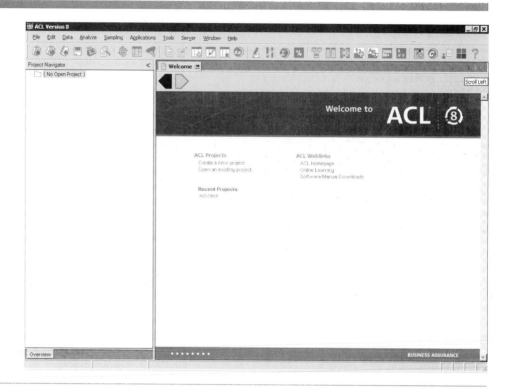

1. Plan the project—identifying the objectives of the project.

2. Acquire the data—identifying the location and format of the data needed for the project.

3. Access the data—adding the data to your project as tables.

4. Verify the data—determining the integrity of the data.

5. Analyze the data—finding any exceptions in the data.

6. Report results—reporting the findings of your project analysis.

RESEARCH TOOLS

Internet

FARS

LexisNexis

AICPA reSOURCE

PwC Edgarscan

Thomson ONE

RIA Checkpoint SE

ACL

i2

Analyst's Notebook. This software package, developed by i2 Inc., is a visual investigative analysis product that assists investigators by uncovering, interpreting, and displaying complex information in easily understood charts. In many investigations, one must carefully analyze large amounts of multiformatted data gathered from various sources. The software provides a range of visualization formats showing connections between related sets of information and in chart form reveals significant patterns in the data. This visual presentation is a powerful tool to use in discussions of the case with legal counsel and in presenting findings in court. For example, if the fraud examiner has a complex investigation chart of individuals and locations of suspects and legal counsel is interested in one particular individual, the software can immediately produce a smaller chart showing only the information relating to that one individual. The software is excellent for extracting sections from large and complex investigation charts in order to produce smaller, more manageable presentation charts. Figure 10-5 provides an example of i2's charting capabilities of a drug cartel investigation.

In a fraud investigation, the Analyst's Notebook can aid the fraud examiner in developing building blocks that support the key issues of how and why. The software can help manage the large volume of information collected; help in understanding the information

Practice Exercises   *ALC Software*

1. Complete Chapters 2 and 3 of the "ACL in Practice" tutorial and determine the following:
   a. How many duplicate card numbers are there in the "Employee List"? _____
   b. Using the Agents_Metaphor table, how many employees are from Michigan? _____
   c. Verify the Acceptable_Codes table. Were any data validity errors detected? _____

2. Complete Chapters 4 and 5 of the "ACL in Practice" tutorial and determine the following:
   a. How many transactions are for amounts greater than $500? _____
   b. Of the credit card numbers that have a PASTDUEAMT greater than $200, how many have an expiration date of February 1, 2005, or earlier? _____
   c. What are the total expenses for hotel stays? $ _____

3. Complete Chapters 6 and 7 of the "ACL in Practice" tutorial and determine the following:
   a. What can you do with the Join and Relations commands? _____
   _____
   _____

   b. What are the four methods used to combine information from two or more tables?
   _____
   _____
   _____
   _____

by providing a link analysis to build up a picture (chart) of the individuals and organizations involved in the fraud; help in the examination of the fraudsters' actions by developing a timeline analysis as to the precise sequence of events in the fraud case; and help in the discovery of the location of the stolen money or assets. Figure 10-6 provides an example of a timeline chart of the famous "Bonnie and Clyde" investigation.

Typical investigations using the Analyst's Notebook include money laundering activities, securities fraud, credit card fraud, insurance fraud, and organized crime cases. Additional tools available to the fraud investigator from i2 Inc. include iBase and iBridge. iBase is a state-of-the-art database software tool that not only captures, but also controls and analyzes, multisource data in a secure environment. With iBase, one can quickly build a multiuser investigative database that can provide information in a unique visual format. iBridge serves as a connectivity solution that provides the user with a live connection to multiple databases throughout one's organization. It provides connection to a variety of relational databases for data retrieval and analysis by the fraud investigator. Accompanying this text at the authors' web site (*http://weirich.swlearning.com*) is a tutorial provided by i2 Inc. that presents an excellent overview of this unique product for the fraud examiner. Please review this tutorial to prepare for answering selected end-of-chapter questions.

RESEARCH TIPS

Use Analyst's Notebook to help chart your fraud investigation.

Public Databases

Given the enormity of public records (including information sold to the public for a fee), the fraud examiner or investigator in certain cases may not need anything else in gathering evidence. These public databases include, among other information, records of lawsuits, bankruptcies, tax liens, judgments, and property transactions from all over the United States and, in certain cases, from around the world. If the examiner cannot locate

FIGURE 10-5 | I2'S CHART OF A DRUG CARTEL INVESTIGATION

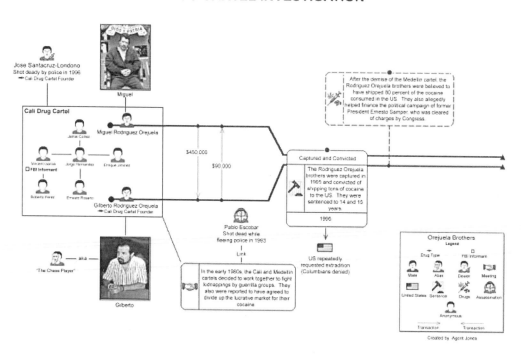

DRUG CARTEL INVESTIGATION

the information via computerized databases, he or she can still locate the necessary information by personally visiting courthouses, recorder's offices, or city halls.

The fraud examiner/investigator heavily relies on public records/databases. Because public records are in the public domain, usually there are no restrictions in accessing the information. Business intelligence literature commonly cites the fact that 95 percent of spy work comes from public records/databases. Additional reasons for utilizing public records include the quick access time and the inexpensive search costs.

Some of the commonly used public records/databases include courthouse records, company records, online databases, and the Internet. Figure 10-7 presents a summary listing (not all inclusive) of typical records/files or databases available to the investigator.

"Courthouse" Records. Every county has a courthouse and a place to file real estate records. In both small towns and large cities, lawsuits, judgments, and property filings are found at the courthouse. In addition to county records, those same types of records are filed at federal courts, which also contain bankruptcy filings. These records address the basic questions of a business investigation: Is the subject currently in a lawsuit? Are there unsatisfied judgments? Is there a criminal history? Has the subject filed for bankruptcy?

The existence of these courthouse records tells the investigator something, but buried within the case jackets and docket sheets is even more information. Looking for financial

RESEARCH TIPS

Use public databases that include courthouse records, company records, online databases, and the Internet

FIGURE 10-6 | I2'S TIMELINE CHART OF THE "BONNIE AND CLYDE" INVESTIGATION

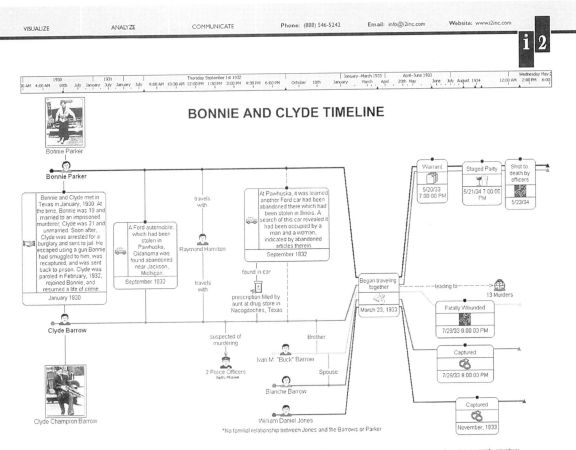

BONNIE AND CLYDE TIMELINE

*No familial relationship between Jones and the Barrows or Parker

information, the investigator can examine the mortgage on a subject's home. Divorce filings and bankruptcy filings are business investigations themselves. They will contain records on assets and liabilities, employment histories, and pending suits.

Company Records. The common starting point in many business investigations is public filings made with the Securities and Exchange Commission (SEC filings), accessible on the EDGAR database at the SEC's web site. Unfortunately, the great majority of privately held companies need not file with the SEC. This leaves two primary sources for company information. First, Dun and Bradstreet compiles data on millions of companies. Experienced investigators recognize D&B's shortcomings, but know that reports make great starting points. Second, all businesses file some form of report within either the state or the county where they are located. Proprietorships and partnerships typically file local "assumed name," "d/b/a," or "fictitious name" filings. Corporations, limited partnerships, and limited liability companies (LLCs) file annual reports in their states of registration. These reports will typically identify the officers and registered agent of the company, but most reports will not list ownership data or financial information.

Other sources of company information include the various public records and courthouse records discussed previously. Uniform Commercial Code filings (UCCs) and real estate filings can provide details missing in basic business filings. An investigator may

> **RESEARCH TIPS**
>
> Examine company records and other relevant documents from online databases.

FIGURE 10-7 | INVESTIGATIVE RESOURCES

State Records
Driving Records
Workers' Compensation Claims
Department of Education Records
Licensing Boards (i.e., bar and
    accountancy boards)
Corporation and Securities Commissions
    Filings
UCC Records—documents the record of
    a loan or lease with secured assets
State Tax Liens
Vehicle ID
Ownership/Property Records
Criminal and Civil Records
Social Security Number Records
Vital Statistics—birth, death, marriages
Driving Records—MVR
Bankruptcy Records

Locator Records
Phone Directories
Zip Code Directories
Surname Directories

Federal Records
Military Records
Federal Aviation Records
SEC Filings
UCC Filings
Library of Congress
Federal Tax Liens

Educational records
Degrees Awarded
Attendance Records
Teacher Certification

Databases
Full Text
    LexisNexis
    Dow Jones/The Wall Street Journal
    DIALOG
    Datatimes

Public Records
    PACER
    Information America
    CDB Infotek

Credit
    Experian (formerly TRW)
    Trans Union
    Choicepoint (formerly Equifax)

Other
    Demographic
    Biographical
    Internet

tie an individual to a company because both the individual and the company are co-debtors in a secured agreement. Detailed financial information on private companies often can be gathered from litigation records over contracts, trade secrets, and other issues. Different regulatory bodies may have information on companies, even when they are closely held. State insurance commissions, for instance, have files for the public on companies that sell insurance in their states. Companies awarded government contracts also have to make certain information public. Investigators should try a variety of public records to acquire relevant information on the company under investigation.

Online Databases. Many investigators use commercial databases to acquire the majority of their information. As described above, commercial databases give investigators the ability to quickly pull information from all over the world without alerting the subject. The speed and depth of commercial databases make them a "must have" for business investigators.

Online databases come in four basic formats. The first type of database is the "full text" database. Full text means the database stores, for retrieval, the full text of articles. Several databases now have articles from newspapers and magazines from around the world. Databases also carry the full text of transcripts of television and radio broadcasts. LexisNexis, Dow Jones News Retrieval, and Datatimes are examples of full text databases.

Many online databases are now conveniently available on the Web. The online database world provides the majority of information now used by the business investigator.

The second type of database is the public record database. Database companies provide access to many different types of courthouse records as well as company records. Access to federal litigation and bankruptcy records is obtainable through the "PACER" system. Major vendors of public record databases include Information America, CDB Infotek, and LexisNexis.

A third type of database is the credit and demographic database. The Fair Credit Reporting Act (FCRA) restricts the use of consumer credit information, but credit bureaus also offer data not covered by the FRCA. Other databases act as national phone books, providing names and addresses across the country. Credit Bureaus include Experian (formerly TRW), Trans Union, and Choicepoint (formerly Equifax). Suppliers of demographic data such as names and addresses include Metronet and DNIS.

Finally, there are databases that provide additional types of information. Vendors like Dialog and LexisNexis also provide company directories, abstracts, and biographical records such as Who's Who.

The Internet

Fraud examiners/investigators utilize the Internet, beyond accessing commercial databases. Searching the Internet is generally not as precise as searching most commercial databases. Thus, investigators tend to stick with LexisNexis and Dialog. However, Internet online magazines often provide breaking news stories not covered elsewhere. Newsgroups and mailing lists contain raw (but often erroneous) data on companies. Finally, the first source of information on a company these days is often provided on its own corporate web site. For example, companies place detailed background information on themselves as well as profiles of their key executives on their web sites.

A few of the Internet web sites utilized by fraud examiners/investigators include KnowX, Switchboard, and others, as described in the following paragraphs.

KnowX (*http://www.knowx.com*). Many of the previously listed public documents are currently accessible via the Internet. KnowX, an online public record service, is available via the Internet. This web site provides the fraud investigator inexpensive searches, and, depending on the search, does not charge a fee. Typical searches available include aircraft ownership records, a business directory, corporate records, date-of-birth records, lawsuits, real estate tax assessor records, stock ownership records, and watercraft ownership records.

Switchboard (*http://www.switchboard.com*). Switchboard is a free white- and yellow-pages service that contains primarily U.S. listings. Anyone can use this to search the database for people or businesses by going to Switchboard's home page and clicking on Find a Person, and then typing the information into the respective fields and clicking search. Business searches are similar to individual searches.

The web sites indexed in the Switchboard search engine are gathered by an intelligent search tool that helps one find information related to any topic or web site address (URL) specified. One can locate information in the following ways: (1) by entering keywords in the search fields; (2) by entering a URL in the search field; or (3) by using the A–Z letter bar to browse through topics. A user can also click the more button, which will provide a list of web sites with similar content. This Switchboard web site is a quick way for the fraud examiner/investigator to search for individuals and/or businesses that are under investigation.

Other Web Sites. Other specific Internet sites related to fraud include:
- Association of Certified Fraud Examiners (*http://www.cfenet.com*). This web site provides information on fraud and the Certified Fraud Examiners Program.

QUICK FACTS
Online databases include full-text documents, public records, credit information, and other valuable information.

RESEARCH TOOLS
Internet
FARS
LexisNexis
AICPA reSOURCE
PwC Edgarscan
Thomson ONE
RIA Checkpoint SE
ACL
i2

RESEARCH TIPS
Use notable web sites to assist in finding helpful research information.

- Online Fraud Information Center (*http://www.fraud.org*).
- Fraud Information Center (*http://www.echotech.com/fmenu.htm*).

FRAUD INVESTIGATION REGULATIONS

Many different types of information exist for fraud investigations. One must gather the information legally in order to provide the evidence in a court of law. Some federal acts that govern access to information are the Freedom of Information Act (FOIA), the Fair Credit Reporting Act (FCRA), and privacy laws.

The Freedom of Information Act increased the availability of many government records. Typical information available under the Act include tax rolls, voter registration, assumed names, real property records, and divorce/probate information. Information not available under the Act includes such items as banking records, telephone records, and stock ownership.

The Fair Credit Reporting Act regulates what information consumer reporting agencies can provide to third parties. Under the Act, an individual cannot obtain information about a person's character, general reputation, personal characteristics, or mode of living without notifying that person in advance. Thus, a fraud examiner/investigator needs to be careful as to the legality of evidence gathered.

Privacy laws may also restrict the type of information that organizations may provide.

> **QUICK FACTS**
>
> Conducting a professional fraud investigation requires following the law.

SUMMARY

As discussed in this chapter, fraud is a major risk to society. As fraud increases, businesses are turning to fraud examiners/investigators to help fight it. Therefore, professional accountants are offering additional services to clients in the area of forensic accounting or litigation support services related to the audit. This chapter presented an overview of fraud and the steps involved in a fraud examination/investigation and of software and database tools to use in order to help the professional gather some basic knowledge for such engagements.

DISCUSSION QUESTIONS

1. Describe four different examples of fraud engagements.
2. Define "forensic accounting."
3. Define fraud and identify four examples of fraud.
4. What are the three components of the fraud triangle? Of what concern are they to the fraud examiner?
5. What is a risk factor or red flag?
6. Differentiate between management fraud and employee fraud.
7. What are some risk factors associated with management fraud and employee fraud?
8. Identify the basic steps of a fraud examination.
9. Provide two examples of a business/due diligence investigation.
10. Describe three computerized tools used by the fraud examiner/investigator.

11. Explain the difference between data mining software and public databases.

The following questions relate to the "ACL in Practice" tutorial:

12. Before one proceeds with analyzing the data, what ACL commands can be utilized to verify the data?

13. What is the purpose of a filter in your analysis of the data?

14. What are the different ways one can utilize the "Analyze" function?

EXERCISES

1. Review i2's Analyst's Notebook tutorial at the authors' web site (*http://weirich. swlearning.com*) and view the Financial Fraud segment. Explain how the Analyst's Notebook was utilized in the investigation.

2. Review i2's Analyst's Notebook tutorial at the authors' web site (*http://weirich. swlearning.com*) and view the Insurance Fraud segment. Explain how the Analyst's Notebook was utilized in the investigation

3. View the iBase segment of the Analyst's Notebook tutorial at the authors' web site (*http://weirich.swlearning.com*) and briefly explain how it can be used in an investigation.

4. Access the KnowX web site (*http://www.knowx.com*) and enter a free search. Discuss what you searched for and what you found. Provide two examples of how the fraud examiner/investigator can utilize this web site.

5. Access Switchboard (*http://www.switchboard.com*) and search for a business. What were your results?

6. Access the Fraud Information Center (*http://www.fraud.org*) and locate and describe three types of fraud reported by the Center.

7. Review the ACL materials and explain how an auditor can utilize ACL to detect or search for:
    a. Purchase fraud
    b. Vendor fraud
    c. Inventory fraud

8. Access ACL's web site (*http://www.ACL.com*) and locate three examples of how ACL assists in fraud detection.

INDEX